Templars, Hospitallers
and
Teutonic Knights

TEMPLARS, HOSPITALLERS
AND
TEUTONIC KNIGHTS
IMAGES OF THE MILITARY ORDERS,
1128–1291

Helen Nicholson

Leicester University Press
Leicester, London and New York

Distributed exclusively in the United States
and Canada by St. Martin's Press

Leicester University Press
(a division of Pinter Publishers)

First published in 1993

Editorial offices
Fielding Johnson Building, University of Leicester,
Leicester, LE1 7RH, England *and*
Room 400, 175 Fifth Avenue, New York, NY 10010, USA

Trade and other enquiries
25 Floral Street, London, WC2E 9DS, England

British Library Cataloguing in Publication Data

A CIP catalogue record for this book is available from the British Library

ISBN 0–7185–1411–4

Library of Congress Cataloging-in-Publication Data

Nicholson, Helen.
　　Templars, Hospitallers, and Teutonic Knights: images of the military orders, 1128–1291/Helen Nicholson.
　　　　p.　cm.
　　Includes bibliographical references and index.
　　ISBN 0–7185–1411–4
　　1. Military religious orders — History. 2. Templars. 3. Hospitalers.
　4. Teutonic Knights.　I. Title.
　CR4701.N53　1993
　271′.05–dc20　　　　　　　　　　　　　　　　　　　　　92–44121
　　　　　　　　　　　　　　　　　　　　　　　　　　　　　CIP

Typeset by Mayhew Typesetting, Rhayader, Powys
Printed and bound in Great Britain by Biddles Ltd., Guildford and King's Lynn

CONTENTS

LIST OF FIGURES

LIST OF TABLES

PREFACE

This is a study of twelfth and thirteenth-century attitudes towards the military religious orders. It centres on the three major international military orders: the knighthood of the Temple of Solomon of Jerusalem, the Hospital of St John of Jerusalem, and the Hospital of St Mary of the Teutons in Jerusalem, which I shall refer to throughout as the Temple, the Hospital and the Teutonic order respectively.

Most of the evidence concerns these three orders, although there were many other military orders which will be mentioned where evidence exists. Although the Hospital was arguably the most successful of the military orders during our period, there is more evidence for attitudes towards the Temple, which obviously made a greater impact on people's imaginations. We shall discuss the reasons for this during the course of this study.

A problem with a study of this kind is how to render names: whether in the original form (usually Latin), the modern form or a modern anglicized form. The last of these three options is currently the norm for historical studies covering this period, and I have adopted it. However, as satirists and writers of romances are usually cited in their own language (e.g., Guiot of Provins, Jean Renart, Hugo von Trimberg) I have made an exception for these writers so that students can find them easily in libraries.

This book is adapted from my Ph.D. thesis, 'Images of the military orders, 1128–1291' (Leicester, 1989) which was researched and written with the assistance of an open research scholarship from Leicester University Research Board. My travelling expenses and some other expenses were also assisted by grants from the Research Board.

I must acknowledge the immense help I received from the staff of Leicester University Library, especially the staff of inter-library loan, and the staff of the British Library, London. Without their patience and persistence much material would have been unavailable to me. I am also most grateful to Malcolm Barber, Tony Luttrell, Aubrey Newman, Jonathan Riley-Smith, Elizabeth Siberry, Judith Upton-Ward, John

Walker and Danny Williams for their advice and suggestions. Norman
Housley, who supervised my Ph.D. research, has been an invaluable
source of inspiration and guidance. David Tattersall generously drew the
maps. My husband, Nigel, has been a great source of strength, a valued
critic and computer expert. Finally, I must acknowledge the efforts of my
toddler son Gawain, without whom this book would have been
completed much sooner.

For the discussion of literary sources in the introduction and chapter
five, I am grateful for the views and comments put forward following
my paper, 'Literary sources as historical sources: problems and
possibilities,' on 26 February 1992 in the Early Medieval Seminar at the
Institute of Historical Research, chaired by Brenda Bolton, Michael Clan-
chy, and Janet Nelson. Chapter six is adapted from a paper presented to
Jonathan Riley-Smith's crusade seminar in May 1990, and some of the
comments then received have been incorporated into the chapter.

The map of the Holy Land on page xvi is reproduced from *The Atlas
of the Crusades*, London, Times Books, 1991. Figures 4, 5, 6 and 7 are
reproduced with the permission of the British Library. I am also grateful
to the Deputazione di Storia Patria per l'Umbria and to Francesco
Tommasi for permission to reproduce figures 4 and 6 from his article
'L'ordine dei Templari a Perugia,' *Bolletino della Deputazione di Storia Patria
per l'Umbria* 78 (1981) (plates 6 and 7, figs. 10 and 11, following page
64). Figures 3 and 8 are reproduced with the permission of the Bibliothèque Nationale.

ABBREVIATIONS

AOL	*Archives de l'orient latin*, publiés sous le patronage de la Société de l'orient latin, 2 vols. (Paris, 1881—4)
BEC	*Bibliothèque de l'école des chartes*
BEFAR	Bibliothèque des écoles françaises d'Athènes et de Rome
BLVS	Bibliothek des literarischen Vereins in Stuttgart
CFMA	Classiques Français du moyen age (Paris, 1912ff.)
CGH	*Cartulaire Général de l'ordre des Hospitaliers de S. Jean de Jérusalem, 1100—1310*, ed. J. Delaville le Roulx, 4 vols. (Paris, 1894—1905)
CM	Matthew Paris, *Chronica Majora*, ed. H. R. Luard, 7 vols., RS 57 (London, 1872—83)
GRL	Gesellschaft für romanische Literatur
HDFS	*Historia diplomatica Fridericii Secundi*, ed. J. L. A. Huillard-Bréholles, 6 vols. in 11 (Paris, 1852—61, reprinted Turin, 1963)
MGH	*Monumenta Germaniae Historica*, ed. G. H. Pertz *et al.* (Hanover, Weimar, Stuttgart and Cologne, 1826ff.)
MGHC	*MGH Constitutiones et acta publica imperatorum et regum*, ed. L. Weiland, 3 vols. (Hanover, 1893) in *MGH Legum Sectio IV (Leges 2. Quarto)*
MGHES	*MGH Epistolae saeculi XIII e regestis pontificum Romanorum selecti*, ed. G. H. Pertz and K. Rodenburg, 3 vols. (Berlin, 1883—94)
MGHL	*MGH Legum*, series in folio, ed. G. H. Pertz, vol. 2 (Hanover, 1887)
MGHS	*MGH Scriptores*, ed. G. H. Pertz *et al.*, 32 vols. (Hanover, 1826—1934)
PL	*Patrologiae Cursus Completus, Series Latina*, ed. J. P. Migne, 217 vols., and 4 vols. of indexes (Paris, 1834—64)
PPTS	Palestinian Pilgrims' Text Society
RHC	*Recueil des Historiens des Croisades*, pub. L'Académie des

	Inscriptions et de Belles-Lettres, 16 vols. (Paris, 1841—1906)
RHC DocArm	*RHC Documents Armeniens*, 2 vols. (Paris, 1869—1906)
RHC Occ	*RHC Historiens Occidentaux*, 5 vols. (Paris, 1841—95)
RHC Or	*RHC Historiens Orientaux*, 5 vols. (Paris, 1872—1906)
RHGF	*Recueil des Historiens des Gaules et de France*, ed. Bouquet *et al.*, new edition ed. L. Delisle, 24 vols., (Paris, 1878)
RIS NS	*Rerum Italicarum Scriptores: Raccolta degli storici Italiani dal cinquecento ad millecinquecento*, ed. L. Muratori: new edition ed. G. Carducci, V. Fiorini, P. Fedele (Citta di Castello, Bologna, 1900ff.)
ROL	*Revue de l'orient Latin*, 12 vols. (Paris, 1893—1911)
RRH	*Regesta regni Hierosolymitani*, and *Additamentum*, ed. R. Röhricht (Innsbruck, 1893, 1904)
RS	Rolls Series. Rerum Britannicarum Medii Aevi Scriptores, 99 vols. (London, 1858—1911)
SATF	Société des anciens textes français
SHF	Société de l'histoire de France
SOL	Société de l'orient latin
TLF	Textes Littéraires Français, 1ff. (Geneva, 1949ff.)
TRHS	*Transactions of the Royal Historical Society*
UB	Urkundenbuch

Figure 1. Europe in the mid thirteenth century

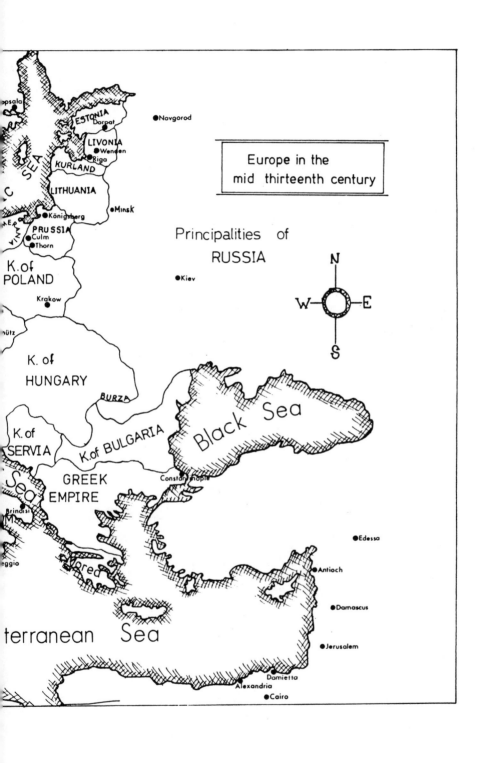

Europe in the
mid thirteenth century

psala

ESTONIA
Dorpat

Novgorod

LIVONIA
Wenden
Riga

KURLAND

LITHUANIA

Minsk

Königsberg

PRUSSIA
Culm
Thorn

K.of
POLAND

Krakow

Principalities of
RUSSIA

Kiev

N
W   E
S

nütz

K. of
HUNGARY

BURZA

K. of
SERVIA

K.of BULGARIA

Black Sea

Sea

GREEK
EMPIRE

Constantinople

Brindisi

M

Edessa

eggio

red

Antioch

Damascus

terranean   Sea

Jerusalem

Damietta
Alexandria
Cairo

Figure 2. The Holy Land and Cyprus in the mid twelfth century, showing principal towns and fortresses. (From *The Atlas of the Crusades*, London, Times Books, 1991)

INTRODUCTION

The Templars, the Hospitallers, the Teutonic knights: what images these names conjure up in the imagination! Modern images of the military orders are many; but these images are often distorted, even mythical. And modern perceptions of the military orders are far from the images which the orders enjoyed during their careers in the Holy Land — careers which ended with the fall of the last Christian citadel, Acre, to the Muslims in May 1291.

This study sets out to examine the images which various contemporaries held of the orders between the first official recognition of a military order in 1128 and the immediate aftermath of the loss of Acre in 1291, during much of which time they were seen as principally responsible for the defence of the Christians in the Holy Land. Of course, we cannot establish 'public opinion', because the bulk of the population left no records. We may only establish individual opinions, but even these can tell us a great deal, building up a consistent picture across time and society. However, as so little is generally known about the military orders nowadays, and so few good histories are available in English,[1] this introduction will explain the background to the study.

(a) What were the military orders?

The military orders were religious foundations, akin to monastic orders, and closely bound to the papacy. Unlike many other religious orders, they were lay orders, where most of the members were never ordained to the priesthood. This was because of their military function; priests are forbidden to shed blood. The orders were founded for peaceable and charitable causes: the protection and care of Christian pilgrims in the Holy Land.

The first military order was the order of the Temple, which was founded by a group of knights who had come to the Holy Land on pilgrimage. They made vows of obedience, chastity and poverty, and the patriarch of Jerusalem commanded them, 'in remission of their sins', to defend the pilgrim routes from Muslim bandits. The brothers received some land next to the Lord's Temple on Temple Mount in Jerusalem, and the adjoining royal palace in the former al-Aqsa mosque, known as the Temple of Solomon.[2]

On this all the chroniclers agreed; but they were unsure when it occurred. Some of the earliest sources dated it to the aftermath of the first crusade, that is, around 1099.[3] William, archbishop of Tyre from 1175 to 1184, the great historian of the Latin kingdom of Jerusalem, stated that the group was first set up around 1119. In any case, it received papal recognition and an official rule at the Council of Troyes, in Champagne, in January 1128.[4]

The fact that some early commentators confused the foundation of the order with the end of the first crusade may indicate that military brotherhoods existed in the Holy Land even before the order of the Temple, made up of ex-crusaders. The life of such groups could have been very short, either because they were destroyed by the Muslims or because the members split up, some to go into more conventional religious orders and others to return home. In any case, a decade after the order of the Temple received official recognition, the Hospitallers are recorded hiring mercenaries to protect pilgrims.[5] The work was too much for one order alone.

The orders soon extended their role, to the defence of the Latin kingdom of Jerusalem itself against the Muslims. The Hospitallers were undertaking the defence of part of the frontier of the kingdom as early as 1136.[6] The Templars did not take on such responsibilities in the south of the kingdom until 1149, when they acquired the fortress of Gaza, but in the 1130s they were given a number of castles on the northern frontier with Cilician Armenia.[7]

The concept of the military order was greeted with enormous enthusiasm by laypeople and clergy in the Holy Land and Europe. It was particularly welcomed in Spain, where Christian and Muslim were engaged in continual hostilities. Count Raymond Berengar IV of Barcelona, ruler of Aragon, tried to persuade the Templars to set up a house in Aragon to assist him in defending his frontiers against the Muslims. But for many years the Templars were unwilling to commit themselves in Aragon, perhaps because they felt that the order could not afford the strain on its men and other resources.[8] Several other military orders were set up in Spain by the 1170s: such as the orders of Calatrava, of St James, and of Mountjoy.[9] These 'home grown' orders had the advantage over the international orders that their loyalties and resources were concentrated entirely on one object, and almost entirely on one king.

It was probably for this reason that the bishops supporting the

'Christianization' of the Baltic states and Prussia in the thirteenth century preferred to set up their own military orders, based on the Templars' rule, rather than call upon the help of the international orders. These orders suffered from lack of men and money, and were incorporated into the Teutonic order during the 1230s. But already the Livonian order of 'Swordbrothers' had made itself as unpopular as the international military orders through the brothers' greed for land.[10]

The Teutonic, or German, order was re-launched as a military order in 1198, eight years after its foundation as a German hospital at Acre.[11] It owed a great deal of its subsequent development to the patronage of the Holy Roman emperors. In the Holy Land, the order was never as rich or powerful as the older orders of the Temple and Hospital. Most of its property was held within Germany, and most of its members were Germans.

Perhaps because of its weak power base in the Holy Land, even early in its existence the Teutonic order was eager to take on territory, privileges and responsibilities elsewhere. In 1211 King Andrew of Hungary gave the order the deserted land of Burza, frontier territory between his own domains and the pagan Cuman tribes to the south east. The king hoped that the order would defend his kingdom and also bring colonists into the area, building towns and bringing unproductive land under the plough. Under its greatest master, Hermann of Salza (master from 1209 to 1239) the order pressed on enthusiastically with this. But in 1225 King Andrew drove the order out; it had become too powerful, and its productive territory and fortresses too tempting.[12] In the following year Conrad, Duke of Masovia and Cujavia (in Poland) offered the order the land of Culm, in Prussia, which he did not own but wished to conquer. This gift was confirmed by the Holy Roman emperor, Frederick II, who did not own Prussia either.[13] Hermann von Salza, however, hesitated until 1230, when the order secured greater concessions which guaranteed its autonomy in Culm; he did not want a repetition of the order's experiences in Burza. The Teutonic knights then began military operations in Prussia, and subdued the pagans to Christianity with remarkable speed. Their hand was strengthened when in 1237 the brethren and property of the Swordbrothers of Livonia were incorporated into the Teutonic order, enabling the order to attack the pagans on a double front. Peter of Dusburg, historian of the order, wrote in the 1320s that by 1283 all the peoples in Prussia had been attacked and exterminated so that not one was left who did not bow to the Roman Church.[14]

The three major military orders rapidly became major landowners, with property scattered across Europe. Territories were either given to them by their patrons or purchased. Some of these, especially in the Holy Land, were given to the brothers for them to defend; but the majority were to enable them to finance their work in the Holy Land. The Teutonic order held most of its property within the Holy Roman empire, but also received some lands in eastern and southern France, and in Spain,[15] as well as the Latin empire of Constantinople after the fourth crusade, and the north-east frontier of Europe. The Hospital held property across Europe, from Ireland to Hungary, from Sweden to Sicily. The Temple was less successful in this respect; it was slow to attract donations within Germany, making little progress until the thirteenth century, as I shall discuss in chapter two. It never obtained possessions in Norway or Sweden.

Obviously the orders faced a vast problem in holding together their enormous organizations. They were not entirely successful in overcoming localizing tendencies.

The general organization of all three orders was similar. Each was governed by a master, who was usually based in the Holy Land, with his convent of brothers, whose role (in theory) was to advise him. In practice he was advised by a smaller group of older and more experienced brothers.

The overseas territories (i.e., outside the Holy Land) were divided into provinces, each governed by an official, known confusingly as a master in the order of the Temple, a prior in the Hospital, and a land commander in the Teutonic order. Below these in the chain of command came the local houses, or convents, commanded by a preceptor, prior, or commander.

Although the orders were always associated with knights, most of the brothers were not knights but 'sergeants', fighting men who had not been knighted, less skilled and less heavily armed than knights. While at the beginning of our period it was possible for a sergeant to be knighted if he showed sufficient prowess on the field, by the end of the thirteenth century only the sons of knights or of knights' daughters had the right to be knighted, and the orders were very particular in ensuring that no brother was admitted out of his correct class. The orders in the Holy Land also contained knights and squires who were serving for a period only, servants, and slaves (Muslims captured in battle). The Teutonic order admitted women as servants, and in practice also as sisters. The Hospital admitted women as sisters, but only in enclosed houses. The Temple claimed not to admit women at all, but in practice it did.[16]

The military orders played a vital role in every military expedition to the Holy Land from 1128 onwards, and assisted in invasions of Egypt from the Holy Land. They played no military role in the fourth crusade's capture of Constantinople in 1204, nor in the Albigensian crusade against the Cathar heretics in the Languedoc during the first few decades of the thirteenth century. They did, however, give moral support to the conquest of Constantinople on the grounds that it would assist the recapture of the Holy Land.[17] During the Albigensian crusade, the Templars and Hospitallers assisted the crusaders in a non-fighting capacity, as did other religious orders. The situation was, however, an embarrassment for them, as many of their patrons were Cathar sympathizers and thus were under attack from the crusaders. The position was particularly difficult for the Hospital, as Count Raymond VI of Toulouse, a major Cathar sympathizer (although not a Cathar himself) was a patron of the order and in 1218 became a *confrère*, or associate member. When he died, still excommunicate, in 1222, the order took away his body for burial, although excommunicates were not entitled to Christian burial.[18]

As the military orders were dependent on support and aid from the political powers of Europe in order to fulfil their vocation in the Holy Land, conflicts of loyalty were inevitable. In particular, the loyalty of the Temple and Hospital towards the papacy strained relations with the emperor Frederick II during his crusade of 1229. The emperor, having promised to go on crusade, had delayed for so long that the pope, Gregory IX, had at last excommunicated him just as he embarked. The Templars, Hospitallers and other religious and secular leaders in the Holy Land then faced the dilemma of working alongside an excommunicate crusader without offending the pope, and each side blamed the other for the problems which resulted. The Hospital was successful in healing the breach, the Temple less so. The Teutonic order had no such problem: the order supported the emperor, even when this meant estrangement from the pope.

Another such dilemma arose in 1267. Count Charles of Anjou, brother of King Louis IX of France, had come at papal request to oust Frederick II's grandson Conradin from Sicily. Pope Clement IV urged the military orders to give the count military support: the local Hospitallers did so, but at great cost to the order.[19]

So far we have examined only the major international military orders, and a few of the national ones. There were also other international orders, in particular the order of St Lazarus, which began as a leper hospital outside the walls of Jerusalem, probably in the 1130s. The order is first specifically recorded playing a military role at the battle of La Forbie, in 1244. Probably those lepers who were knights had been determined to continue fighting for the Christian cause in the Holy Land, and able-bodied knights had joined them. In Europe, however, it was seen primarily as a leper order which admitted both men and women, and its military functions were scarcely known.

Another such was the order of St Thomas, a purely English order, dedicated to St Thomas à Becket, and founded during the third crusade. It did not become a military order until the late 1220s. Because it was founded late, having to compete with international orders (while the promised support from the English monarchy never materialized), it never became significant, and is never mentioned by chroniclers in battles against the Muslims.[20]

(b) The importance of their image

The image of the military orders in the eyes of their contemporaries is a matter of great historical interest, which has never been systematically and objectively investigated.

The historical interest derives largely from the orders' close connections with crusading. Changing attitudes to crusading during the thirteenth century remain a hotly debated subject among crusade historians. It used to be accepted that the popularity of crusading declined during the thirteenth century. But this view has been disputed in recent studies by Norman Housley and by Elizabeth Siberry.[21] Their arguments have in turn been heavily criticized by Hans Mayer.[22] A better understanding of changing attitudes towards the military orders should assist our assessment of changing attitudes towards crusading.

The interest of this subject also derives from the trial and destruction of the order of the Temple between 1307 and 1312, instigated by King Philip IV of France. Historians have long attributed the destruction of the order to its unpopularity. Possibly the order was unpopular because of the abuses of which the brothers were accused during the trial, leading to a public outcry which prompted Philip IV to act. Possibly the order was unpopular for reasons unconnected with the trial, but this unpopularity enabled Philip to destroy it for his own ends.

The accusations against the order in 1307 may be summarized as follows. The brothers were accused of idolatry; sodomy; various abuses at the admission of new brothers to the order, such as denying Christ; and various errors of belief such as not believing in the mass, or other sacraments, and believing that lay officials of the order could absolve their sins (a power reserved for priests). They were also accused of excessive secrecy in their admission ceremonies and chapter meetings, and not making charitable gifts or practising hospitality as they should. Again, it was not reckoned a sin in the order to acquire properties by illegal means, or to procure profit for the order in any possible way, or to commit perjury in order to do this.[23]

In this book, I shall examine praise and criticism of the military orders until the end of 1291. In the conclusion, we shall consider whether these abuses existed or were as widespread in the orders as was claimed in 1307, and why the order of the Temple in particular was vulnerable to attack.

A limited amount of research has already been carried out into the images of the military orders during the twelfth and thirteenth centuries. Jonathan Riley-Smith has noted major sources of criticism of the Hospital and Temple; Marie Luise Bulst-Thiele has made a brief examination of criticism of the Templars. Joshua Prawer, Marian Melville, and Peter Partner have all made useful contributions to the question, but their studies were brief or narrow in scope.[24]

In 1986 Judith Upton-Ward completed an M.A. thesis on the subject of attitudes towards the Templars from 1119 to 1312. This was the most thorough and balanced study of the subject to date, but it dealt with only one military order, and was relatively brief.[25]

(c) Evidence and its use

Let us first define 'image'. Of course there was no single image of the military orders at any one particular time. There were concepts, ideals and rumours which circulated, formed by the turn of events, the pre-conceptions and prejudices of onlookers, and the orders' own deliberate efforts; but even establishing the nature of these is difficult. Four problems confront us.

Firstly, we must study at least the three major military orders: the Templars, Hospitallers and Teutonic knights. This will reveal how far the military orders shared a common image, and how far donors distinguished between them.

Secondly, we must examine the orders' image over nearly two centuries. This will show how criticism of the orders changed and developed.

Thirdly, our investigations must cover the whole of Europe, as well as the near east: everywhere that opinions of the orders were recorded. Opinions differed from one region to the next: for instance, in Germany and eastern Europe the concept of the military order was not welcomed with the same enthusiasm as it was in western Europe. However, as reactions to the military orders in Spain have been included in the extensive research carried out by Alan Forey and by Robert Burns,[26] I will not discuss them in depth.

Fourthly, we must investigate the views of as wide a range of the population as possible, laity as well as clergy. This requires the use of a very wide range of source material.

Charters of donation are the most obvious source of information, as they cover all classes of society, directly or indirectly. (Even some serfs asked to be given to a military order.) But charters of donation must be used with care.

A simple act of donation to the order of the Hospital, for the sake of the donor's soul, tells us only that the donor thought the Hospital worthy of a donation. Donations in alms were given in exchange for prayers for the souls of the donor and his or her family. As it was believed that God heard the prayers of the holy, but not of sinners, donors were anxious to obtain the holiest prayers they could find. During our period, potential donors could choose from many apparently virtuous orders and individuals, and so they would not 'waste' alms by giving to an unworthy order.

We do not know how many times the Hospitallers had to ask before a donation was made, or whether it was spontaneous. We do not know why a donor preferred the Hospital to another order. Perhaps he was a friend of the local prior, or he needed money and the donation is really a sale.[27] Perhaps the Hospital was a fashionable order at the time. Even where the charter gives a motive for the donation, it is likely that the Hospital's scribe wrote the charter and these are not the donor's choice of words.

We may only say that the donor approved of the Hospital as a religious order, as he considered the Hospitallers' prayers for him to be effective.

When we come to the order of the Temple there is a still greater problem, in the lack of charter evidence. The central archive of the Temple was lost after the dissolution of the order. This is a particular problem as charter evidence is usually favourable.

Sources which directly represent lay opinions are difficult to come by. Charters of donation and sale, administrative and legal records, and chronicles, were usually written in Latin, by monks or secular clergymen. Only a few were written in the vernacular, such as French, Provençal, or German, although the number increased as the thirteenth century progressed. Hence these sources give very little insight into the views of the laity, for very few of them could read or write Latin.

Much of the source material produced by the laity was non-factual in nature: love poetry, epic poetry and romances (the 'novels' of the period, including Arthurian romance). Traditionally, historians have been suspicious of such material. However, it has gradually been recognized that we cannot make a sharp distinction between Latin 'factual' and vernacular 'literary' sources. The writing of history was not an independent activity in the Middle Ages. Histories, like epics and romances, were written to entertain and instruct in moral truths.[28] In fact historians have yet to define the meaning of the term 'historia' during our period.

Of course we face serious problems in analysing the historical value of literary works. The author, intended audience and date of writing are often unknown and sometimes hotly disputed by philologists; where the experts are in agreement, I have accepted their conclusions. It is difficult to ascertain how widely literary works circulated. Unlike writings in Latin, vernacular verse often had a much greater circulation than the surviving number of manuscripts indicates, for verse was easy to memorize, and was circulated by word of mouth as well as on parchment.

Whose opinions are reflected in literary works? Even those who listened to an epic might not understand its message or endorse it. Even the patron might not approve of the finished work; and usually we do not know who he or she was. Yet often we cannot say much more of the opinions expressed in a monastic chronicle. Every form of historical evidence presents its own problems.

Yet we can say that, unlike the documentary sources and many of the chronicles, literary works were written to appeal to some part of the laity, and so give a general impression of their attitudes and expectations. Hence the skilful historian can draw a great deal from literary sources which could never be learned from the supposedly more 'factual' sources.

However, because of the nature of the evidence they offer, I have considered obviously 'fictional' works separately from other sources, along with 'facts' recorded by chroniclers which actually appear to be legends. (See chapter five.)

A further problem is in organizing the evidence obtained. Generally, I found that the views of the clergy were quite different from those of the laity, and have divided them accordingly. However, they do overlap to some extent: for instance, the bishops and princes who ruled north-eastern Europe agreed that the military orders were useful colonizers, and thus there is duplication of their views in chapters three and four. Some clerks in minor orders, who could marry and whose lifestyle was hardly different from that of the laity, held views very similar to those of the laity, and have been included with them, in chapter four.

I shall begin the study with a chronological survey of attitudes over the period, providing a framework for the detailed evidence discussed in chapters two to four.

CHAPTER 1

A CHRONOLOGICAL SUMMARY OF ATTITUDES TOWARDS THE MILITARY ORDERS, 1128–1291

The military orders attracted praise and criticism throughout our period. The praise remained substantially the same: the brothers were knights of Christ who laid down their lives for their brothers and for the defence or extension of Christendom. But the criticism changed. Early doubts over the validity of a military religious order faded as the orders became an established feature of the religious landscape, and as new orders and groups appeared which were still more controversial: such as the friars and Beguines. In the late twelfth century the major criticisms of the orders centred on their privileges, disputing the basis of these privileges and criticizing the orders' abuse of them. In the thirteenth century these criticisms were generally redirected on to the friars.

Until the emperor Frederick II's crusade of 1229, periods of praise and criticism alternated, and were mutually exclusive. Before the second crusade (1148), most writers were full of praise for the new military orders, and the only criticism came from those who doubted that a military order could be a valid religious order.[1] After the second crusade, from the late 1150s until Saladin's capture of Jerusalem in October 1187, there was little praise and a great deal of criticism, most of which was prompted by the orders' increasing possessions and their abuse of their extensive ecclesiastical privileges.[2] Some commentators, notably John of Würzburg and the Würzburg annalist, criticized the Templars for their alleged part in the failure of the second crusade.[3]

The courage displayed by the Templars and Hospitallers during their defeat near Nazareth on 1 May 1187, and in the face of martyrdom after Saladin's victory at Hattin on 4 July 1187, won them considerable praise from clerical and lay writers in Europe.[4] Likewise, they gained much admiration from reports of their courage during the Christian siege of Acre, between August 1189 and July 1191.[5] Onlookers lauded their courage and steadfast faith in the face of the Muslim threat, and overlooked their rashness, pride and greed.

However, the failure of the third crusade to recover the city of

Jerusalem, and the disappointments and disasters of the years which followed, seem to have reflected badly on the prestige of the Templars and Hospitallers. During the two decades from 1191 to 1210, the tale of the enchanted gold was first applied to them,[6] and writers as diverse as Roger of Howden, a Yorkshire parson, Guiot of Provins, a trouvère-monk, and Pope Innocent III expressed their dissatisfaction with the orders' worldliness.[7] These criticisms did not affect the newly-formed and relatively unknown Teutonic order.

After the fifth crusade embarked for Syria in 1217, recorded attitudes again became more favourable, particularly in the letters and sermons of James of Vitry, bishop of Acre from 1216 to around 1228, and in the works of Oliver, at that time the *scholasticus* at Cologne cathedral but later bishop of Paderborn. Both these churchmen had been among the preachers who urged the laity to support the fifth crusade, and both were eye-witnesses of the crusade itself.

However, opinions became sharply divided during the dispute between the emperor Frederick II and the papacy. Reporting Frederick's crusade of 1229, writers representing the opinions of the Palestinian Franks (Europeans living in the Holy Land) favoured the orders of the Temple and Hospital. These included the unknown chronicler whose work was incorporated into the history of the Holy Land written for Bernard the treasurer at Corbie Abbey in 1232;[8] and Philip of Novara, layman and poet and a supporter of the Ibelin family, which dominated the politics of the Holy Land at this period.[9] Opponents of the emperor also favoured the Temple and Hospital: such as Philip Mousket, a Flemish poet, writing a history of the kings of the French.[10] Supporters of the emperor, on the other hand, tended to denigrate the Templars and Hospitallers, as did Matthew Paris, chronicler of St. Albans abbey from around 1236 to 1259, and Conrad of Lichtenau, provost of the abbey of Ursberg from 1226 to 1240.[11] In contrast, these two writers praised the Teutonic order, which faithfully supported the emperor.

This period was a low point in the popularity of the military orders. Various other events acted to tarnish the military orders' image. The treaty of Paris, in 1229, which ended the Albigensian crusade against the Cathar heretics of the Languedoc, brought some criticism upon the Templars and Hospitallers for not supporting their patrons against the crusaders.[12] The lacklustre crusades of 1239–40, and the final loss of Jerusalem in 1244, led to much disillusionment in Europe. Finally, the rising popularity of the newly-created, austere friars distracted patronage away from the military orders, who seemed spiritually second-rate in comparison.

The events of Louis IX of France's first crusade (1249–50) helped to redress the balance in the orders' favour. The defeat of the crusaders at Mansourah was widely recognized to have been due to the rashness of the king's brother, Robert of Artois, rather than the orders' failure. Usually such defeats were blamed on the military orders. The Templars and Hospitallers in fact won considerable praise from some writers for their courage in the battle, and from others for their prudence in attempting to dissuade the count of Artois from attacking the Muslims.[13]

After the failure of this crusade, expressions of criticism or praise became rarer. There was some criticism of the orders in connection with the second council of Lyons, of 1274. Pope Gregory X called this council in order to prepare a great crusade to recover the Holy Land, and he asked churchmen to submit reports on the state of the Church for consideration at the council. One of the surviving reports, by a Franciscan friar, Gilbert of Tournai, contains some criticism of the military orders (copied from James of Vitry, writing half a century earlier)[14] but two others, by Bruno, bishop of Olmütz, and Humbert of Romans, a Dominican friar, make no mention of the military orders.[15] The orders' failure to mobilize their resources for effective action in the east was criticized at the council by Richard Mepham, dean of Lincoln,[16] and King James I of Aragon, but James admitted that the orders were supported by the majority of the members of the council.[17]

Praise and criticism fluctuated in accordance with events outside the military orders' control. During a period without crusades, particularly after the failure of the second crusade, the military orders' faults came to the fore: spiritual failings, their abuses of their privileges and their worldly wealth. During a period of crusading, attention was fixed on their prowess and their faults were overlooked, unless the crusade met with problems, when they were blamed, as guardians of the Holy Land. The Templars and Hospitallers took more blame than the Teutonic order, which never achieved the fame or notoriety of the two older orders in the Holy Land. Given that the military orders never commanded crusades, only giving military support and advice, they seem to have had little control over the events which shaped their image.

There were other, underlying influences on the military orders' image, which we should consider at this point.

One of these was the changing perception of the Church during our period. Lay criticism of all aspects of the Church was constantly growing, attacking the papacy, secular clergy (parish priests to archbishops) and regular clergy (clergy living under a rule, such as monks). Criticism of the regular clergy also came from the secular clergy: in the twelfth century the schools-educated secular clergy, such as John of Salisbury and Walter Map, attacked the privileges of the regular clergy and denied that they were spiritually superior, as they claimed. Alongside this criticism, revealing the same dissatisfaction with the state of the Church, the concept of the 'religious life' was evolving new forms.[18]

At the beginning of our period the standard form of the religious life was that of the monk or nun. Regular canons were a relatively new development: these were priests living together under a rule, who spent time in prayer and contemplation and could also perform valuable work amongst laypeople. Some men and women seeking a life totally dedicated to God became hermits or anchorites. During our period, a much greater variety of forms of religious life appeared. These included various military orders; the mendicant friars, who lived by begging and travelled around, preaching to the laity; the Beguines, laywomen who lived in communities and supported themselves by their own work; and, moving outside the Church, the Cathar heresy, which called a select few to complete purity of life.

The concept of knighthood was also developing rapidly during the twelfth and thirteenth centuries.[19] At the beginning of the twelfth century knighthood as an ideal existed mainly in the minds of clerics who sought to define the ranks of society and lay down the duties of each group within it. Some saw only two orders in society, the chaste clergy and the unchaste laity. Others saw three: those who pray (the clergy), those who fight (the king, nobles and their warriors) and those who work (the peasantry). The duty of warriors was to obey God, the Church, and their lord, and to protect the Church.[20]

In this setting, the military orders appeared a heaven-sent means for knights to win salvation. At the time of their conception they represented the latest trend in the spiritualization of knighthood, and their spirituality was very attractive to many knights and ladies. But as ideals of knighthood developed, some knights came to regard their rank as being in itself blessed by God. There was therefore no need to become monks or even to join the military orders in order to win salvation; they need only practise knighthood.[21] This, at least, was the theme constantly repeated in their literature: the *chansons de geste*, or epics, and the romances. Here we find knights seeking salvation through war waged on the Muslims, through serving their lady[22] or through their own personal search for God, without need for priestly intermediary. Often they take up a religious life towards the end of their lives, but they make poor monks.[23] Many become hermits, spiritual subversives outside the ordered ranks of Church organization. In a romance of *circa* 1230, King Arthur's nephew Gawain wins salvation through knightly almsgiving to the poor.[24] Gawain was the most widely and consistently popular of Arthurian heroes during our period. Another holy knight was St Renaut of Montalban, who, the story said, had rebelled against the emperor Charlemagne. Making his peace with his lord, he became a labourer in penance, assisting the construction of Cologne cathedral; but suffered martyrdom at the hands of his fellow-labourers, because he worked too hard.[25]

The knighthood of the thirteenth century seems a far cry from that of the first crusade. The individual working within the joint discipline of the group is replaced by the lone wandering knight, the rugged asceticism of the early Templars by the worldliness of Tristan.[26] Yet there was also a more fundamental change. The means of finding salvation was different. The new 'mystique' of knighthood described in knightly literature rejected the established structures of the Church as the intermediary between humans and God. Love alone sufficed. This new 'mystique' would therefore undermine support for the military orders, if they were regarded as monks rather than as knights (and therefore alien to knights), and if knights really believed in this means of salvation. This will be discussed further in chapters four and five.

CHAPTER 2

THE RULERS OF CATHOLIC CHRISTENDOM AND THE MILITARY ORDERS

The operations of the military orders were dependent upon the policies of popes, emperors and kings. They organized expeditions to the Holy Land and levied taxes to assist it (or did not), and led the way in patronage or exploitation of the military orders. Rulers' attitudes did much to shape their subjects' view of the military orders. The military orders depended on the rulers of Catholic Christendom for their privileges, the protection of their members and property, and thus for their income and very survival. Although the papacy claimed their first allegiance, in reality the orders depended for their survival on the attitude of those who held power in the localities.

(a) The bases of the relationship

Papacy and monarchs could be effusive in their praise of the military orders. From Pope Celestine II's bull *Milites Templi Hierosolymitani* of 1144 onwards, the Templars were frequently compared to the Maccabees, Biblical warriors who had fought the Gentiles in defence of the Temple and the land which God had given His people.[1] In 1221 Pope Honorius III made a similar comparison for the Teutonic order, as did his successor, Gregory IX, in 1230.[2] Popes Honorius III, Alexander IV and Clement IV applied the compliment to the Hospitallers.[3] Successive popes praised the brothers as *athletae Christi*, champions of Christ.[4] Popes of the second half of the thirteenth century also described them as *pugiles Christi*, Christ's soldiers.[5] Every pope praised the brothers' dedication and self-sacrifice, and their readiness to lay down their lives and property in the service of their fellow Christians. The repetition of these praises in numerous papal encyclicals must have engrained them in the minds of listeners, and was itself vital in shaping the orders' image.

Monarchs also praised the military orders in charters of donation and exemption. Sometimes this was in response to help which the orders had given them while they were in the Holy Land. Following the second crusade, Louis VII of France acknowledged the great services which he had received from the Templars.[6] Likewise, during his brief expedition to the Holy Land of 1217–8, King Andrew of Hungary overflowed with praise for the Hospitallers' hospitality towards him, their charity towards the poor and their battles with the Muslims.[7] In 1194 Richard I of England, confirming the Hospitallers' privileges, wrote glowingly of their works of piety and charity 'beyond belief and beyond the means of the house', which he himself had seen while he was in the Holy Land. His words were repeated in 1268 by his great-nephew, another crusader, Louis IX of France.[8]

Where the same glowing phrases occur repeatedly in preambles, they suggest that a standard form charter was used, either supplied by the king's scribes or the order. Such standard forms created and reinforced a favourable image of the order. In a charter of 1184 the emperor Frederick I referred to the 'religious devotion and assiduous labours' of the Templars; this phrase was repeated by his son and successor Henry VI in a similar charter of 1196.[9] Frederick II used the same preamble of praise for the Teutonic order in three charters of April 1221.[10] Whether or not there was any genuine feeling behind these words, these charters display the importance of the military orders to the monarchies of Europe.

The crusade was of great significance to both papacy and monarchies during the twelfth and thirteenth centuries. The papacy was anxious to protect the Latin Christian settlement in the Holy Land and the pilgrims travelling within it. Successive popes therefore fostered and protected the military orders, urging them to persist in war against the Muslims rather than in making truces or in quarrelling among themselves.[11]

Crusading was also an indispensable part of kingship. Monarchs who were unable to go on crusade could show their dedication to the Holy Land by patronage of the military orders. For instance, Henry II of England sent money over a period of many years to the orders of the Temple and Hospital for the Holy Land,[12] while in 1169 King Wladislas II of Bohemia gave the order of the Hospital a number of properties in Bohemia in thanks for the brothers' offer of hospitality to him at such time as he was able to come to the Holy Land on crusade.[13]

The obligation on Christian kings to protect God's lands was reinforced by the dynastic obligation to follow one's ancestors to the Holy Land. This obligation could be redeemed to some extent by patronage of the military orders. Direct dynastic influences are, however, difficult to prove. In her study of the Templar Inquest in England of 1185, Beatrice Lees concluded that dynastic influences had prompted the generous donations of King Stephen and his wife Matilda to the order of the Temple: Stephen's father (Count Stephen of Blois) and his uncle Robert, duke of

Normandy, had been crusaders, while Matilda was a niece of Godfrey de Bouillon, hero of the first crusade, and of Baldwin I, king of Jerusalem.[14] She did not, however, suggest such motives for the generous welcome which Henry I of England gave to Hugh of Payns in Normandy in 1128, although Henry was himself the youngest brother of the crusading Duke Robert. It is equally likely that such patronage was prompted by piety and a desire to win divine favour through patronizing a new, virtuous order.

In any case, Stephen's successors continued his patronage of the orders of the Holy Land. Besides the Temple and Hospital, other orders based in the Holy Land also received favour from the English king: the order of St Lazarus received an annual pension from around 1184 onwards, and various privileges; the Teutonic order received an annual pension following the marriage of Henry III's sister Isabel to the emperor Frederick II in spring 1235; while the order of St Thomas of Acre claimed Richard I as its founder, and received his successors' patronage as a result.[15] Until the 1240s, the order of the Temple was the most favoured, but after this period the Hospital gradually supplanted it. Perhaps this was a reaction against the great influence of the Temple.[16]

Dynastic tradition could work both ways; not only did it confer an obligation of patronage, but patronage could be used to reinforce dynastic ties. The Staufen emperor Frederick II and his sons made much of the dynastic connection of the Staufen with the Teutonic order, partly based on the order's claim to be the descendant and heir of the German Hospital in Jerusalem prior to 1187.[17] This claim is still hotly debated, and was not accepted by most of the chroniclers.[18] After the destruction of the Staufen dynasty, subsequent kings of the Romans took up patronage of the order, but never to the same extent.

Papal and royal support for the military orders also extended to areas of conflict outside the Holy Land. The papacy was anxious to protect Catholic Christians from non-Catholics, and therefore encouraged the military orders which were set up in Spain, Livonia and Prussia for the defence of Christians against Muslims and pagans, as well as fostering military confraternities which were formed within Europe to combat heresy.[19]

The rulers of the frontiers of Catholic Christendom valued the military orders as a potential source of aid in the struggle against hostile neighbours, or in expanding the frontier into hostile territory. Obviously, the Catholic rulers of the Holy Land patronized the military orders primarily for this reason. The papacy expected the military orders to assist in keeping the peace in the Holy Land and in protecting papal interests there, but not elsewhere. The papacy only once appears to have used the international military orders to promote its interests outside the Holy Land by military force: in 1267, when Pope Clement IV invoked the Hospitallers' military assistance against his enemies in Sicily.[20]

Outside the Holy Land, the international military orders were often unwilling to take up military responsibilities. This could be because they could not afford the additional drain on their resources: possibly this was why the Templars were initially reluctant to send brothers to assist Raymond Berengar IV, ruler of Aragon, against the Muslims.[21] It could be because too many restrictions were placed upon them, as the Hospital apparently decided after making an agreement in 1247 to assist King Bela IV of Hungary against the Tatars.[22] Or it could be that insufficient inducements and guarantees were offered to them, as the Teutonic order seems to have judged in the face of the initial offers from Conrad, duke of Cujavia and Masovia, of territory in the land of Culm.[23] Monarchs, of course, were unwilling to offer more than was absolutely necessary, from a well-founded fear that the order would become too powerful and threaten their own authority.

Remarkably, the international military orders were only viewed as defenders of the frontiers of Christendom. They were never used as defenders of Christendom from heresy within. For defence against heretics or schismatics, as in the south of France, Italy and the Latin empire of Constantinople, rulers did not appeal to the international military orders. Instead, in France and Italy the local ruler or the pope formed local orders, which were more responsive to local conditions and more easily controlled than the great orders.[24] In the Latin empire of Constantinople, no local orders were formed, but all religious orders which were granted territory were expected to perform military service for it, defending the land against the Greeks.[25]

Again, few monarchs saw the military orders as anything more than *defenders* of Christendom; royal charters seldom make any reference to the military orders converting pagans to the Christian faith. I have only found four examples of monarchs making such references. These monarchs were rulers of lands on the frontiers of Christendom, anxious to expand their territories and conquer non-Christian peoples: three rulers of Aragon, Raymond Berengar IV in the twelfth century and Peter II and James I in the thirteenth, and King Andrew of Hungary, in the thirteenth century.[26] According to the chronicler of St Martin of Tours, Philip II of France's generous legacy to the military orders and the king of Jerusalem was intended to convert the Muslims of the Holy Land; but this is not stated in the will, and was probably the chronicler's own interpretation.[27] Likewise, the papacy said little about the military orders actually *converting* the heathen; their task was to protect Christians rather than to create them. However, in the second half of the thirteenth century, Popes Innocent IV and Alexander IV did emphasize the Teutonic order's role in converting the pagan Prussians and Lithuanians.[28]

These were the perceived functions of the military orders. In order to facilitate the brothers' work, the papacy and monarchs granted the orders extensive privileges and exemptions. The papacy granted exemptions from ecclesiastical dues, such as tithes, and the authority of diocesan bishops.[29] In the twelfth century, the only other order to hold such wide privileges was the Cistercians; in the thirteenth century, the friars received similar privileges. All these privileges were greatly resented by bishops and other members of the clergy. Monarchs also gave away generous rights and privileges to the military orders.

These grants were intended to free the orders from the constraints of paying taxes and answering to local authority in Europe, which consumed resources intended for the Holy Land. However, they also reflected the growth and extension of papal and monarchical authority during the twelfth century. Papal authority expanded beyond the diocese of Rome to cover the whole of the Latin Church. The papal reformers of the second half of the eleventh century, eager to restore the Church to its original purity, had stressed the primacy of the See of Rome. Christ had given St Peter the 'keys of the kingdom of Heaven,'[30] and therefore Rome, Peter's see, should be responsible for the whole of Christendom. In the twelfth century this theoretical primacy was gradually transformed into real authority: the papal court became the court of appeal from all ecclesiastical courts, a papal bull was prerequisite to a crusade, papal recognition essential to the cult of a saint. Religious orders were eager to obtain papal approval of their privileges, in order to defend them more effectively against episcopal pressure, while the granting of such privileges underpinned papal authority.[31]

In the same way, monarchs granted privileges both to display and to widen their authority. Throughout this period, monarchs were extending and consolidating their authority over the peoples they ruled and over whom they had influence; as Conrad, duke of Cujavia and Masovia, and the emperor Frederick II sought to do in offering Culm to the Teutonic order.

On the other hand, popes and kings also valued the support of the military orders, who were influential and sometimes powerful allies. Papal favour was particularly great during periods when the papacy was under pressure. Two of Innocent II's three bulls of privilege for the Hospital were granted during his long struggle against a rival, the antipope Analectus II.[32] Marie Luise Bulst-Thiele thought it significant that his great bull of privilege for the Temple, *Omne datum optimum*, was granted immediately after he had gained full control of the papal see.[33]

Alexander III was very much in need of reinforcements to his prestige and authority: forced to flee from Rome immediately after his election, and struggling against both the emperor and a Roman rival. According to Gerald of Wales, he used to declare that he held three orders dearer than all the rest, and wished to protect them: the Templars, the

Hospitallers, and the Cistercians.[34] Three brothers of the order of the Temple held the posts of papal almoner and chamberlains: Brothers Peter, Franco and Bernard.[35] These were positions which could only be awarded to men close to the pope, whom he felt that he could trust implicity. Hence it is hardly surprising that in 1179 the clergy at the third Lateran Council were unable to obtain any lasting measures to restrict the Templars' and Hospitallers' misuse of their privileges.[36] Alexander obviously valued the support of the privileged religious orders more than that of the secular clergy.

Papal reliance on the support of the military orders led to an interesting conflict under Pope Clement IV. He inherited from Urban IV a dispute with the order of the Temple, over the order's failure to dismiss on papal command Brother Stephen of Sissy from the office of marshal. Writing to the master and brothers of the order in March 1265, Clement stated that the problem was not Stephen's original crime but the order's disobedience to the papacy. He warned the brothers not to try his patience any longer, but went on to say that he had decided to absolve Stephen, although the master was to punish him, and amend his own disobedience.[37] In fact, as the master and brothers were no doubt well aware, the pope could not afford to do otherwise than reconcile himself to the order. At the time that this letter was written, Clement was hard pressed by Manfred of Sicily, suffering financial crisis, and was being forced to make large concessions to Count Charles of Anjou in order to secure his military assistance. His lengthy letter of rebuke to the order was his attempt to salvage as much papal dignity and authority as possible from the fiasco. It was not simply a question of what the order of the Temple would do if the papacy was to withdraw its protective arm; what would the papacy do without the services and support of the order of the Temple?

Monarchs also valued the military orders for the influence which could be exerted through them. Frederick II particularly valued the Teutonic order because it protected and promoted his interests in the Holy land.[38] Hans Mayer has argued that the same motives lay behind Henry II of England's donations to the orders of the Temple and Hospital.[39] Charles, count of Anjou and king of Naples and Sicily, seems to have regarded the order of the Temple under Brother William of Beaujeu in a similar light. He may have used his influence to ensure William's election as master; certainly William threw the order's weight behind Charles' interests in the Holy Land.[40] King Leo I of Armenia's affection for the Teutonic order was undoubtedly due to its connection with the German emperor, who had given him his crown.[41] The support given to the Teutonic order by Premysl Ottokar II, ruler and then king of Bohemia, in the second half of the thirteenth century, was prompted mainly by his own determination to gain authority in Prussia, which the brothers were in the process of conquering.[42]

Again, the military orders were often valued supporters of a regime in time of crisis. The Teutonic order remained faithful to Emperor Frederick II throughout his dispute with the papacy. In particular Hermann of Salza, master of the order from 1209 to 1239, was a much valued friend and counsellor of the emperor.[43] For King John of England, who trusted hardly anyone, the Templar master in England, Aimery of St. Maur, was one of the select few on whose counsel he relied.[44] During the minority of his son, Henry III, especially during the early years, the military orders' support was very valuable: both in giving loans and in supplying reliable public servants.[45]

The frequency with which brothers of the Temple, Hospital and Teutonic order appear as personal and public servants of the papacy and monarchies indicates that they valued the brothers' integrity very highly, at least in comparison with other groups and individuals. A Templar and a Hospitaller often appear as papal chamberlains. Brother John of Capua of the Teutonic order appears as papal notary under Alexander IV and Urban IV, while Brother Wultard of the Teutonic order was Urban's chaplain and penitentiary, and Brother Hermann of Livonia, of the same order, was his porter.[46] These three won a number of concessions for their order from the popes they served. Other offices filled by members of the orders include that of marshal under Urban IV, filled by successive Templars; chaplain, held by the prior of the Hospital in Acre under Urban IV; and porter, held by a Templar under Nicholas III, and by a Hospitaller under Martin IV.[47]

Popes also employed the knight-brothers in a variety of other duties fitted only for men of the utmost fidelity. Following the treaty of San Germano between Pope Gregory IX and the emperor Frederick II in 1230, Hermann of Salza, master of the Teutonic order, was entrusted with a number of properties by the emperor which he was to retain, as a neutral party, until the treaty was carried out.[48] Urban IV appointed Brothers Raymond, Berard of Gallerceto and Martin, of the order of the Temple, as custodians of the castle of Perrochio, near Spoleto, Rocca Caesis, Spoleto diocese, and Trebis respectively.[49] Gregory X appointed Brother William of Villaret of the Hospital as vicar of the county of Venaissin in 1274; this appointment was renewed by Nicholas III and Martin IV.[50] Members of the military orders were also used by successive popes as messengers, treasurers and judge-delegates.[51] However, not all the brothers were as trustworthy as the pope believed: one of Villaret's successors in the Venaissin, Brother Raymond of Grassa, was later convicted of adjudging to his order some castles and villages within this county to which his order had no right.[52] In July 1220 Honorius III explained to his legate, Pelagius, that he had entrusted the transportation of a large volume of cash to the Templars and Hospitallers because he had no other messengers whom he could trust better;

although his tone suggests that he and his legate did not entirely trust even the Templars and Hospitallers.[53]

The monarchs of Europe also appointed the knight-brothers to positions of responsibility. They served as procurators and messengers,[54] financial officers, (Templars in particular appearing as royal almoners),[55] and royal ministers, often with great authority and influence.[56]

Yet these close relationships were not wholly to the orders' advantage. Popes could not always enforce the privileges they claimed for the military orders; papal authority was based on canonical claims and prestige, not on force. Popes frequently complained that bishops and clergy ignored papal instructions.[57] Moreover, papal protection came with strings attached. It was granted for the good of Christendom (and, therefore, of the papacy) and not for the order alone, and it was effective only until the papacy saw fit to revoke it. Innocent IV gave some of his legates power to dispense with the privileges of exempt orders if they were disobedient.[58] In the second half of the thirteenth century, when the papacy was in great need of money for its wars, all exempt orders in France had to contribute towards a tithe for Charles of Anjou's Sicilian campaign.[59] Nicholas IV refused the military orders' claim to an exemption from a similar tithe despite their pleas that a third of their revenues were used to help the Holy Land. He granted them exemption only from the tithe on that third.[60]

The same problems faced the military orders in their relations with monarchs. Royal patronage gave them rights on parchment, but in practice they remained at the mercy of the monarch's whim. Individual brothers were given temporary power and influence, but this did not necessarily benefit the order in the long term or at an international level. Monarchs expected service in return for their favours. Yet, the brothers apparently accepted this as natural and honoured their royal patrons as their lords, although in theory their only earthly lord was the pope.[61]

(b) Knighthood: a valid basis for a religious order?

Popes and monarchs had differing views on this question.

When in 1128 Pope Honorius II recognized the order of the Temple as a religious order, his decision seemed to be a natural development. In the previous century the Church had already been recruiting warriors in its own defence.[62] In 1053, Pope Leo IX had led a military expedition against the Norman threat to the papal territories, and his successors had readily used force to repel force. In early 1128, Honorius himself was engaged in promoting a war against Roger of Sicily.[63] Moreover, the military religious order may have seemed a natural succession to the first crusade.[64]

Yet there were certainly doubts among the clergy as to whether such an order was valid. While it was agreed that knights could win remission of sins by using their weapons in God's cause, this was only in the context of a single campaign, such as a crusade. To transform these laymen into members of a permanent religious order, living in a community under a rule, was a new development, which threatened the exclusiveness of monasticism.[65]

Probably Honorius approved the concept of the military order because he recognized its usefulness. The military orders offered a means of defending pilgrims in the Holy Land and could encourage knights to help the Church rather than attack it. Bernard of Clairvaux hinted at such considerations in his letter of encouragement to the first Templars, *De laude novae militiae*. He stated that the Saracens had to be killed in order to prevent them from attacking Christians; and pointed out that the new order recruited undesirable troublemakers, thereby ridding Europe of them.[66]

Yet the papacy regarded the military orders' lifestyle as less spiritually advanced than the lifestyles of contemplative religious orders such as the Benedictines or the Cistercians. Although the military orders possessed privileges which forbade the brothers to leave their order without their master's permission, the pope would generally grant such permission when a brother wished to enter another religious order, because this would advance his spiritual life.[67] Again, the papacy was slow to recognize that the Hospital was becoming a military order,[68] and protested against the change. Twice between 1168 and 1180 Pope Alexander III wrote to urge the brothers to continue in their original vocation, rather than taking up arms, except in emergencies.[69] He argued that they should follow the customs set by their forefathers, and that love and mercy for the poor was better defence for them than strength of arms. In other words, serving Christendom with weapons was inferior in spiritual terms to caring for the poor and sick.

Monarchs, however, had no such doubts. Until around 1185, the order of the Temple was more popular with royal donors than the Hospital. A variety of factors may have contributed towards this, but the overwhelming difference between the orders of the Temple and the Hospital at this period was that the Temple was known to be military in function, while the Hospital was not. Its military activities were not generally known in Europe until after the third crusade.[70]

Possibly monarchs considered a military order to be more honest and high-principled than secular clergy or monks. In twelfth century vernacular literature — written for monarchs and the nobility — the clergy are frequently depicted as treacherous, greedy and cowardly. Their service of God in prayer and fasting is shown as being far less valuable than the knight's service for God on the battlefield.[71] Monarchs may have preferred a religious order which operated according to their own system of values, rather than following the traditional monastic lifestyle. In the Holy Land in particular, where the Latin Christian rulers were always short of fighting manpower, fighting men would have seen the military religious orders as being far more useful than praying orders. The rulers of the Holy Land made no objection to the militarization of the Hospital and the Teutonic order in the twelfth century, or of the order of St Lazarus and the order of St Thomas in the thirteenth; on the contrary, they probably encouraged it.

In Germany and eastern Europe, however, the military order initially aroused little enthusiasm. In the twelfth century, the order of the Temple received little patronage, except in Lorraine, Bavaria and Brunswick.[72] In contrast, the Hospital attracted so much patronage within Germany in the first half of the twelfth century that by 1158 the order was seeking from the emperor Frederick I a general confirmation of its liberties and privileges within his estates. Frederick's first such confirmation for the order of the Temple was not issued until November 1184, again indicating that the Temple accumulated estates in Germany much more slowly than the Hospital.[73]

The earliest royal donation in Hungary to the Hospital was made by King Stephen III in 1168; the Temple apparently received nothing from the king until 1198, when King Henry gave the order in Hungary liberties and exemptions. In his will he gave two thirds of his property to the Temple and the Hospital, for the Holy Land.[74] The first gift by a ruler of Bohemia to the Hospital in Jerusalem was made by King Wladislas II in 1169;[75] the order was particularly favoured by his successors, who praised its charitable work in their charters, but made little mention of its military activity. The Temple did not receive a royal donation in Bohemia until the 1220s.[76]

The initial indifference to the order of the Temple in these areas was clearly not caused by indifference towards the Holy Land. It is possible that the Templars were viewed with hostility because the order was predominantly French, or because of its close connections with the papacy. Yet the order of the Hospital was also predominantly French and its connections with the papacy were equally close.

We might suggest that in the twelfth century the order of the Temple held no appeal for German patrons as a knightly order. The knights of Germany were legally unfree, like serfs, and in the early twelfth century knights do not appear to have had the 'class awareness' of knights elsewhere in Europe. Hence 'knighthood' had no great prestige in Germany. Not until the late twelfth century, when the ideals of knighthood began to filter in from France, would German knights have begun to regard their social order with pride. The German nobility then took up the concept of the military order with enthusiasm, but, preferring things German to French, they founded their own German order, reforming the Teutonic hospital at Acre into a combined military/hospitaller order of the kind they had admired in the Hospital of St John.

However, Jean Flori has recently argued that the concept of knighthood was far more developed among German clerical writers in the twelfth century than it was among French clerical writers, and that the Church deliberately encouraged the growth of a knightly ethic within the empire because of the dispute between the papacy and emperor, transferring to knights the moral duties traditionally ascribed to the emperor. Hence German knights may have been aware of the individuality and importance of their own 'class' long before French knights.[77]

The solution is unlikely to be simple and clear-cut, and probably lies in a combination of factors. It may even be that the Templars, lacking the resources to penetrate into Germany, did not attempt to solicit donations in this area until the thirteenth century.

By the thirteenth century, attitudes had changed. The papacy seems to have come to terms with the necessity of the military orders in the defence of the Holy Land, perhaps in the wake of the third crusade. No objections were raised by Pope Innocent III to the militarization of the Teutonic hospital in 1199,[78] or by Gregory IX to the gradual militarization of the order of St Lazarus, or the reform of the order of St Thomas.[79]

(c) Criticism

As we would expect, criticism was dominated by the demands of policy. The military orders were more likely to be criticized because they upset a ruler's political strategies than because they offended his moral scruples.

This is well illustrated by attitudes of popes Honorius III and Gregory IX towards the Teutonic order. Although relations had often been bad in the past, these two popes made a serious effort to maintain good relations with the emperor, in order to cooperate in areas of mutual concern. Until papal-imperial relations finally broke down in March 1239, with Pope Gregory IX's second excommunication of Emperor Frederick II, these popes favoured the Teutonic order because of its close connections with the emperor.

As a result, the order of the Temple received strong criticism from Pope Honorius III in 1222, because the brothers had been troubling the Teutonic brothers over the latters' white mantles. The Templars claimed that these mantles were too like their own, and were causing confusion between the two orders (which they were).[80] Honorius' predecessor, Innocent III, had supported the Templars' case.[81] But Honorius declared that the Templars' complaint was ridiculous, and was making their order a laughing-stock.[82] Likewise, in September 1230 his successor Gregory IX ordered the Templars to stop troubling the Teutonic brothers over their white mantles.[83] However, in an identical case involving a different order, the pope upheld the Templars' complaint.[84]

Gregory IX had been involved in a bitter dispute with the emperor, but this had been resolved in July 1230, in the treaty of San Germano. The pope was now determined to improve relations with the emperor, protecting the Teutonic order and upholding the emperor's truce with the sultan of Egypt, even forbidding the Templars to attack the Muslims. In return, he urged the emperor to return the property which he had confiscated from the Templars and Hospitallers.[85]

After the second excommunication of Frederick II, in March 1239, relations between the papacy and the Teutonic order became strained. Gregory wrote a number of letters of rebuke and criticism to the order. On 11 June 1239, he wrote rebuking the master and brothers for continuing to support the excommunicate emperor, 'that Sathenas.'[86] On 20 August, he wrote to his subdeacon concerning the Hospital of St Jacob of Andrevida, in the Morea, Greece, which had been given to the Teutonic order by its patron, Geoffrey II of Villehardouin, lord of the Morea. Although Gregory had previously confirmed this concession, he now declared that, because of accusations of fraud against the order, it should be investigated and reversed.[87] On 12 January 1240, the pope wrote to the master and brothers of the order instructing them to prepare and present to him before Michaelmas their reasons for having thrown off the authority of the Hospitallers, in violation of a bull of Celestine II, of 9 December 1143, nearly a century previously! This may have been not only an attack on the Teutonic order, but also a move to win over the Hospital: in June 1239, Brother Bertrand of Barras, prior of the Hospital of St Gilles, had come to an agreement with the emperor.[88]

Finally, on 11 April 1240, Gregory wrote to the bishop and two provosts of Meissen, concerning the 'excesses' of the Teutonic order in Prussia, and listing complaints that he had received from Bishop Christian of Prussia. The bishop claimed that the brothers would not allow converts to be baptized, that they had been torturing new converts who were faithful to the bishop, forcing some to relapse, and that when the bishop was held prisoner by the pagan Prussians the brothers had not tried to rescue him, but invaded his land and carried off his chattels. This was not the first letter of rebuke which Gregory had sent to the Baltic, but it was the first dealing solely with the Teutonic brothers.[89]

It seems unlikely that the Teutonic order had suddenly declined in virtue. Rather, until his final break with the emperor, the pope had not been willing to entertain criticism of the order; now he used every means at his disposal to attack it, and so to undermine one of the emperor's most faithful supporters.

Conversely, Frederick II attacked the orders of the Temple and Hospital for their support of the papacy. In 1228 Gregory IX complained that the emperor was disputing the papacy's privileges and struggling to subject the Hospital and Temple to imperial jurisdiction.[90] In 1231 he accused the emperor of taking the orders' property because they refused to act contrary to their duty.[91] This was presumably a reference to the orders' obedience to the papacy. Frederick apparently believed that the Temple and Hospital, as papal supporters, tried to betray him to the Muslims during his crusade, in 1229. He referred in a letter of 1240 to a papal plot to kill him while he was in the Holy Land. No contemporary writers report this incident, but Matthew Paris recorded it a decade later, and another fifty years on the antipapalist Bartholomew of Neocastro had heard a similar tale.[92]

Other monarchs also attacked the military orders for disloyalty. In 1160 Louis VII of France exiled three Templars who had been entrusted with the safekeeping of three castles in the Vexin, a frontier area disputed between himself and Henry II of England. These Templars had surrendered the castles to Henry II, in suspicious circumstances. They fled to England, where Henry welcomed and promoted them.[93] In 1288, Alfonso III, king of Aragon, wrote in fury to the marshal and convent of the Hospital because, despite the favour which his ancestors had shown the order, brothers of the Hospital had assisted the French during their invasion of Aragon in 1285, and the order was currently persecuting his friends and relatives.[94] Such conflicts of loyalty were inevitable for an international order whose members were trusted by rival monarchs as officials and ministers.

The major royal complaint against all privileged religious orders by the end of the twelfth century was that they had become too wealthy and powerful. This resulted from the generous donations made to the orders earlier in the century.

Monarchs began taking steps to prevent privileged religious orders from acquiring inheritable property. Frederick II confiscated some of the military orders' properties in Sicily; other properties were taken under an ordinance forbidding the Temple and Hospital, or any exempt religious order, from acquiring any inheritable property.[95] This was also applied to the Teutonic order. When challenged on his confiscations by papal delegates in 1238, Frederick replied that some of the confiscated properties in Sicily had been given to the Temple and Hospital by his enemies; and that the others were held contrary to the ancient constitution of the kingdom of Sicily. If they were allowed to acquire these, 'in a short time they would buy or acquire the whole kingdom of Sicily, which they consider more suited to their needs than other regions of the world.'[96]

Frederick II was not alone in fearing that the Templars and Hospitallers were undermining his authority. William of Tyre recorded that, according to rumour, in 1173 King Amalric I of Jerusalem intended making a complaint to the kings 'of the globe' about the Templars' defiance of him over his negotiations with the Assassins.[97] A century later, in 1276, Hugh of Lusignan, king of Jerusalem and Cyprus, left his capital (Acre) in a fury because, as he informed the kings of Europe, he could not rule in Acre because of the 'insolence' of the communes, the confraternities and the religious: especially the Templars.[98]

Some of the earliest confiscations in Europe occurred in Hungary, where King Andrew (1205–1235) made donations to the Temple in 1219,[99] Hospital in 1217–18 and 1225,[100] and Teutonic order in 1211.[101] By 1225 he had revoked the donations to the Teutonic order,[102] while his successor, Bela IV (1235–70), immediately revoked the donations to the Temple and Hospital.[103] The order of St Lazarus also suffered. The Teutonic order lost its possessions because it had become too powerful; the later confiscations, which affected all religious orders, were necessary (according to Bela) because of the poverty of the kingdom following the Tatar invasions.[104]

The kings of England also took steps against religious orders acquiring vast estates, culminating with the statute of mortmain of 14 November 1279.[105] Matthew Paris recorded Henry III of England declaring to the prior of the Hospital in England in 1252 that the clergy in England, especially the Templars and Hospitallers, had so many liberties and charters that they had grown mad with pride. The only solution, he said, was to revoke what had been so imprudently conceded to them.[106] Much as Matthew Paris was inclined to place his own opinions in the mouths of others, these words are compatible with Henry's general policy of recovering rights granted away by himself and his predecessors to the Church, and probably represent his actual opinion.

In Germany, Rudolf of Habsburg, soon after his election as king of the Romans in 1273, issued a general commission to his officials to recover all imperial property which had been given away by his predecessors; but he instructed them not to trouble the Teutonic order.[107]

In France, King Philip II and his successors gave little to the Temple and Hospital and took steps to recover what had been given.[108] Louis IX and his son Philip III did not even include the orders in their wills.[109] They obviously considered that these orders were already sufficiently endowed, and less meritorious than the friars and hospitals to whom they made the bulk of their bequests; although the military orders were still valued highly as royal servants.

We need not doubt the assertion of Richard Mepham, dean of Lincoln, at the second council of Lyons in 1274, that many kings and princes considered that the military orders had no need of further financial assistance, as they had vast possessions which would be quite adequate to support an army, if they were turned into cash.[110] Why should they have to continue giving, when their ancestors had already given the orders more than enough?

In Bohemia the situation was different. Patronage towards the Teutonic order and the Hospital continued, although the Temple received little. The Teutonic order was particularly favoured because the rulers of Bohemia had a great interest in acquiring property in Prussia. In a confirmation charter of 1251, Premysl Ottokar II referred to the 'continual labour which the brothers faithfully and frequently perform in overseas parts and also in Prussia for the Church of God against the barbarity of the pagans'.[111] In 1254 he led a crusade to Prussia and worked in cooperation with the Teutonic order, financing the building of a fortress in Samland, named Königsberg in his honour. In contrast, favour for the Hospital seems to have been based entirely on its charitable work, giving food and drink to the poor.[112]

Popes and monarchs were also concerned that the spiritual standards of the military orders were not what they should be, or not what they had been. Popes from Alexander III onwards constantly nagged the orders for abuses of their privileges and sharp practice. Pope Innocent III in particular rebuked the military orders for abusing their privileges of almscollecting and confraternity. In 1198 the Hospitallers were reproved for appointing as almscollectors uneducated laymen who brought the order into disrepute, and appointing unknown and unapproved men as priests.[113] In 1207 the Templars were sharply reprimanded for abusing their privileges during interdicts, allowing anyone to collect alms for them, admitting all and sundry to their confraternity (including adulterers, open usurers and other criminals) and for ignoring the orders of papal legates.[114]

At the same time as Innocent III was composing his rebukes, monarchs were uttering their first complaints against the orders' spiritual standards. However, these seem to have sprung from dissatisfaction with the spiritual standards of the clergy as a whole rather than with the military orders in particular. The Yorkshire priest Roger of Howden, a former king's clerk, recorded in his 'Chronicle' an anecdote of King Richard I of England responding to a rebuke from the famous preacher Fulk of Neuilly. Fulk had advised him to marry off his three daughters: Pride, Greed and Sensuality. Richard retorted that he would give Pride to the Templars, Greed to the Cistercians, and Sensuality to the prelates.[115] This tale was repeated soon afterwards by Gerald of Wales, in the mid-thirteenth century by Matthew Paris, and in the fourteenth century by Walter of Guisborough, with some variations: for instance, Gerald, an aspiring prelate himself, substituted the Benedictines for the prelates.[116] While the military orders' knighthood was initially an important factor in attracting or discouraging royal patronage, this anecdote suggests that by the end of the twelfth century the order of the Temple was regarded as just another religious order in the same category as the Cistercians and Benedictines.

By 1250 the Hospital was also being included in such criticism. The so-called 'satirical will' attributed to Frederick II on his deathbed regards the Templars and Hospitallers as religious men, no more and no less troublesome than other prominent religious orders. According to this, as Frederick lay dying, the religious orders came pestering him for some legacy. He therefore drew up a will, bequeathing, firstly, pride to the Templars and Hospitallers, discord to the Friars Preacher and Minor, avarice to the grey and black brethren, and sensuality to the white monks.[117]

It is unclear how far such criticisms of the military orders affected contemporaries. Onlookers were probably well aware that royal criticism was prompted by political motives as much as by dissatisfaction with the orders' standards. Certainly Matthew Paris, no friend of the Temple and Hospital, shows no sympathy for King Henry III's case in recording his outburst against the orders. At the second council of Lyons, James I of Aragon criticized the Templars' lack of enthusiasm for a crusade; but the rest of the delegates supported the Templars rather than the king. Perhaps they suspected that James' criticism was designed to enhance his own image as an eager crusader and faithful servant of the pope; he was hoping that the pope would crown him.[118]

Some criticism sprang from the orders' actions during a crusade. Conrad III of Germany seems to have had the military orders in mind, as well as the Frankish nobility of the Holy Land, when he complained at the end of his crusade, in 1148, that the siege of Damascus had failed because of treason from those he had least feared.[119] The emperor Frederick II remarked drily that he would not speak about the sort of aid which the patriarch and the masters and brothers of the military orders ('the religious houses overseas') had given him in the Holy Land, except to contrast it with the devoted assistance which he had received from the Teutonic order.[120]

The papacy was very concerned that the military orders performed well during crusades, and for this reason was anxious to stamp out abuses in the orders which would undermine their economic, military and spiritual strength. Moral abuses weakened the brothers, for God would not help them if they were sinful. In March 1238, when a French crusade was in preparation and Gregory IX was trying to secure the emperor's assistance for the crusaders,[121] he wrote two letters of rebuke to the military orders. He had heard that the Templars were failing to carry out their duty of protecting the pilgrim routes, and that pilgrims were being ambushed by Saracens. If the brothers could not protect the pilgrims, he had instructed Count Walter of Brienne to provide safe escorts. The pope had evidently forgotten that in 1231 he had ordered the Templars to cease hostilities against the Muslims, and to respect the truce with Egypt.[122]

The Hospitallers, on the other hand, were rumoured to be guilty of far greater abuses. The pope had heard that the brothers kept harlots in their villages; owned private property; received thieves, murderers of pilgrims, and heretics into their confraternity; assisted the Greek emperor-in-exile against the Latin empire of Constantinople; were reducing their alms to the poor; altered the wills of dying men in their own favour; and committed many more 'enormities'. Several of the brothers were also suspected of heresy. The pope gave the Hospitallers three months to reform themselves, before he sent the archbishop of Tyre to reform them.[123]

No other source mentions these allegations. Their spitefulness is reminiscent of Frederick II's later accusations against the Templars, and it is possible that Frederick had made such allegations to account for his unwillingness to assist the forthcoming crusade.

In a similar way, in July 1275 Gregory X, planning a great crusade, wrote to the Hospitallers, ordering them to cease their quarrels with other religious orders in Acre, which were harming the Holy Land.[124] However, a very similar letter from Nicholas III in 1278 to the Hospital, Temple and Teutonic order, was not intended to precede a crusade but to remind the military orders that they were responsible for the protection of the Holy Land and that they could expect no help from the papacy. In this case, the pope seems to have been deflecting blame for the state of the Holy Land from himself on to the military orders.[125]

The military orders' failings also brought the papacy into disrepute. As Gregory IX informed the Templars and Hospitallers of the provinces of Bordeaux and Tours in 1236, many claimed that abuses occurred because of 'the excessive favour which we do not cease to expend on you.'[126] Certainly, Gerhoh of Reichersberg, writing 1160–62, William of Tyre and Walter Map, writing in the 1180s, and Roger Bacon, writing 1266–8, complained that the Hospitallers and Teutonic order had excessive influence over the papacy. Gerhoh, William of Tyre and Walter Map thought that this was achieved by bribery, Bacon by subtle persuasion.[127]

If the military orders' abuses damaged the reputation of the papacy, papal policy could also damage the military orders' reputation. In the second half of the thirteenth century, the papacy gave priority to installing a friendly regime in Sicily and crushing heresy before launching a crusade to the Holy Land. The military orders were expected to assist in papal policy as required, understanding that only when Christian opponents in Europe had been crushed could Christendom go to the assistance of the holy places. Yet this policy was disastrous for the Templars and Hospitallers. Firstly, it took papal resources from the Holy

Figure 3. A Templar sergeant pleads his case before the pope, while the master of the Franciscans looks on, from Jacquemart Giélée's *Renart le nouvel*, BN MS Fr. 25566 f. 173. (Phot. Bibl. Nat. Paris.)

Land. Secondly, it took two of these orders' best officers, Brother Amaury of la Roche of the Temple and Brother Philip of Eglis of the Hospital, away from the posts where they were most useful to their orders, in order to serve papal and royal convenience.[128] Thirdly, by involving the military orders in the popes' Sicilian wars, it won them many enemies. In 1267, Pope Clement IV authorized Brother Philip of Eglis, now prior of the Hospital in Sicily, and his brothers to take up arms against the enemies of Charles of Anjou, king of Sicily and Naples. Like the brothers' battles against the Muslims in the Holy Land, this was to be in remission of their sins.[129] They did so, but in retaliation the Sicilians destroyed the Hospital's house in Sicily, cutting down the fruit trees and vines.[130] In addition, the Hospital suffered considerable loss due to the loans which, as prior in France, Brother Philip had raised for

Charles of Anjou's benefit, secured on the Hospital's possessions; and then failed to repay.[131] At the end of the thirteenth century, Bartholomew of Neocastro, a judge of Messina, criticized Brother Philip for forgetting the cross which he bore on his habit in acting thus against the wretched Sicilians.[132] Fortunately for the order's reputation, its involvement in the war does not appear to have been known outside Sicily.

Even where royal intentions were good, they could backfire against the orders. Between 1268 and 1272, Charles of Anjou succeeded in making the usually inoffensive order of St Lazarus extremely unpopular by enforcing in Sicily a law that all lepers must be segregated from healthy persons and be compelled to live in the houses of the order of St Lazarus. The lepers' property would pass to the order. Not surprisingly, the lepers' families violently resisted the enforcement of this law.[133]

(d) Chapter summary

In general, popes, emperors and kings regarded the military orders as a Good Thing. Although there were some initial reservations over the validity of their vocation among the popes and the monarchs of eastern Europe, by 1200 their vocation received general and enthusiastic support. The orders were praised, patronized and used by papacy and monarchs alike.

But despite the exemptions showered on them, it was impossible for the military orders to remain unaffected by the policies of papacy and monarchs. This often resulted in a conflict of loyalties which hindered the orders' activities and damaged their reputation.

Most expressed criticism was similar to that directed at other religious orders of the period, particularly the royal complaint that they were growing too rich and privileged, and that their moral standards were therefore declining. Popes constantly complained that they abused their privileges and quarrelled between themselves, but this was not mirrored in monarchs' recorded remarks. The most serious criticism was that aimed at the Temple, Hospital and Teutonic order during the disputes between Pope Gregory IX and Emperor Frederick II.[134] The criticism aimed at the Teutonic order was later echoed by Roger Bacon, but the other criticisms were never repeated during our period, and appear to have been prompted purely by the dispute.

More serious for the orders was the change in attitude towards the Holy Land emerging in papal policy by 1250. Popes increasingly subordinated the needs of the Holy Land to their own need for territorial security; the Sicilian problem had to be solved before a crusade could be launched. Gregory X was the last pope seriously to plan a great crusade, but his plans died with him in 1276. It is also debatable how many kings apart from Louis IX seriously considered the option of a crusade after 1250, despite the protestations of James I of Aragon. Kings paid lip-service to the need for crusades, but seem to have judged that they had more pressing commitments at home.

CHAPTER 3

THE VIEWS OF THE CLERGY

Good relations between military orders and clergy existed side by side with criticism throughout our period, although evidence for criticism diminishes after the middle of the thirteenth century. It falls into three main categories.

Firstly, there was fundamental criticism of the concept of a military order. This sometimes sprang from contempt for the knightly class and a belief that religious men should not shed blood. Some of the more educated and deep-thinking clergy believed that violence had no place in the extension of Christendom. Such views were held by members of both secular and regular clergy, but were seldom expressed.

Secondly, and partly as a result of the first, there was criticism of the military orders' privileges. This was voiced particularly by those involved in the administration of the Church; mainly the secular clergy, but also those monks whose interests came into conflict with the orders' privileges. It also came from those schools-educated clergy, such as John of Salisbury and Walter Map, who protested against the privileges of all the regular clergy on canonical grounds.

Thirdly, there was criticism voiced by chroniclers, ostensibly based on the orders' failings in the Holy Land, but bolstered by a plethora of personal and national prejudices. These chroniclers included both secular and regular clergy, men of widely divergent historical and literary talent. Some, such as William, archbishop of Tyre, were writing for the edification of Christendom; many others were monastic annalists, writing primarily for the information of their own house. Nevertheless, because history had a moral purpose, the opinions expressed by chroniclers in general were remarkably similar.

(a) Initial praise and fundamental criticism

The surviving evidence indicates that the clergy greeted the creation of the first military order enthusiastically. In 1128, soon after the Council of Troyes, Guigues, prior of La Grande Chartreuse (principal house of the Carthusian order), wrote to Brother Hugh of Payns, master of the

Figure 4. Spiritual warfare: Templars in white conventual dress defy the lion (Satan). From a fresco in the Templars' church of San Bevignate, Perugia, Italy. (Phot. Francesco Tommasi.)

Temple. Addressing Hugh as an equal, he admitted that he knew nothing of physical battles, but encouraged him and his brothers in their spiritual battle. Wishing him a complete victory over the physical and spiritual enemies of the Christian faith, he ended by asking the Templars to remember him and his monks in their prayers 'in the holy places which you protect'.[1] Some years later Gauchier, a Cistercian monk, expressed similar sentiments when writing to a Templar friend in the Holy Land: 'daily you walk about the buildings of our redemption, and adore in the place where His feet stood', asking him to pray for 'your Gauchier' as he went around the holy places.[2] This monk saw his own position in France as inferior to his friend's: 'There is a great abyss established between me and you, so that you cannot descend to me or I ascend to you'.[3]

Although he calls him a knight, Gauchier makes no reference to his friend fighting the Muslims. Other clerics, however, placed more emphasis on the brothers' fighting and less on their prayer. This did not necessarily dampen their enthusiasm for the new order. Simon, bishop of Noyons, and the canons of St Mary of Noyons, in a charter for the order of 1130 or 1131, gave thanks to God for restoring the order of knights, 'which had perished'.[4] Simon, a monk of St Bertin of Sith, writing around 1135–7, described them as ex-crusaders who had made vows of poverty and only used weapons to defend the land against the Muslims when necessity demanded.[5] Sometime between 1128 and 1136, Bernard, abbot of Clairvaux, wrote a letter to encourage the Templars, at the request of Hugh of Payns: here he called the order 'a new kind of knighthood', and declared that the brothers' desire was to die for Christ against the infidel. They lived, he said, a simple life, peaceful at home, fierce in battle, and were both monks and knights.[6]

Although this was not one of Bernard's best-read pieces (thirty-three manuscripts survive) it appears to have influenced many other early commentators on the order. Orderic Vitalis, a monk of St Evroul in Normandy, writing before 1141, referred to the brothers as 'admirable knights' who 'face martyrdom daily'.[7] Otto, bishop of Freising, writing his *Chronicon* between 1145 and 1147, described the order as 'a new kind of knighthood'.[8] Richard of Poitou, a monk of Cluny, wrote in 1153 of the order as 'a new kind of knighthood', and added: 'there are some who say that, if it had not been for them, the Franks would have lost Jerusalem and Palestine long ago'.[9] Anselm, an Augustinian canon and bishop of Havelburg, wrote in his *Dialogues* at some length in praise of the order, in terms very similar to St Bernard, but calling the brothers 'holy laymen'. He stated that Pope Urban II had approved the order; a more illustrious pope than Honorius II, and responsible for calling the first crusade.[10]

According to Anselm, the pope had confirmed that the new order was of equal merit to monks and regular canons. Obviously some doubted this. St Bernard himself seems to have set out to refute critics who claimed that the Templars were murderers and that knights could never be the spiritual equals of monks. He retorted that the brothers were 'malicides', not homicides, because they hated the evil in the Muslims, not the men themselves; and that they were quite different from the knights of the world. This was a new knighthood, whose brothers could not be told apart from monks.[11]

Another letter to the Templars of about the same period, written by one 'Hugh the sinner', states that certain persons had been undermining the brothers' self-confidence by saying that their vocation was invalid and harmful, a sin and an obstacle to their spiritual advancement. Hugh urged the brothers to persevere in their vocation. Although their order was not as glamorous as others, it was vital for Christendom. Their role was like that of the roof of a house, which is exposed to the rain and hail and wind, but protects the beautiful painted panelling inside. He also denied that they were guilty of the sin of hatred: 'you do not hate the man but the sin', and of the sin of greed in taking spoils, because the workman earns his pay.[12] These allegations, he said, although they seemed good, were the work of Satan, disguised as an angel of light.[13]

This Hugh has been identified as either Hugh of Payns or Hugh of

Saint-Victor. Whatever the author's identity, the letter shows that there was considerable criticism of the concept of the military order during the early years of the order of the Temple, and that this undermined the brothers' morale.

None of this criticism survives at first hand. But a letter of Peter the Venerable, abbot of Cluny, written around 1148, expresses similar doubts about the spiritual value of the military order. Peter was writing to Ebrard of Barres, master of the Temple, asking him to release from his vows Humbert of Beaujeu, a local lord who had become a Templar. He began his letter by assuring Ebrard of his love and admiration of his order, but went on to state that Humbert would be doing better work for God in subduing the 'Christian' troublemakers in the region around Cluny than in subduing the Muslims who were threatening the holy places. Furthermore, writing to Pope Eugenius II on the same matter, he stated that he and many of his monks considered that if Humbert had left an order of canons, monks or hermits, any old-established order, he would deserve to be punished for leaving, but since he had only changed 'from one knighthood to another', turning from attacking Saracens to attacking false Christians, 'worse than Saracens,' he should be allowed to leave.[14]

This letter indicates that not all the educated clergy believed that a religious order could carry on the profession of knighthood, or that knights could be the spiritual or social equals of monks. As the papacy and St Bernard approved of the order, it is hardly surprising that such doubts were seldom expressed in writing. But the vast volume of donations given to the order by the clergy indicates that most of the clergy approved of the concept. The critics were in the minority.

Doubts over the vocation of the military orders remained throughout our period. But those who spoke out against either the concept or the orders' actual activities were mostly notable individualists from remote corners of Europe whose work had only a small circulation. They cannot be taken as representative of the clergy in general.[15]

Those who opposed crusading would naturally dislike the concept of the military orders. Certainly the Würzburg annalist, who was totally opposed to the second crusade, also criticized the Templars for pride, fraud and jealousy.[16] Yet Ralph Niger, an English cleric who opposed the third crusade, exonerated the military orders from all blame for the disasters in the Holy Land.[17]

Isaac of l'Étoile, another Englishman, a Cistercian philosopher and theologian, expressed misgivings about 'a certain new knighthood' which used force to convert pagans: following a fifth gospel, Isaac remarked (since they were not following any of the other four). He was probably describing the Templars, for although the order did not set out to convert Muslims, crushing them and converting them went hand in hand.[18] Isaac went on to assert that using force was more likely to deter converts than to encourage them.[19]

Over a century later, his opinion was repeated by the Franciscan Roger Bacon, also an Englishman, in his *Opus Maius*, written on the command of Pope Clement IV in 1266—8. Although Roger was not opposed to using force against pagans, he declared that the military orders' desire for domination over the pagans had rendered the latter inconvertible.[20] In particular, he claimed that the pagans of Prussia would have been converted long ago if the Teutonic order had allowed this. But the brothers wanted to conquer and enslave the Prussians, and they were deceiving the Roman Church in this matter.[21]

Such accusations were not new. In 1222, Pope Honorius III had ordered the Teutonic order's predecessors in Livonia, the Swordbrothers, not to harass the new converts.[22] In 1240, Pope Gregory IX recorded that Bishop Christian of Prussia had complained that the Teutonic order would not allow converts to be baptized, and were torturing new converts who were faithful to the bishop.[23] In 1258, Duke Semovit of Masovia and the Franciscans of Thorn wrote to Pope Alexander IV to defend the Teutonic order against various accusations, including that the brothers had been forbidding the preaching of Christianity to the Prussians, the building of oratories or appointment of ministers, that they had been destroying old churches, impeding the sacraments and enslaving the new converts.[24]

Probably these accusations had been brought against the brothers by Bishop Bartholomew of Lukow and the Polish princes Kasimir and Boleslaw, who had initiated a peaceful Franciscan mission to the pagan Prussians.[25] Roger Bacon's accusations may well derive from these.[26]

Ramon Lull, however, a Majorcan mystic who shared Bacon's concern to convert the infidel, did not share his aversion to the military orders' methods. Writing in the 1280s, he advocated that the orders be united into one and the brothers educated in disputation, so that they could go into Saracen lands and defeat the Saracens both in deeds of arms and words, so converting them.[27]

For modern readers, the obvious criticism of the military orders' use of force is that it contravened Christ's preaching of non-violence. Only one such criticism actually survives, in *De nugis curialium*, written in the 1180s by Walter Map, a cleric in the household of Henry II of England, archdeacon of Oxford, canon of St Paul's and Lincoln, *raconteur* and satirist. Only one manuscript of his work is known, and no contemporaries refer to it; although, as Map was famed as a *raconteur*, his opinions would have been well known among his own circle.[28]

Of course we may never be certain when Map was being serious, and when he was joking. But others certainly held this view seriously, especially heretical sects such as the Cathars and Waldensians, who laid stress on non-violence. James of Vitry, bishop of Acre, referred to such opinions in his thirty-eighth sermon, representing them as belonging to heretics. He condemned them for misrepresenting Scripture, continuing: 'If we did not resist the Church's enemies, the Saracens and heretics would have already devastated the whole Church'.[29] However, even Thomas Aquinas considered that there was sufficient doubt about the matter to discuss it: he concluded that a religious institution could be validly founded for military service, provided that it was acting on behalf of others, in the service of God.[30]

Other intelligent clergymen had no criticisms of the military orders for using violence, even though some of these belonged to the same school of humanist thought as Walter Map. Writing in 1159 in his *Policraticus*, John of Salisbury was bitterly critical of their privileges, but conceded that the Templars were almost alone in waging legitimate war. This did not, however, give them the right to usurp ecclesiastical duties.[31] Following Saladin's defeat of the Christians in 1179, Nigel of Long-champs, a Benedictine of Christchurch, Canterbury, mocked the Templars' rash self-sacrifice. He did not say, however, that a religious order should not fight.[32] Some three decades later, Guiot of Provins, former trouvère turned Cluniac, declared his great admiration for the order of the Temple: 'It is the order of knighthood'; the brothers were like a wall against the Turks, and never fled in battle. He rebuked them for their pride, but admitted that he himself would never have the courage to join them. Although he criticized the Hospital for its militarization, this was because the order seemed to have forgotten its original purpose and its charity.[33]

In his *Expositio in Apocalypsim*, completed in 1249, one Alexander the Minorite identified the 'armies which are in Heaven' of Revelation chapter 19 verse 14 with the military orders. He discussed their forma-tion and role and declared that they fought 'both spiritually and bodily for the Lord.' His approval may be a reflection of his hostility towards the emperor Frederick II, whom he identified with the Beast of chapter 13.[34]

Nevertheless, Alexander added that spiritual knighthood is greater in the Lord's eyes than bodily knighthood. This was the general opinion of the clergy. Although the Templars' and Hospitallers' harsh discipline was widely admired,[35] their rules were not considered to be particularly strict.[36] Despite their austere lifestyle, those entering a military order did not have to change their attitudes or priorities greatly. In comparison to the monks of Grandmont or Chartreuse, their life was comfortable; as they always had to be fit to fight, excessive fasting and vigils were forbidden, and it was recognized that brothers would often have to miss services. Although they underwent great deprivations on campaign, these were common to all active knights and would not win them particular approval from the clergy. In fact, as James of Vitry made clear, poorer knights' lifestyle improved when they entered a military order.[37] In addition, they lacked the learning which marked other religious orders,[38] and few of the brothers were priests.

It is likely that there was also an element of jealousy in this attitude. The novelty and spiritual prestige of the orders' vocation, the defence of the Holy Land, held a great attraction for lay donors and led to their acquiring wealth and privileges which far outstripped those of many longer-established houses.[39]

(b) Criticism of privileges

A conviction that military orders were inferior to traditional forms of the religious life, and doubts over the principles underlying the military orders, must have heightened criticism of the military orders' privileges.

Such criticism was not aimed only at the military orders. The secular clergy greatly resented the privileges granted to the regular clergy by the papacy, claiming that these not only undermined the income and authority of the secular clergy, but were also contrary to canon law and Biblical teaching.[40] The Cistercians' privileges in particular aroused anger, resentment and fear during the twelfth century.[41]

Yet, as the secular clergy at the third Lateran council (1179) singled out the Templars and Hospitallers by name for their abuse of their privileges and flouting of episcopal authority, evidently their privileges were considered to be especially unreasonable.[42] Clergy who believed that the new military orders were inferior to traditional orders would not have accepted their entitlement to exemption from payment of tithes and from interdict, or the right to build their own chapels and to bury their own confrères.[43]

In addition, by 1179 it was obvious that the military orders were not fulfilling their function in the Holy Land with complete success. In particular, the order of the Temple had been blamed by some clergy for the failure of the siege of Damascus during the second crusade.[44] No doubt William, archbishop of Tyre, and his fellow-delegates from the kingdom of Jerusalem, made much of the orders' military failings in the east and the Hospital's refusal to render obedience to the patriarch of Jerusalem.[45]

There were other factors which combined to arouse the bishops' anger against the orders. They were recently founded, in an age when tradition was of great importance; they were everywhere, not only owning property all over Europe, but also sending out alms-collectors on a regular basis; their work was done far away, across the sea, where few had the opportunity to see its effects, and they were constantly claiming that they were impoverished and in need of larger and larger sums of money. In the mid-thirteenth century, Matthew Paris complained that the Templars and Hospitallers swallowed up enormous sums from Christendom for the defence of the Holy Land, as if they had dropped them into the abyss.[46] Despite a constant stream of newsletters from the Holy Land to Europe, the European clergy were unable to appreciate the worsening situation in the Holy Land, and preoccupied with their own pressing needs.

Complaints against the military orders' privileges continued throughout the twelfth and thirteenth centuries, both from the bishops and from rival religious orders. The complaints made at the third Lateran council were repeated by some later councils and synods, national and international. The council of Westminster of 1200 reiterated the relevant decrees of the third Lateran council virtually verbatim.[47] The fourth Lateran council (1215) repeated them again, but without mentioning the military orders by name.[48] A synod held at Nimes sometime between 1242 and 1272 repeated them more briefly, as did the decrees of the council of Riez in 1285 and the synodal decrees of Cahors, Rodez and Tulle in 1289.[49]

Two bulls of Pope Alexander IV, of 1256 and 1257, asserting the rights of the French diocesan bishops in the face of abuses by the Hospitallers, Templars and other religious,[50] indicate that the contention was still as great as ever and that the military orders' privileges were still at its centre despite the even more hated privileges of the friars. Yet it is possible that, by the mid-thirteenth century, this emphasis was due to tradition, not the actual situation. When specific complaints were made, as they were in 1274 by Bruno, bishop of Olmütz, no mention was made of the military orders.[51]

Significantly, most of the complaints of abuses came from the French clergy. By the second half of the thirteenth century, relations were particularly strained in France and in the Holy Land, where the orders had been longest established and their privileges were most entrenched. In the Holy Land, disputes were embittered by a shortage of land, as most Christian territory had been lost to the Muslims.[52] In France, the situation was aggravated by the royal policy of recovering alienated crown rights and lands, many of which had fallen into ecclesiastical hands. The evidence indicates an increasing number of disputes between the Hospital or the Temple and other religious houses in France during the second half of the thirteenth century, notably a particularly bitter case which began in 1289, involving the Hospital, Temple and Franciscans in a dispute over papal privilege claimed by Raymond, abbot of St Gilles.[53]

While the bishops continued to attack the military orders' privileges, the orders continued to fear the bishops. When faced with a recalcitrant military order, popes frequently threatened to revoke its privileges, thereby leaving it at the bishops' mercy.[54] In 1274, at the second council of Lyons, the Templars and Hospitallers were particularly afraid of this, pleading that if they were subjected to the bishops, they would have more to do defending themselves against them than against the Saracens.[55]

The orders' fears, however, were apparently unfounded. When the bishops had their opportunity to destroy the military orders' privileges, they failed to take it. At the Church councils of early 1292, called by Pope Nicholas IV in order to discuss the recovery of the Holy Land, no one suggested the abolition of the military orders' privileges. The prelates' concern was that the orders' resources should be properly used and that the brothers should work together efficiently.[56]

(c) Other criticism

The military orders also suffered criticism for other reasons, most of which was recorded by chroniclers seeking to draw a moral message from recent events.

The orders' most criticized vice was pride, the greatest of the seven deadly sins. The Hospitallers' pride was first noted and condemned by a German priest, Gerhoh of Reichersberg, in 1160–2.[57] The first to condemn the Templars for pride was another German, the Würzburg annalist, Gerhoh's contemporary and fellow-critic of the second crusade.[58] In the 1180s, William of Tyre and Walter Map repeated the criticism, the former condemning both orders, the latter the Templars.[59] In the thirteenth century the criticisms continued: Guiot of Provins criticized the Temple for pride, James of Vitry's criticisms were probably aimed at the Temple, while Matthew Paris condemned both the Temple and Hospital for pride and Ramon Lull noted it as a problem in both orders.[60]

Pride was a deadly sin, but it was a widespread problem. A more specifically damaging accusation was that the military orders were more eager to win wealth than to advance Christendom. This accusation must have been partly a backlash against the orders' constant and pressing alms-collecting in Europe, and their exploitation of their privileges in order to obtain the maximum possible income; but it was also the result of defeats in the Holy Land.

One of the earliest accusations of this kind was recorded by the chronicler of the Benedictine abbey of Egmont in Frisia, probably from information provided by Norwegian crusaders, concerning the siege of Ascalon in 1153. The chronicler records that the Templars were at first rather reluctant to fight, because they used to obtain a large revenue from attacking the relief caravans which the emir of Cairo sent regularly to the city. However, when the Templars realized that their reputation in the Christian camp was suffering, they were ashamed and attacked the city at dawn, killing an enormous number of Saracens.[61] William of Tyre had heard a different version of this story; he depicted the Templars impeding the capture of the city through their greed for booty.[62] He also told two other tales showing the Templars preferring booty to converts, concerning in one case Nasr ed-Din, and in the other the Assassins.[63]

William's stories enjoyed a wide circulation. Walter Map used them as illustrations of the problems caused by the Templars' love of war, rather than their greed.[64] In the 1190s, Guy of Bazoches, a veteran of the third crusade who died as cantor of St Étienne de Chalons in 1203, wrote a history drawing on William's work. He repeated William's story of the Templars and the Assassins, but rejected his version of the tale of Nasr for a version more favourable to the Templars. His work was copied in around 1240 by Alberic, a monk of Trois Fontaines.[65] In 1279 a Franciscan friar, Thomas Tusci, repeated William's tale about the Templars and the Assassins, although with details altered.[66]

Similarly, some chroniclers heard that the Templars had deliberately sabotaged the siege of Damascus in 1148 in exchange for Muslim gold.[67] By the beginning of the thirteenth century, this tale had been incorporated into a legend which told how the Templars, or Templars and Hospitallers, had accepted a bribe of false gold in order to raise the siege of a Muslim stronghold.[68]

Another potentially damaging accusation was that the military orders were more eager to make peace with the Muslims than to fight them, thus preventing Christian advance. Menko, abbot of Werum in Frisia, writing in the early 1270s, was of the opinion that this was the result of cowardice; Odo, bishop of Tusculanum and papal legate on Louis IX's first crusade, seems to have considered that it revealed the orders' political ineptitude.[69] The incident he described, when the master of the Temple and marshal of the Hospital attempted to make peace with the sultan of Egypt before the crusade arrived, was recorded later in the thirteenth century by both John Columna and William of Nangis, and in the fourteenth in the 'Chroniques de Saint-Denis.' The last of these adapted the story to depict the master of the Temple deliberately attempting to halt Louis' crusade; but the earlier writers do not seem to have put such a sinister interpretation on events.[70]

Some chroniclers apparently repeated such tales more from love of a good story and scandal than from conviction. Yet Matthew Paris indicates that lurking beneath the scandal lay a constant suspicion that the military orders could not be trusted. He complained that the Christians could not believe reports of good news from the Holy Land even when they came, because of 'the ancient infamy of the Templars and

Hospitallers, for it is said they always procure discord between Christians and Saracens in order to prolong the war and so collect money from the pilgrims coming from everywhere'.[71] Such suspicion would have been prompted partly by the traditional distrust of orientals, among whom the military orders lived.[72]

Xenophobia affected many chroniclers. The writings of two Germans, the priest John of Würzburg and the monk Otto of St Blasien, show that they resented French domination of the crusades and of the Holy Land. When they accuse the Templars of treachery, it is tempting to blame their suspicions on their hatred of the French; particularly as Otto of St Blasien blamed both Templars and Hospitallers for fraternizing with the Muslims, but carefully exonerated the Teutonic brothers from blame for events during the third crusade.[73]

French chroniclers also suffered from such prejudice. The chronicler of Limoges was the only contemporary chronicler to blame the loss of the Templars' castle of Saphet in 1266 on treachery from within; however, he took care to record that a Syrian and an Englishman were the guilty parties.[74] It seems as if he hated the Syrians and English as much as he hated the Muslims.

Finally, political suspicion of the military orders could become suspicion of all their activities. This is very marked in the cases of William of Tyre, Matthew Paris and German chroniclers during the dispute between the papacy and the emperor Frederick II.

William of Tyre supported the principle of military orders. Although he believed that clergy generally should not fight, he approved of the military orders provided that they fulfilled their function effectively, and were obedient to their bishops.[75] His dislike of the Templars may have been aggravated by the political conflicts within the kingdom of Jerusalem during the reign of Baldwin IV (1173—85).[76] However, this would not have affected his attitudes towards the Hospital.

As archbishop of Tyre and former royal chancellor, William believed that the military orders' defiance of royal and/or patriarchal authority had brought great harm on the kingdom of Jerusalem and on Christendom. As religious men, the brothers were bound to obey the divinely-ordained authorities, but as they became wealthy they had grown proud and rebellious. William devoted six chapters of the eighteenth book of his 'Historia' to describing how the Hospital acquired independence from the patriarch of Jerusalem, the troubles that this brought on the Church, and contrasting their present contumacy with their past obedience.[77] As for the Temple, although he made only general accusations that this order defied the patriarch, he cited a number of incidents to demonstrate that the Templars' refusal to submit to royal authority had brought great damage on the kingdom.[78]

William wrote for a European audience, in defence of the Latin kingdom of Jerusalem.[79] He intended to show Europeans that the kingdom could be saved by the Palestinian Franks, if only they had European support; not through foolish outsiders, such as Philip, count of Flanders, or Guy of Lusignan, nor through the military orders. So he revealed the harm which the military orders were doing to the kingdom, portraying them as proud, rash, quarrelling between themselves and refusing to cooperate with the Palestinian nobles; not only failing to defend the Holy Land, but actually weakening it. He seldom mentioned their successes, minimized their positive role, and emphasized their failures.[80]

The 'Historia' had a very wide circulation, both in Latin and in French translation, and it was used by many other chroniclers. Yet William failed to make his message understood: Europeans continued to blame losses in the Holy Land on the Palestinian Franks.[81] Nonetheless, European chroniclers adopted his derogatory tales about the order of the Temple, and these seem to have been at least half-believed.

In general, William of Tyre was a careful historian, sifting his evidence and distinguishing between reliable and unreliable sources. In contrast, Matthew Paris was a bigoted, undiscerning scandal-monger. Yet these two historians had very similar opinions of the Templars and Hospitallers.

Matthew Paris (c.1200–1259) was a monk of the Benedictine abbey of St Albans. From around 1245, he wrote four major historical works, as well as a number of minor pieces, such as a biography of the abbots of St Albans. His greatest historical work, the *Chronica Majora*, did not have a large circulation, although it was used by a few English chroniclers late in the thirteenth century. The shorter, more racy *Flores Historiarum*, however, was very popular, surviving in nineteen manuscripts, and was widely used by other English chroniclers.[82] Thus Matthew exerted considerable influence on English clerical opinion through his writings, and some influence on secular opinion, as he had many friends among the nobility.[83] This was unfortunate for the orders of the Temple and Hospital, as Matthew criticized them in virtually all that they did.

In some instances, he was merely repeating the opinions of his informants, such as Richard, earl of Cornwall. Elsewhere, he laid out his own opinions, often claiming that they were general opinion; which was only sometimes true. Matthew was not a great thinker; unlike John of Salisbury, Walter Map or William of Tyre, he had not been educated at one of the great schools of Europe. He was opposed to all earthly authority beyond that of his own abbot, so hated both pope and monarch. He supported the emperor Frederick II, however, because he opposed the papacy. He was concerned about the protection of the Holy Land; so he supported Frederick II's policies in that area. Although his vision was broad, covering events from Ireland to the Far East (in this he is unique among contemporary chroniclers), his major concern was the interest of his own house, and he generally hated foreigners.

Matthew believed that the Templars and Hospitallers had weakened the Christian cause in the Holy Land by their opposition to the emperor Frederick II. He regarded the Templars and Hospitallers as proud, treacherous, and envious of each other and of others who threatened to surpass them, such as the emperor. They did not make proper use of their resources, and were eager to prolong the war with the Muslims in order to make money.[84] They were often rash, they sometimes preferred alliance with Muslims to peace with Christians, their quarrels promoted the Muslim cause, and their reports should not always be believed.[85] But he also disliked them for other reasons. They represented a departure from traditional monasticism, and were composed largely of foreigners. They were faithful servants of the papacy and of the monarchy. His particular dislike fell on the order of the Temple, which was especially close to King Henry III until the mid 1240s and which failed to come to any agreement with the emperor Frederick II.

It is interesting to contrast these opinions with his remarks on the less powerful military orders. Matthew favoured the Teutonic order, a faithful supporter of Frederick II.[86] He noted the reform of the order of St Thomas by Peter of Roches, bishop of Winchester (although incorrectly)[87] and losses suffered by the order of St Lazarus in the field.[88] Few other chroniclers made any mention of the order of St Lazarus, which was apparently hardly recognized in Europe as a military order.

Matthew did admit that the Templars and Hospitallers had courage, refusing to submit to the Tatars, fighting to the death at Darbsak (Trapesac) and Mansourah.[89] He spoke well of Thierry, prior of the Hospital in England, perhaps because he was a friend of Earl Richard of Cornwall, a patron of Matthew.[90] With the benefit of hindsight, he realized that the notorious Brother Geoffrey the Templar, royal almoner, had exercised some beneficial restraint on King Henry III, and, under pressure from his informants or patrons, he was prepared to admit that the stories told against the military orders were untrue.[91] Most of his more favourable remarks were recorded after 1250, by which time the emperor was dead, the order of the Temple was no longer as prominent in royal favour as it had formerly been, the Temple and Hospital were suffering at King Henry's hands, and papal policy (Matthew thought) was harming the Christian cause in the Holy Land far more than the military orders had ever done. Moreover, old age may have made him more wary of attracting enemies.

Yet there were no favourable remarks in the *Flores*, Matthew's most influential and best-read work. Here he had very little to say of the Hospital or other military orders, but much to say against the Temple. This was apparently due to the criticism which the Temple had received from the emperor Frederick II; but scandal also made good reading. Here his readers were given the impression that the Hospital was a nonentity, with little significance or influence in the Holy Land except for its presence in Christian defeats, and that the Temple was largely to blame for these defeats. Nevertheless, none of the chroniclers who used Matthew's work before 1291 repeated his stories against the military orders.

The dispute between the papacy and Frederick II also influenced some German chroniclers against the Templars. The 'greater annals' of Cologne were written contemporaneously, so that they praise the Templars during the fifth crusade (following the work of Oliver, scholasticus of Cologne), but for 1237 record with relish that the emperor Frederick refused to give any assistance to them after their defeat at Darbsak. On the other hand, the annalist publicized a miracle at the tomb of St Elizabeth of Marburg, for the glory of the Teutonic order (and, thus, the emperor).[92]

Another critic was Conrad of Lichtenau, provost of the abbey of Ursberg from 1226 to 1240. He blamed the papal legate, the Templars 'and other governors' of the army for the failure of the fifth crusade; they had rejected the sultan of Cairo's favourable terms because of their pride. According to Conrad, the emperor Frederick II had put up with a good deal of trouble 'as they say' during his crusade from the perfidious treachery of the Templars, and only the Teutonic brothers faithfully assisted him.[93]

(d) Changes in attitudes after 1250

Criticism did not remain constant throughout our period. Evidence for hostility towards the military orders diminishes in the second half of the thirteenth century.

There were two major reasons for this. Firstly, in the early thirteenth century the new mendicant orders replaced the military orders as the latest and most radical religious development. As the friars acquired wealth and privileges, they became even more unpopular than the Cistercians or the military orders. In 1274 Bruno, bishop of Olmütz, writing to Pope Gregory X, protested at length about the friars usurping priestly functions, but made no mention at all of the military orders.[94]

Secondly, the public profile of the military orders fell during the second half of the thirteenth century. This may be seen in the writings of Gilbert of Tournai, Friar Minor, and Humbert of Romans, Friar Preacher, who show little actual knowledge of the military orders.

Gilbert, writing a report for Gregory X in the same way as Bruno of Olmütz, criticized every part of the Church in turn: the bishops were defective in many respects, there were many irregularities among monks (although he had little to say against the friars), nuns were very corrupt and Beguines were condemned out of hand. However, when he came to the military orders, he had nothing of his own to say against them: he took his entire critique from James of Vitry's thirty-seventh sermon, sometimes verbatim, sometimes in summary. As a result, he referred to the Swordbrothers of Livonia as an order still in existence, whereas in fact they had been incorporated into the Teutonic order some forty years previously. He said little of the Teutonic order; like most Frenchmen, he probably knew virtually nothing about it.[95]

Humbert of Romans, fifth master-general of the Dominican order (1254–63), also used the works of James of Vitry when compiling his instruction manual on preaching, but he used the *Historia Orientalis* more than the sermons.[96] He recommended particular points to be included when preaching to particular groups: for the Hospitallers, the need to preserve discipline and for humility rather than pride; for the Templars, to learn to be good warriors in spiritual battles as well as physical; and for the Teutonic brothers, not to offend their patroness the Blessed Virgin Mary, to concentrate on spiritual improvement as well as caring for the poor and warfare, and to provide for the salvation of their fellow-Germans as well as for their bodily needs, as St Paul did for his fellow-countrymen. He made no reference to their work in Prussia, which is hardly surprising, as even German chroniclers hardly mentioned it. He was apparently ignorant of the complaints that they were obstructing the conversion of pagans, and appears to have believed that the order was still pure in spirituality and devoted to the bishops (numerous papal bulls indicate that this was not the case).

Likewise, Humbert had nothing of contemporary relevance to say of the order of the Temple; his account was based on the *Historia Orientalis* and St Bernard's letter to the Templars. Much of his description of the Hospital was also taken from the *Historia Orientalis*.[97] But he omitted James of Vitry's criticism of the Hospital's wealth, instead emphasizing the brothers' discipline and humility. His tone throughout was approving and encouraging.

Apparently neither of these friars knew of the criticism of the military orders voiced by the friar Roger Bacon. Although Bacon was not thrown into prison until 1277, he had been under supervision in Paris since 1257 and this would have inhibited the circulation of his works and ideas.[98]

The profile of the military orders fell as the plight of the Holy Land became overshadowed by the papal Sicilian wars and the internal affairs of the European kingdoms, such as disputes between the king and his barons in England, or rivalry for the crown in Germany. Although Europeans received frequent pleas for help from the Holy Land, few chroniclers mentioned it.

We may suggest two reasons for this. Firstly, because of the conflicts in Europe, few crusades were actually going to the Holy Land. Hence chroniclers had to rely on letters for news, which were not nearly so interesting as eyewitness reports. There was little or no personal involvement with the Holy Land among writers in Europe, and therefore little appreciation of the actual situation. Secondly, the news that came from the Holy Land was almost invariably bad. A generation grew up thinking the military orders incapable of winning a battle against the Muslims, and watching crusades going to Sicily rather than Acre. The fact that the few crusades which did reach the Holy Land achieved little only served to reinforce this image. The real state of the Holy Land was too bad to think about; writers preferred to fantasize, to treat the Holy Land as if it were a land of fable and legend, rather than a real place with real problems.[99] Hence events in the Holy Land, and the deeds of the military orders, faded out of the chronicles, not to return until the loss of Acre again jolted Europe into concern.

This change would account for the relative increase in popularity of the military orders amongst clerical commentators during the second half of the thirteenth century. There were few hostile comments by chroniclers after the death of Matthew Paris. The most serious critic was the second Bury chronicler, who twice accused the Templars of treachery. He was writing between 1285 and 1296, that is, possibly after the loss of Acre; certainly the inaccuracies in his work indicate that he wrote a long time after the events he describes.[100] The evidence of charters and episcopal registers indicates that, outside the Holy Land and France, where the orders had been established longest, relations were usually peaceful and sometimes very good.

(e) Good relations

There is evidence of good relations between the military orders and the clergy throughout their history.

In the Holy Land, the orders won the praise of some of the clergy who worked alongside them. James of Vitry, an Augustinian canon and bishop of Acre from 1216 to around 1228, while recognizing that the Temple and Hospital had serious faults, such as pride, greed and usurping bishops' rights, believed that they were necessary for the defence of Christendom, and should be encouraged to reform themselves.[101] He praised the Templars' hard work and expense in building Castle Pilgrim, and their courage during the siege of Damietta.[102] He praised the Teutonic order as still free from the faults of pride, wealth and litigation.[103]

Fidenzio of Padua, provincial vicar of the Franciscans in the Holy Land from around 1266 to 1291, had close and friendly relations with the order of the Temple, giving a long and sympathetic account of the loss of the Templars' castle of Saphet in 1266, in which he depicted the executed defenders as martyrs. Nevertheless, he blamed the military orders for contributing towards the general disorder by quarrelling among themselves and refusing to obey the king.[104]

Another friar, the Dominican Burchard of Mount Sion, also deplored the treachery which had led to the loss of Saphet. He was probably refer-ring to the treachery of the Sultan of Egypt, although he may have been repeating the tale recorded by the chronicler of Limoges, that a Syrian brother betrayed the fortress. Burchard visited the Holy Land only briefly, sometime between 1274 and 1284. He blamed the state of the Holy Land on the Palestinian Franks, not the brothers.[105]

Some clerical pilgrims to the Holy Land were greatly impressed by the military orders. The priest John of Würzburg, who visited the Holy Land around 1170, was full of praise for the hospitality and military work of the Hospital, but was less enthusiastic about the Temple, which he suspected of implication in the failure of the second crusade at Damascus.[106] In contrast, the priest Theodoric, who was in the Holy Land around 1172, was full of praise for both orders.[107] An anonymous pilgrim of the late twelfth century, probably a cleric, was particularly impressed by the courage and discipline of the Templars; he also admired the Hospitallers, but had less to say about them.[108]

Clerics who were present during crusades generally received a favourable impression of the military orders. This was the case for Odo of Deuil during the second crusade, and during the fifth for a certain Italian cleric in the entourage of the papal legate and for Oliver Scholasticus. Odo praised the discipline and courage of the Templars;[109] the Italian praised both the Temple and Hospital, but particularly the Temple, whose brothers appear in one vivid scene proclaiming Christ and calling upon St George to come to their help against the blaspheming Muslims who had just broken into the Christian camp. This writer may have been anxious to prove the Templars' integrity, in view of rumours circulating during the crusade against them, the Hospitallers and King John of Jerusalem. His work has not survived, but we can reconstruct it from the work of several other writers who drew on it.[110]

Oliver, as revealed in his *Historia regum Terrae Sanctae* and *Historia Damiatina*, was almost invariably favourable towards the military orders. Although following William of Tyre in his history of the Holy Land, he modified or removed William's attacks on the Templars and Hospitallers. In his history of the fifth crusade, most of which he witnessed himself, he had only praise for the Templars, Hospitallers and Teutonic knights, especially the Templars.[111]

Oliver's work enjoyed a wide circulation. A copy of the *Historia Damiatina* reached the St Albans chronicler, Roger of Wendover, and hence Matthew Paris.[112] It was also used by the annalist of Cologne, by the author of the *Gesta crucigerorum Rhenanorum*, who may have come from Cologne, by the annalist of the abbey of St Rudbert of Salzburg, by the chronicler of St Peter's of Erfurt, and, slightly adapted, by the author of the *Historia Damiatina* attributed to James of Vitry.[113] It must have done much to restore European confidence in the military orders after the failures of the late twelfth and early thirteenth centuries. Although they might be unsuccessful, their integrity, faith and courage were beyond reproach. So favourable was Oliver's work towards the Templars that Matthew Paris apparently thought that a Templar had written it.[114]

Those clergy who were concerned for the defence of the Holy Land also had an interest in the military orders. In a typical donation, in 1261 Bishop Volrad of Halberstadt gave two pieces of land which his sister Margaret had conferred on the cathedral to: 'our beloved brothers in Christ of the knighthood of the Temple, having inspected their constancy of faith, fortified with which they do not fear to oppose themselves manfully day and night against the barbarous nations'. In contrast, a gift to the Teutonic order was given from reverence to the order's patroness, the Blessed Virgin Mary.[115]

In a charter of 1261 Hermann, bishop of Kammin, praised the Templars still more enthusiastically. Quoting from a bull of Alexander IV, he spoke of their self-sacrifice for the defence of the eastern Church and their heavy losses in the field, describing the brothers' deaths as martyrdom. In a charter of 1285 he referred to the brothers' services to him, and their alms to the poor.[116] However, Hermann's principal interest in the Templars was not as defenders of Christendom but as cultivators of uncultivated land, bringing tithes into his coffers. The same motive prompted the friendship and donations of the bishops of Lebus towards the order of the Temple between 1232 and 1244.[117] On the underdeveloped, underpopulated northeastern frontier of the Empire, the economic usefulness of religious orders to the bishops outweighed their inconvenience, at least until the land was settled.[118]

The military orders were also assured of the support of the secular clergy in areas outside the Holy Land where they defended the land against pagan attack, and, in some cases, because they assisted in their conversion. Henry of Livonia, a German priest working in Livonia in the early thirteenth century who became the pastor of the newly-converted Letts, worked alongside the Knights of Christ of Livonia, or Sword-brothers. In his chronicle of Livonia, written between 1225 and 1228, he had much praise for their courage and tenacity, as well as the piety of individual brothers, although he did not condone their mistreatment of the converts, nor their quarrels with the bishop.[119] Bruno, bishop of Olmütz, professed a great affection for the Teutonic order, not only because of its hospitable work but also because of its defence of Christendom.[120]

Although, by the second half of the thirteenth century, there is little evidence of good relations between French bishops and the military orders, some does survive. For instance, the register of Eudes Rigord, archbishop of Rouen 1248—1269, shows him lodging with the Hospitallers or at the Paris Temple, and installing the candidates of both Templars and Hospitallers to their churches, without argument.[121] In the twelfth century relations had often been amicable.

In the Holy Land also, relations could be good even in the difficult conditions of the thirteenth century: the archbishop of Caesarea in the 1230s was friendly towards the orders of St Lazarus and the Temple,[122] while Paul of Segni, a Dominican friar, bishop of Tripoli in the 1270s, was a Templar *confrère*.[123] In 1259 Henry, archbishop of Nazareth, took the order of the Hospital under his protection and came to an agreement with the order whereby the order would protect the Church's property against the Muslims.[124]

The registers of the English bishops indicate that relations here were usually peaceful and sometimes even friendly. Robert Grosseteste, bishop of Lincoln 1235—1253, not only instituted the Templars' and Hospitallers' presentees to their churches without objection, but also gave the order of the Temple the church of Rothley under certain conditions; although Matthew Paris depicted him in lengthy and fruitless dispute with the Templars, Hospitallers and other exempt orders over their privileges.[125] In 1279, Walter Giffard, archbishop of York, gave the Hospital the church of St Felix, referring to the brothers' hospitality, honour and support for the downtrodden poor, and their constant and generous liberality.[126]

The Franciscan John Peckham, archbishop of Canterbury 1278—1293, seems to have held much respect for the order of the Temple. As he was a man of great integrity and personal austerity, this is an interesting reflection on the order's own standards of holiness. He used the order's house in London as a meeting place for councils and synods, while in his work *Defensio Fratrum Mendicantium*, written before he became archbishop, he had set the order of the Temple alongside the order of Grandmont. A century before, Walter Map had considered the latter to be the only pure order still in existence. While admitting that both these orders, as well as canons and friars, had declined from their original high ideals, John Peckham maintained that it was still better to enter one of these orders than to remain a layman, in order to obtain salvation.[127]

The best relations between bishops and military orders by the second half of the thirteenth century are found in Germany. The Teutonic order, naturally, received the most patronage.[128] However, there was little reference to the Holy Land in donations. In 1278 Witego, bishop of

Meissen, gave the Teutonic order the monastery of Zschillen, but specified that any surplus income was *not* to be sent to the Holy Land, Prussia or Livonia.[129]

Friendly relations also existed between the military orders and other religious orders, although records are few as good relations seldom merit record. The connections between the Cistercians and the Templars are well known. These did not cease with the death of St Bernard, as is shown by a letter from Brother Philip of Plessis, master of the Temple, to Arnold I, abbot of Citeaux, in 1202. Philip asked for the Cistercians' prayers, adding that 'since our house took its institution from yours', the Templars were especially bound to help the Cistercians, and the Cistercians should in turn love the Templars.[130] The general chapter of the Friars Preacher in 1243 referred to the Templars as 'devoted friends of the order'. In 1251–2 officials of the Hospital in the Holy Land sent three newsletters to Brother Walter of Saint Martin, Friar Preacher, in England, addressing Walter as a friend of their order.[131]

Friendships also existed between individual houses. For example, around 1180, the canons of Osney and the Templars of Cowley drew up a charter of 'special love' by which each would support the other; this was a result of the friendship which one of the canons, Master Gaut, held for the Temple before he entered Osney.[132] In 1274, the Teutonic brothers took the nuns of Quedlinburg into their confraternity, because of the nuns' friendship towards the brothers and their works of charity; the nuns would receive not only a 'share' in the Teutonic order's masses, vigils, etc., but also in the brothers' loss of blood in the Holy Land, Livonia and Prussia 'for the amplification of the Catholic faith'.[133] In the Mark of Brandenburg, in 1289 the monks of the Cistercian monastery of Lehnin took the Hospitallers of Werben into their fraternity.[134] The orders benefited not only from each others' sanctity but also from their power and influence.[135]

There were also friendly relations between the more radical religious movements and the military orders. In the twelfth century, a few hermits were recorded admiring the spirituality of the orders of the Hospital or Temple; Godric of Finchale preached to the sick in the Hospital during his second visit to Jerusalem, before 1100,[136] while Geoffrey, a hermit near Cirencester, granted his house at Mosehud to the Templars, 'the poor brothers of Solomon'.[137] Again, a few knight-brothers became hermits. In 1288 and 1291, two Beguines gave the Hospital money with which to buy property, while in 1291 another gave some property to the Teutonic order at Marburg.[138]

(f) Chapter summary

Three principal points emerge.

Firstly, in the later thirteenth century the worst relations between the military orders and the rest of the clergy were found in France. This was also the area of least opposition to the arrest of the Templars. In contrast, the English prelates, traditionally more friendly towards the orders, were unenthusiastic about the arrest, especially in the province of York.[139]

Secondly, there was no general condemnation of the military orders from the direction where we might most expect it: from the austere and idealistic friars. Humbert of Romans, John Peckham and Fidenzio of Padua all showed respect and even friendship for one or more of the military orders. Perhaps this was because all religious orders were under attack from the laity for their failings by the end of the thirteenth century; so that they felt it wiser not to attack each other. Yet even Gilbert of Tournai, who did criticize the military orders, had far greater criticism for the bishops and the older religious orders.

Thirdly, the most savage criticism of the military orders came from the regular rather than the secular clergy. The bishops were forced by their office to be pragmatic, realistic and tolerant; monks could afford to be more idealistic and to take a higher moral stance. But there were notable exceptions.

Many of the conflicts between the military orders and the bishops and other religious were common to all religious orders. Many of those who criticized the military orders had even greater criticism for other sections of the Church, as did John of Salisbury, Nigel of Longchamps, Walter Map, Matthew Paris or Gilbert of Tournai. The greatest criticism of their privileges was expressed during the twelfth century, while the greatest criticism of their moral standards appeared during the first half of the thirteenth. After 1250, as the military orders slipped out of the public eye, so did their vices.

Much of the criticism was the result of factors outside the orders' control, or unavoidable if they were to discharge their duties effectively. Their particular function led to their being singled out as the butt of scandalous tales from the Holy Land in some monastic chronicles. Exemption from episcopal authority was essential for their efficient operation; but these exemptions aroused hostility from the bishops and from those clergy opposed to such exemptions on canonical grounds. The fact that they followed an active rather than a contemplative lifestyle and shed blood won them the disdain of a few clergy and lowered their status in the eyes of some others.

Yet, nevertheless, their function was recognized to be essential for Christendom. Although James of Vitry complained that they abused their privileges and grew proud, while the bishops at the councils of 1292 bemoaned the inefficient use of their resources and their quarrels among themselves, the solution was always seen to be reform, not abolition. At the grassroots, in the localities, relations between houses and between brothers and bishop were as often good as they were bad, and perhaps the scandalous stories were not taken particularly seriously. As Walter Map drily remarked

Perhaps many lie when they tell these stories about the lords Templars; let us ask them themselves and believe what we hear. How they behave at Jerusalem I do not know; here with us they live harmlessly enough.[140]

CHAPTER 4

THE VIEWS OF THE LAITY

The evidence for lay opinions of the military orders is fragmentary and scattered. Virtually none of the laity set their opinions of the military orders down in writing in the twelfth century, and relatively few even in the thirteenth. It is therefore difficult to build up a consistent picture of opinions held of the orders, even within groups holding similar interests, such as merchants or the higher nobility.

Most of the lay opinions which survive or which can be deduced belonged to members of the major landholding classes, the nobles and knights. Many of the influences on monarchs' opinions, as discussed in chapter two, also affected their noble and knightly subjects: crusading, dynastic tradition, and knighthood. Again, patterns of patronage in Germany and eastern Europe were different from those elsewhere. However, we must also consider the views of those outside the knightly/noble class, the free and unfree peasantry, and merchants, as far as these can be deduced.

It is impossible to draw a precise division between knightly and non-knightly landholders, so I have considered them together. Again, although some knights might be merchants, I have considered merchants and other towndwellers separately. It is also interesting to examine opinions expressed outside Roman Catholic Christendom, as these were surprisingly similar to opinions held within it.

(a) The lay landholding classes in western and eastern Europe

Some evidence for opinions may be found in nobles' appointments of members of the military orders to positions of responsibility. Brothers were frequently appointed as counsellors and servants, to positions of great power and influence; and friendships often developed between members of the nobility and individual brothers. This would indicate that the brothers were held in very high esteem by the nobility.

At his death in 1219 William Marshal, count of Striguil and Pembroke, had a Templar, Brother Geoffrey, as his almoner, while his biographer commented on the great friendship which existed between Marshal and

Table 1.   Donations to the military orders, 1128—1291

	Sandford	Provins	Beauvoir[a]	Thuringia[b]	Hesse[b]	CGH
1130—39	4	1				29
1140—49	11					44
1150—59	11	1				45
1160—69	10	1				52
1170—79	8	1				69
1180—89	17					68
1190—99	31	4				59
1200—09	18	1		2	1	65
1210—19	26	20	2	7	2	55
1220—29	38	6	13	10	7	53
1230—39	16	14	10	5	10	54
1240—49	20	5	4	12	3	39
1250—59	21	2		12	16	45
1260—69	9	1	2	19	16	52
1270—79	21[c]		2	38	20	34
1280—89				62	20	41
1290—91				7	4	9

[a]   Lalore, ed., 'Chartes de la commanderie de Beauvoir de l'ordre Teutonique', *Collection des Principaux Cartulaires du diocese de Troyes*, 7 vols. (Paris/Troyes, 1875ff.) 3 pp. 177—328. The first donation to the Teutonic order at Beauvoir was made in 1219.
[b]   The earliest charters date from the first decade of the thirteenth century.
[c]   Nineteen of these are very small grants of land by one donor.

the master of the Temple in England, Aimery of St Maur.[1] Thierry of Nusa, prior of the Hospital in England from 1236, was a friend of Richard, earl of Cornwall, and Simon of Montfort, earl of Leicester.[2] In the 1250s Brother Heidenreich, of the Teutonic order, commander of Zwatzen, was a close friend of Dietrich, burgrave of Kirchberg.[3] There are many other examples.

However, the evidence for such relationships is fragmentary, and only concerns the higher nobility. While Georges Duby has contended that between 1180 and 1220/30 the division between lords and knights vanished, so that all nobles were knights and all knights nobles, he also conceded that in France an ancient 'nobility of blood' remained, seen as superior to other knights. This is certainly the impression given by the romances, which stress the difference between the noble knight and the common *vavassor*.[4] Obviously, we should prefer evidence from a wider group. It is also impossible to know why a particular friendship developed; it may have been based on character rather than an individual's membership of a military order.

At the other end of the scale, we can only draw generalized conclusions about the non-knightly classes' views of the military orders. There are indications that, because their privileges were extended to their tenants, the military orders were generally regarded as good landlords.[5] However, there are also records of bitter disputes.[6] Some peasants made donations to the military orders; some unfree peasants even requested that their lord should transfer them to the service of a military order.[7]

One indicator of the orders' popularity at any point in time is the number of donations being made. Table 1 gives a summary of donations to individual military orders in the twelfth and thirteenth centuries, taken from several cartularies: the Sandford cartulary (Temple, England), the Provins cartulary (Temple, France), the Beauvoir cartulary (Teutonic order, France), the Thuringian cartulary (Teutonic order, Germany), the Hesse cartulary (Teutonic order, Germany) and the general cartulary of the Hospitallers, CGH. These cartularies were selected as those covering the longest period, and a broad geographical area, but pose some problems: the cartulary of Provins becomes fragmentary after 1240, while the dating of many charters is uncertain or approximate. The analysis includes only donations, exemptions and privileges given in alms, and excludes papal charters. There are, of course, problems in identifying donations, as discussed in the introduction.

Although these cartularies include donations by monarchs and clergy as well as the laity, this does not materially distort the results as patterns of donation were fairly consistent across society. Donations varied 'vertically' rather than 'horizontally', that is, between high nobility and poor knights rather than between the high nobility and high clergy.

Table 1 suggests that, while donations in England and France fell after 1240 or 1250, donations in Germany continued to rise. This may be confirmed by an analysis of the Hospitallers' cartulary for the thirteenth century, shown in Table 2.

By separating out donations in Germany and eastern Europe, we may see that donations elsewhere were steadily declining from the beginning of the century. There seems to have been a rise during the 1230s, but the general trend continued again after 1240. Michael Gervers noted the same pattern in his analysis of gifts to the Hospital in Essex.[8]

Does this indicate changes in the popularity of the military orders? Michael Gervers suggested a link between the influx of donations during the 1230s and the fact that Jerusalem was in Christian hands from 1229 to 1244: success overseas improved the order's image in Europe. But it is also possible that the influx was the result of an alms-collecting drive by the Hospital to compensate for their loss of revenue in Sicily following the confiscations of the emperor Frederick II.[9] Again, the influx may be more apparent than actual, a distortion due to the uncertain dating of many charters.

Table 2. Analysis of the Hospitallers' cartulary for the thirteenth century

	Germany and Eastern Europe	Elsewhere	Total	% German
1200—09	10	55	65	15
1210—19	14	41	55	25
1220—29	18	35	53	34
1230—39	10	44	54	19
1240—49	17	22	39	23
1250—59	24	21	45	53
1260—69	30	22	52	58
1270—79	18	16	34	53
1280—89	29	12	41	71
1290—91	4	5	9	44

In order to consider this question further, we must consider factors which would have made the military orders attractive to lay donors, and how these changed during our period.

(i) Factors influencing donations. Perhaps the most obvious influence on patronage of the military orders was *crusading*. Throughout our period, noblemen and women gave to the military orders in order to assist their defence of Christendom in the Holy Land.[10]

Some donors gave as a direct result of their experience of the military orders while on crusade. Nigel of Amundeville, a member of a prominent Lincolnshire family, made a donation to the order of St Lazarus in 1242 or 1243 in return for the great honour which the order had done him overseas.[11] Others were moved by the extent of the brothers' military commitments. Leopold IV, duke of Austria, was said to have given at least six thousand silver marks to the Teutonic order on his departure from the fifth crusade in 1219, and fifty gold marks to the Templars to assist in the construction of Castle Pilgrim. Ranulf, earl of Chester, gave the Templars five hundred silver marks for the same purpose. Both had seen the construction work at first hand and realized its value for Christendom.[12]

Yet, although crusading interests accounted for some of the most spectacular donations, at a local level, and in individual houses, few donors expressed crusading motives. This was particularly noted by John Walker in his study of motivation for donations to the order of St Lazarus.[13] Among donors to the Teutonic order's Thuringian commandery, only the noblest of donors considered the order's work in the Holy Land to be worth mentioning.[14] Even the Teutonic order's military activity in Prussia was seldom mentioned by donors to the order.[15] It may be that donors considered its defence and expansion of Christendom in this area too obvious to mention, but it is also likely that the Teutonic order's nationality was more important to donors than its activities.

Again, few German donors to the Hospital mentioned the Holy Land. One exception appeared in 1268, when Conrad I, count of Fribourg, gave a concession to the Hospital because of the Hospitallers' religious way of life and hospitality, and their work to increase the Catholic faith; in honour of God, the Blessed Virgin Mary, St John the Baptist and all the saints; and to help the Holy Land. This is one of the few lay charters indicating that the Hospital's role should include the conversion of non-Christians.[16]

It is difficult to separate interest in crusading from *dynastic influences*, as crusading tended to be a family tradition. Families with a tradition of crusading, such as those of St Omer in Flanders,[17] Beaujeu[18] and Brienne[19] in France, and Mowbray[20] in England, were among the greatest patrons of the military orders.

Dynastic influences are always difficult to prove, but sometimes donors were specific. In 1274 the Vogts of Gera, the brothers Henry and Henry (*sic*) made a donation to the Teutonic order, represented by their 'beloved uncle, Brother Hartmann of Heldrungen' who was then master of the order.[21] In 1265 Sophie, dowager duchess of Brabant, daughter of the Blessed Elizabeth of Thuringia, whose body was in the possession of the Teutonic order at Marburg, gave some tithes to that house, because, she said, it had been propagated by her ancestors and endowed by her uncles.[22] Sometimes family tradition can be deduced as a motive for donation, as patronage continues from one generation to the next.

Ties of lordship could also prompt patronage of a military order. Many servants of kings who patronized the order of the Temple entered this order, such as Thierry Galeran, servant of Louis VII of France.[23] In 1244 Henry III of England made arrangements for the conferral of knighthood on Thomas of Curtun, a young man in his service, although the lad planned to enter the order of the Temple. It might appear strange that the king would go to the considerable expense of knighting a lad only to lose him to a religious order, but perhaps he and Thomas viewed his entrance to the order as admittance to an élite government department, a sort of diplomatic corps.[24] Two masters of the Temple had served the kings of Jerusalem before joining the order: Eudes of St Amand, marshal and then constable of the city of Jerusalem under King Baldwin III, and butler of his successor, Amalric I; and Gerard of Ridefort, who had been royal butler under King Baldwin IV.

Dieter Wojtecki has contended that a major factor prompting *reichministeriales* (knights bound to the imperial family) to patronize the

Teutonic order was the order's connection with the imperial Staufen family.[25] Few donors stated this specifically, but in 1274, Henry Russe, vogt of Plauen, stated that his donation was partly prompted by the patronage of past Holy Roman emperors.[26]

In contrast to the clergy, there were no doubts among lay landholders over the validity of a religious military order. As with monarchs, the orders' *knighthood* was a great attraction for donors, although not in Germany and eastern Europe until the thirteenth century, as discussed in chapter two. The epics of the twelfth century, written for a noble, lay audience, indicate that the spirituality of the lay nobility, although deep, considered itself far removed from the spirituality of traditional monasticism.[27] The differences were immortalized in *Le moniage Guillaume* and *Le moniage Rainouart*, written between 1180 and 1200, in which first the renowned warrior William of Orange, and then his brother-in-law Rainouart, enter monasteries in order to make their peace with God, but make very poor monks. Although both knights and monks in these tales are caricatures, they must reflect the real resentments and fears of their audience.

In contrast, early charters for the order of the Temple indicate that the spirituality of the military orders was very attractive to laymen and women.[28] When one Azalais gave herself and her land to the order of the Temple in 1133 she did so from traditional religious motives, to serve God under obedience to the master of the order, in poverty 'because my Lord deigned to be poor for me'.[29] But Azalais would probably have found the military order more accessible than more traditional religious orders. The depiction of the military orders, particularly the order of the Temple, in the literature of the knightly classes, indicates that the orders were believed to share the interests of the knightly classes to a far greater degree than other religious orders. They fought alongside lay knights in their battles against the Muslims, and were sympathetic to lovers.[30] This image seems to have been based on the fact that although the military orders were religious orders, most of the brothers were laymen, not priests. Indeed, most of the brothers were not even knights, but simple 'sergeants', men-at-arms.

On a more practical level, the military orders had other aspects to recommend them to the poorer knightly classes, who had few prospects of travel or promotion in the world. They were not exclusively noble orders, and most of their members were uneducated, able to read their own language but not Latin. Hence ordinary knights and non-knights could hope to gain admittance more easily than into traditional religious orders. They offered the opportunity of travel; for one clerk this was his express motive for joining the Hospital.[31] The lure of the holy places must have been a particular attraction. Yet travel also offered the certainty of escape from difficult home circumstances; Hugh, count of

Champagne, who joined the order of the Temple in its early days, seems to have been anxious to escape from his wife.[32] This aspect of the military orders' vocation became a recurring theme in romantic poetry and literature.[33]

The majority of the orders' recruits came from the less noble knightly and free peasant families; in Germany, from the *ministeriales*, the knightly class, who were still legally unfree.[34] For such men and women, entrance into a military order would lead to an increase in social standing, and open doors to hitherto unimaginable opportunities.[35] Ubaldesca, a poor farmer's daughter, believed that no religious order would accept her, because her parents could not afford to pay a dowry; admitted to the Hospital of St John at Pisa in 1151, she became an outstanding sister and was canonized soon after her death.[36] Men such as Brother Garin of the Hospital, who rose to be bishop of Senlis under Philip II of France and chancellor of France under Philip's son and grandson, and Hermann of Salza, master of the Teutonic order (1209–1239), advisor and friend to Emperor Frederick II, came from obscure backgrounds to international influence.

But even noble knights sometimes joined a military order from such motives. In 1170, Roger, bishop of Worcester, protested to his cousin Henry II of England that because the latter had given no help to his younger brother, 'an active knight', he had been driven by poverty to join the Hospital of Jerusalem.[37]

The military orders were not only favoured because of their military function. Most of the military orders, with the notable exception of the order of the Temple, had originally been founded as hospitals, and many donations were given primarily *to aid the poor and sick* in the orders' care. In a particularly eloquent charter of 1183, Godfrey III, 'the courageous', duke of Lorraine, praised the Hospital, whose work he had seen during a recent pilgrimage to Jerusalem: 'seeing in it the indescribable anointings of the Holy Spirit, which are poured out and humbly bestowed on the poor and imbecile and infirm'.[38] This was the most obvious motive for donations to the order of St Lazarus, particularly where a family member contracted leprosy. Around the year 1194 Elias of Amundeville, elder brother of the Nigel of Amundeville mentioned above, gave some land at Carlton, Lincolnshire, to the house of St Lazarus, so that the order would admit his daughter, who was suffering from leprosy. But Elias was not the first donor to the order in his family; in 1180, Ralph of Amundeville, his father or grandfather, had provided for the order to support four lepers at Carlton.[39]

Geography appears to have been another important factor in encouraging donations. Many lesser donors in particular appear to have been less interested in the orders' vocation than in their spirituality. Their concern was to find a holy order which they could endow in order to provide a lamp to burn in their name, or to support a chaplain to say mass for their soul.[40] For other donors, their immediate concern was the orders' willingness to provide cash when they needed it, and to provide assurance of security in their old age through membership of the confraternity. Such people would give to the nearest available religious order. Analysing the cartulary of the order of St Lazarus at Burton Lazars, John Walker noted that just over forty percent of the donors whose names are recorded came from an area within four miles of the house, fifty percent from within five miles, and a further twenty percent from between five and ten miles of the house.[41] The military orders had many small houses, scattered across Europe, and were therefore well-placed to benefit from local donations.

As for all religious orders, *economic motives* could also prompt donations. This was particularly important in eastern Europe, where landowners hoped to bring unproductive land under the plough and raise their own revenues by bringing in religious orders who would improve agricultural methods and encourage colonization.[42]

However, donors generally declared that they were giving this land to assist the defence of Christendom in the Holy Land. Before November 1291 Duke Premislaw II of Greater Poland gave the order of the Temple a vast gift of uninhabited land around the lake of Drawiczka in support of the land of Jerusalem.[43] In March 1280, Henry IV of Silesia, in the presence of Rudolf I, king of the Romans, and Hermann of Brunshorn, grand preceptor of the Hospital in Germany and Poland, gave the Hospital the right of patronage of the church of Brieg, in support of the Holy Land, 'for which the aforesaid brothers show themselves incessantly to be a wall of defence and a tower of strength against those blaspheming the Christian name and the orthodox faith'.[44] These words seem anachronistic in 1280, when the order had only Margat remaining of its castles in the Holy Land. Rudolf I, a patron of the Hospital, may have influenced the wording of the charter; the duke may have hoped to flat-ter Brother Hermann of Brunshorn, towards whom he was well-disposed. Perhaps he also hoped to compensate with generous words for the fact that his donation was less generous than those of his ancestors. Or, again, these words may have been suggested by the order, as they were repeated by the dukes Bernard of Silesia and Boleslaw of Oppeln in their charters for the Hospital in 1281 and 1285.[45]

(ii) Changes during the thirteenth century. In most of Europe, all donations to religious orders declined during the course of the thirteenth century. But, comparing the Hospitallers' general cartulary with the local cartularies of Sandford and Essex, it appears that whereas donations from the more noble families, (represented in the Hospitallers' general

cartulary) began to decrease from around 1210, those from lesser landholders, knightly tenants and free peasants (represented in the local cartularies), did not begin to fall until 1250/60.

It is likely that the smaller landowners, anxious to underline and stimulate their rise in social status by charitable donations to the most prestigious causes, continued to give generously even after their lords had ceased giving. But eventually even these donations declined. The obvious cause for this was the various mortmain regulations being introduced by monarchs and local lords in various parts of Europe during the thirteenth century.[46] However, donations were declining even before legislation was introduced, and, in England at least, donations continued after the statute of mortmain of 1279.[47]

In Germany and eastern Europe, the military orders continued to attract generous donations throughout the thirteenth century from all classes; the Teutonic order was particularly popular. It does appear, however, from the evidence collected by Michael Schüpferling, that the Temple acquired the bulk of its property in Germany and eastern Europe before 1250.[48] He did not attempt to assess whether donations from the laity to the Temple in Germany were affected by the dispute between the pope and the emperor Frederick II.

The decline may also have been exacerbated by changes in the factors we identified above as influencing donations.

As among the clergy, interest in the *crusading* in the Holy Land appears to have changed after c.1240—50. Following the crusades of 1239—40 and 1249—54, and the final loss of Jerusalem and defeat at La Forbie in 1244, it is hardly surprising that the laity began to show disillusionment with crusading. Matthew Paris openly declares that this was the case.[49] Elizabeth Siberry has argued that this despondency was considerably less than that following the defeat of the second crusade,[50] but hopes for the second crusade were higher than they were by 1250, and therefore the reaction was greater.

Crusading remained popular, but the crusade to the Holy Land was supplanted by new and less daunting crusade opportunities. As early as the second crusade, would-be crusaders were offered alternative campaigns against the Wends in Slavinia and the Muslims in Spain. But in the second half of the thirteenth century, the papacy put the crusade to Sicily before the crusade to the Holy land: the Church in Italy must be defended before a crusade could be launched overseas, while papal control of Sicily was an essential part of the organization of any crusade. Norman Housley has shown that the Italian crusades sometimes received as much support from potential crusaders as the crusade to the Holy Land.[51] In 1265 the Templar poet Ricaut Bonomel complained that crusaders were going to Lombardy rather than to the Holy Land, with devastating effects on the Christian cause.[52]

The Holy Land still held a tremendous attraction to lay imagination, but although there was no lack of information coming from the east, lay people preferred to hear of the successes of the past, not the losses of the present. William of Tyre's 'Historia' was avidly read in castles and cities across Europe,[53] while the epic crusade cycle was copied and recopied, but nothing was written on current events. Past successes in the Holy Land came to be seen in an almost mythical light, as though the Latin kingdom of Jerusalem was already past history.[54]

Yet, at the same time, the military orders' connection with the Holy Land was of decreasing importance to donors. By 1250 the Teutonic order was well established in Livonia and Prussia, and would-be German crusaders could more easily join the crusade there than travel to the Holy Land. For all the military orders, in most of Europe, their vocation was of less importance than their spirituality. As they became an established part of the religious landscape, donors seem to have viewed them less in the light of events in the Holy Land, and more simply as traditional religious orders. Jean Richard has drawn attention to the will of Dannon, lady of Villy, of 1249, in which she set the Hospitallers and Templars alongside the Cluniacs and Cistercians, stating: 'It is not to the combatants of the Holy Land ... that her legacy is addressed. It is to pious men who practise the rule of the Temple, a rule of Benedictine and Cistercian inspiration, and who are men of prayer'.[55]

There is evidence that *dynastic traditions* of donation became less important among noble families in western Europe during the thirteenth century, just as they had in monarchical families. In a study of the Clare family in England, J. C. Ward noted that the family's flow of monastic endowment was reduced towards the end of the twelfth century, and suggested that the family felt that sufficient land and revenues had been given to monasteries.[56] No doubt many other noble families felt the same. Some families, however, did continue their traditions of patronage of the military orders, such as the counts of Brienne,[57] Forez,[58] Urgel,[59] and the viscounts of Béarn.[60] Although ties of *lordship* continued to be important, vassals would be less enthusiastic donors to an order when their lord was no longer giving. In Germany, dynastic tradition and ties of lordship remained important factors in prompting donations throughout the thirteenth century.[61]

Attitudes to *knighthood* were also changing throughout our period. As discussed in chapter one, by the end of the twelfth century some writers were claiming that knighthood alone was sufficient to win knights salvation, without entering a religious order. But the image of knighthood was also changing. By the second half of the twelfth century, the writers of romances were declaring that knights should avoid senseless violence, and should be ruled by reason and self-control. Evidently this was the self-image of their patrons (or, more often, patronesses). Thus, during the first decades of the thirteenth century, the knight Raoul of Houdenc depicted his hero Meraugis de Portlesguez esteeming character above beauty and defeating his enemies through brain rather than brawn; while one of the continuators of Chrétien of Troyes' *Perceval* declared that a wise knight did not fight voluntarily, but only when he was forced to do so. Around the year 1230, the author of the prose *Tristan* depicted his courageous and intelligent knight Kahedin refusing to fight for the honour of the lady he loved or to win honour for himself: 'if it should happen by some chance that you should throw me dead to the ground at the first blow, what honour will you do me then? And this could very well happen!'[62]

At the same time, the warlike values of the military orders were also coming under fire. By the thirteenth century, lay observers were tempering their admiration for the orders' selfless courage with criticism for the disastrous defeats which resulted. Ernoul, historian of the Holy Land, blamed the disaster of 1 May 1187 on the pride of Gerard of Ridefort, master of the Temple.[63] Guiot of Provins, trouvère turned Cluniac, was of the opinion that the Templars fought too fiercely: 'I would rather be a coward, and alive, than dead and the most admired man in the world'.[64]

This attitude was also expressed in a debate between Adam of Givenci and William the Vinier, probably at Arras, Flanders, early in the thirteenth century. Although the debaters and the judge, Peter of Corbie, were all clerics, the subject matter was secular and the discussion entirely secular in nature, and therefore we shall consider it here. Discussing whether there is more value in the consummation of love or in hope for future consummation, Adam stated the case for consummation:

> ... a man loves for what he will enjoy, not for something that he will never enjoy. You wish to serve like a Templar, for nothing. Hope alone serves to repay your service ...[65]

With one stroke, Adam dismissed the ethic of martyrdom glorified by St Bernard and the *Chanson de Roland*. The Templars fought for the remission of their sins, but Adam declared this worthless.

Flanders was at the centre of the patronage of the military orders and of chivalric ideals. Adam and William were the descendants of those who had supported the first Templars with great enthusiasm. But fashions in chivalric ideals had moved on from the ethic of the military orders. This would have affected donations, as well as prompting criticism.

Donations continued to be given to the hospitaller military orders *to aid the poor and sick*. However, during the thirteenth century, they increasingly suffered in comparison to the new, more virtuous and austere mendicant orders, which many donors saw as more deserving of alms.

Geography continued to be an important factor, more so as poorer donors predominated, whose horizons were limited and who saw no further than the nearest religious house.

Economic motives remained important, but for different reasons, in that in some areas, such as Essex,[66] a shortage of surplus land seems to have contributed to the decline in donations. In eastern Europe after 1250 lay and clerical lords began to pressurize religious orders to surrender the lands which they or their ancestors had given them. Now that their boundaries were secured and the land had been brought under cultivation and was profitable, landholders wished to recover what had been granted away. All religious orders suffered.[67] Nevertheless, some donations were made.[68]

Changing attitudes were also reflected in the growth of criticism.

(iii) Criticism. As crusading was important in encouraging patronage to the military orders, we would expect it to be also a focus for criticism. However, as most criticism was recorded by clerical historians, it incorporates clerical prejudices, and must be used with care. Accounts of the crusades written by crusaders were generally written in the epic tradition, which took a favourable view of the military orders.[69]

An exception is Ernoul's account of events in the Holy Land from 1184 to 1197. During this period, Ernoul was a squire of Balian of Ibelin, one of the leading barons of the Latin kingdom of Jerusalem, and an opponent of King Guy.[70] He therefore wrote from the viewpoint of the Palestinian nobility. Ernoul had a great respect for the courage of the Temple and the Hospital, and regarded the Teutonic order with much sympathy.[71] However, he regarded Gerard of Ridefort, master of the Temple, as being chiefly to blame for the destruction of the Latin kingdom, because of his bad influence on King Guy, his arrogance, and his hatred of Count Raymond of Tripoli. He criticized the Templars and Hospitallers for not giving enough of their wealth to ransom the poor Christians of Jerusalem when Saladin captured the city, and he criticized the Templars for oppressing the Cypriots, causing them to revolt.[72] Like William of Tyre, Ernoul was anxious to show Europeans that the Temple and Hospital, particularly the Temple, had done a great deal of harm to the kingdom of Jerusalem.

Following the defeat of the French crusaders at Gaza in 1239, Philip of Nanteuil, one of those captured by the Muslims, complained bitterly that the military orders had not come to the crusaders' assistance. However, the rest of the crusading host, who had not taken part in the ill-fated expedition, blamed its failure on the rashness and greed of its instigators, and even Matthew Paris eventually conceded that the military orders had tried to rescue the French.[73]

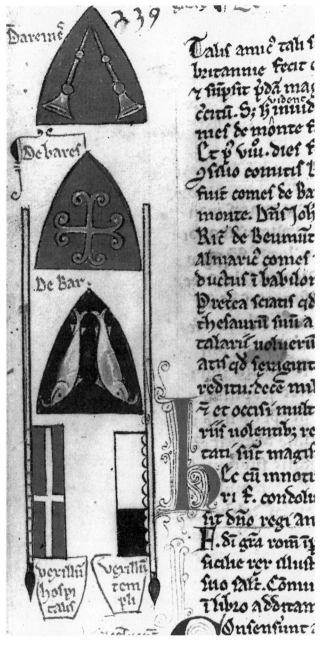

Figure 5. The banners of the Hospital and Temple join those of the nobility thrown down in defeat at Gaza in 1239: from Matthew Paris' *Historia Anglorum*, BM Royal MS 14 C vii f. 130v.

John, lord of Joinville, writing his account of Louis IX's first crusade, had only praise for the military orders' prowess in the field, with the exception of the order of St Lazarus, whose knights were suicidally reckless.[74] But he was intensely irritated by the Templars' bureaucracy (the order mislaid forty pounds which he had deposited) and the arrogance of their treasurer.[75] He is unlikely to have been the only European aggravated by such matters.

There was very little lay criticism expressed of the Teutonic order during the Prussian crusade. However, in the first half of 1258, reports reached the papal court that the brothers had been oppressing the newly-converted Prussians.[76] These complaints probably originated with Duke Kasimir of Cujavia and Lesznc (son of the Duke Conrad who had given the order Culm) and Duke Boleslaw of Krakaw-Sandomir. They had become alarmed at the Teutonic order's rapid expansion into Prussia and were striving to win some territory there for themselves, either through peaceful conversion or through an alternative crusade.[77] Kasimir had opposed his father's donation of Culm to the Teutonic order.[78]

Criticism of a different sort appears in the English Hundred Rolls (begun in 1284—5), which catalogue usurpations of royal rights. They were made up of the depositions of local juries of 'lawful men': preferably knights, but in any case free men. Amidst the juries' countless complaints that laymen and religious orders had damaged royal interests and interfered with local administration, the Templars and Hospitallers, who had small houses scattered across the country, appear again and again.[79] Yet specific and serious criticism of the Templars and Hospitallers alone was extremely rare. Only in two areas were they singled out for their papal privileges, which 'impede and subvert all common justice and excessively oppress the people.' The Hospital and Temple were so criticized at Wirksworth, in Derbyshire, and the Hospital at 'Routhinton', Warwickshire.[80]

During the *Quo Warranto* investigations which followed, from 1278—94, the juries supported the military orders' claims more often than they denied them. In Sussex, where the orders had been abusing their privileges, the juries did not hesitate to say so,[81] but elsewhere they often secured the orders' acquittal.[82] This suggests that, despite widespread resentment against the orders' privileges, they were not bitterly hated.

Much of the nobility's criticism of the military orders does not survive in such direct statements, but rather in the work of the trouvères and troubadours whom the nobility patronized. It is tempting to see these professional political protesters as expressing the views of a broad band of the population. In fact, they probably expressed only the views of their patron, seeking to mould the opinions of others. Moreover, it is very difficult to determine how widely their songs circulated, as they were circulated orally.[83] Yet, despite all these problems, these poets provide a rare insight into lay attitudes towards the military orders.

The work of some trouvères and troubadours was favourable towards the orders: depicting them as energetic champions of Christ, in contrast to the pleasure-loving, idle and cowardly rulers of Europe, who failed to go to their assistance. Before the second crusade, the troubadour Marcabru made this contrast in his poem 'Pax in nomine Domini,' urging the lords and young knights of the Languedoc to go and help the marquis of Provence and the Templars fight for God in Spain against the Muslims.[84] This poem survives in seven manuscripts, a large number for this type of work. In 1221 the Auvergne poet Peirol made similar complaints, while returning from the fifth crusade. He commended the Hospital, Temple and King John of Jerusalem to God, and criticized the present kings of England, France and Spain, the marquis of Montferrat and the emperor for failing to follow their forebears' example in crusading. Peirol was a poor knight in the service of the dauphin of Auvergne (ruled 1169–1234), who was a generous patron of troubadours; hence he was probably expressing the dauphin's opinions. The poem survives in only two manuscripts.[85] Again, in 1277 the Parisian trouvère Rutebuef concluded a poem bewailing the state of the Holy Land by lamenting to William of Beaujeu, then master of the Temple, that modern knights had no interest in serving God and winning Paradise like the heroes of the first crusade. Elsewhere in the poem he urged the barons to help God, Acre and the Temple.[86] Depicting the master of the Temple as being chiefly responsible for the safety of the Holy Land, Rutebuef made no mention of the other military orders. Unfortunately, it is unclear on whose behalf he was writing: he had a number of patrons, but the patron of this poem is unknown, and it survives in only two manuscripts.

Some criticism was primarily political. Writing in response to the Treaty of Paris, 1229, between Louis IX of France and Raymond VII, count of Toulouse, Bernard Sicart of Marvejols lamented the state of the Languedoc, subjected to the French, and criticized the Templars and Hospitallers and clergy for their part in the humiliation. He declared that he disapproved of the Temple and Hospital because of their pride, arrogance, simony, and great possessions; no one was admitted unless he was rich or had a great inheritance. Their rule consisted of ruses and treachery.[87] These were standard complaints against religious orders. But Bernard's underlying grievance against the military orders was that they had not protected their patrons in the Languedoc against the crusaders, although they had received generous donations there since their foundation. Although Bernard's poem survives in only one manuscript, his anger must have been widespread among patrons of the orders who suffered in the Albigensian crusade.

There was little criticism from professional troubadours of the orders' handling of the defence of the Holy Land. *Circa* 1270, in a poem recounting a debate with God over the state of the Holy Land, the troubadour Daspol depicted himself asking God why the Saracens could not be converted instead of killing so many Christians. God replies that the orders of the Temple and Hospital now did evil instead of good, and were full of pride and avarice. Daspol seems to mean that, if the orders were discharging their duty, the Saracens would not be able to kill Christians; but it is unclear whether the brothers should be killing or converting the Saracens. Possibly Daspol thought they should be doing both.[88]

Only one other poet criticized the Temple and Hospital for not attacking the Muslims, Rostanh Berenguier; and this was not until the early fourteenth century, probably after the arrest of the Templars.[89]

In contrast, Hugh, lord of Berzé, who had seen the orders at work in the Holy Land, declared circa 1220 in his 'Bible', that nothing could be said against the orders of the Temple and Hospital if only they could agree between themselves and work together, 'for they give up their bodies in martyrdom and defend the sweet land where the Lord died and lived'. However, he went on to add that their privilege of giving asylum to criminals had led to many murderers escaping justice. He went on to examine other religious orders and concluded that, despite their grave faults, it is possible to win salvation in a religious house, for the world is even more perverted. His work won some popularity, as five copies survive.[90]

Hugh criticized the brothers not as poor soldiers but as poor monks. His work is one example among many criticizing the Church and clergy composed during the thirteenth century, by both laymen and clergymen in minor orders, most of which do not mention the military orders at all. Where they were criticized, they were criticized as severely as the rest; but many writers seem to have regarded the military orders as the least important of the regular orders, even as peripheral. The exception is Jacquemart Giélée's *Renart le Nouvel*, and this probably reflects the interests of his patron.

Peire Cardenal (1180–1278) was one of the handful of moral critics who mentioned the Templars and Hospitallers. He came from a noble knightly family, and began his education training to be a canon, before taking up a career as a troubadour. Eighty-five *sirventes* (moral or political songs) are attributed to him, but only one of these mentions the military orders: 'Mon chanter vueil retraire', written after 1222. This criticized the whole of society, condemning the clergy for setting a bad example. He singled out specific orders for specific faults, such as pride in the Templars and Hospitallers. This was a stereotyped criticism of these orders, and does not indicate that the poet had any personal feeling against them. It is not known whether this poem was intended for a specific patron, but it enjoyed a wide circulation, as it survives in seven manuscripts.[91]

Two satirical poets also mentioned the military orders. The satire 'Sur les états du monde', written in England in the first half of the thirteenth century, mentions the Templars and Hospitallers briefly at the end of a long tirade against the clergy. The Templars are doughty men, but love money too much; the Hospitallers love their horses too much. 'They have no care for buying women's services, as long as they have their horses . . .'[92] Their horses were also remarked on by another English poet in the early fourteenth century.[93] 'Sur les états du monde' was not a well-known piece, surviving only in a single, incomplete manuscript. An interpolation into Raoul of Houdenc's Songe d'enfer introduces the Hospitallers and Templars among the sinners being devoured at the devils' feast: roasted, alongside false hermits. This interpolation only survives in one manuscript, while the original poem survives in nine.[94]

The most interesting, and possibly the most influential, of the moral critics was Jacquemart Giélée, a Flemish trouvère writing in Lille in 1289.[95] His satirical poem, Renart le nouvel (based on the popular satires of Renart the fox) survives in four manuscripts, all copied in the late thirteenth and early fourteenth centuries. The oldest and most beautiful of these was copied for Guy of Dampierre, count of Flanders, who was related to the master of the Temple, William of Beaujeu.[96] The poem was probably written for Guy, and therefore its remarks on the Templars and Hospitallers are particularly significant. For, although the poem only enjoyed a brief period of popularity, this was during the period covering the loss of Acre and the years before the arrest of the Templars, during which the orders' image was particularly vulnerable. Moreover, the poem was circulating among the nobility of northeastern France and Flanders, the heartland of support for the military orders.[97]

Giélée recounts the triumph of Renart, the epitome of everything dishonourable, over society. The clergy are soon corrupted, but the friars have to call on Renart's help in order to reach the heights of Great Pride. He refuses to become their master, but gives them his sons.[98]

The hermits remain untouched, for their purity of life makes them totally unattractive to Renart. However, the fame of Renart's name reaches Acre, where the Templars and Hospitallers take it up. As both orders are determined to have Renart, they bring a case against each other to the papal court, where Renart agrees to be master of both orders, an honour he had refused the friars.[99] The poem ends with Renart seated on the summit of the wheel of Fortune, with Pride at his right and Guile at his left, clad in the habit of the Templars and Hospitallers.[100]

Giélée appears to assume that until recently the orders of the Temple and Hospital, guardians of the Holy Land, surpassed all others in godliness, representing the last bastion of all that was good in the Church and in the world. This image was echoed in the last decade of the thirteenth century by the schoolmaster of Bamberg, Hugh of Trimberg, when he bemoaned the decline of the 'high order of the Temple'.[101] The subversion of the friars was unimportant in comparison to that of the military orders, which was why Renart gave the friars his sons, keeping himself for the military orders. Their capture by Renart marked the final triumph of evil in the world. This was presumably also the view of Giélée's patron and audience.

Giélée's description of the dispute between the Templars and Hospitallers over Renart is also very illuminating, offering a snapshot of his patron's image of the military orders in 1289. The difference between the two orders is striking. The Templar is not a trained speaker, his argument is simple and unskilfully delivered, repeating again and again: 'we are defenders of the Holy Church', and emphasizing the danger to Europe from the Muslims, which presumably the order had been emphasizing for many years. The Hospitaller is a wise man and a good speaker, and his argument is carefully structured. He not only stresses the service of his order for Christendom, in fighting the Muslims and saving sick pilgrims, but also attacks the Templars, saying that his order has existed longer than theirs, that his brothers do more harm to the Muslims than do the Templars, and blaming the Templars for the Christians' failure in the east, because they are envious of the Hospitallers and are in league with the Muslims. Renart, however, sees each order as being as corrupt as the other, for he is unable to choose between them.

Giélée indicates that the order of the Temple was at a disadvantage in relation to the Hospital in the war of words in Europe.[102] The Hospitaller exploits his order's double role and justifies its policies actively, and aggressively. The Templar can only blame European lords for persecuting his order and declares that, if his order does not receive help, it will have to leave the Holy Land. The brothers had obviously made this threat too many times in the past.[103] This contrast throws some light on the French Templars' inability to defend themselves effectively during the trial of the order.

Moreover, Giélée's description of the quarrels between the Templars and Hospitallers underlines the impact these quarrels made on their lay patrons. Hugh, lord of Berzé, and Richard, earl of Cornwall, had criticized them for their disagreements, as did Matthew Paris, and some later blamed the constant quarrelling for the loss of Acre.[104] Giélée suggests that the Templars' and Hospitallers' traditional patrons were somewhat disillusioned by 1289.

We began by asking how far fluctuations in noble and knightly donations to the military orders were due to changes in the orders' image. Although in western Europe all donations to religious orders were declining during the thirteenth century, attitudes which had previously encouraged donations towards the orders were changing during this period, and some criticism appeared. These factors must have contributed to the fall in donations. In Germany and eastern Europe, however, donations remained at a high level. This may have been related to the fact that the concept of the military order did not become popular here until the beginning of the thirteenth century, and retained a certain novelty when it had become too familiar elsewhere. The relative proximity of the crusade in Prussia and Livonia may also have meant that the orders' vocation seemed more immediate in Germany than elsewhere, although donors seldom mentioned Prussia or Livonia, and often did not mention the Holy Land.

(b) Other groups

(i) Merchant classes. As the merchant and burgess classes grew in wealth and influence, so their donations to religious orders also grew, underlining their rise in status. Despite the knightly basis of the military orders, some merchants also admired their spirituality, giving them donations in alms. As with donations from the knightly classes, few donors mentioned the Holy Land.[105] At Metz the order of the Temple had a thriving confraternity.[106]

The military orders could also be attractive to some from the merchant classes who wished to join a religious order. Dieter Wojtecki has shown that some members of the burger and patrician families of Thuringia joined the Teutonic order, although it was a smaller proportion than from other sections of society; ten brothers from the one hundred and five fully identified in the Thuringian *bailie* (10 per cent) and four from the sixty-eight sent from Thuringia to Prussia or Livonia (6 per cent).[107]

As with the lay landholding classes, relations between the military orders and the merchant classes were often influenced by economic interests. The notorious alliances made during the thirteenth century between the Venetians, Pisans, and Genoese and the individual military orders in the Holy Land[108] arose from the respective parties' power and influence and their mutual self-interest rather than respect for each other's spirituality. In such dealings the orders of the Hospital and Temple and the Teutonic order were regarded by their allies more as international financial and military corporations than as devoted men of God, the 'poor knights of Christ', which the Templars still claimed to be. There were similar motives behind the friendship of the citizens of Riga with the Swordbrothers of Livonia, in the 1220s and 1230s; a friendship which lasted only as long as they shared a mutual enemy.[109]

The three great military orders, especially the order of the Temple, were particularly important to merchants as safe depositories for valuables. They used all religious orders for this purpose, but the international military orders had the advantage that as they were continually sending cash overseas they could also arrange for the transfer of funds. This was a role increasingly shared with the Italian bankers, but relations between the two groups seem to have been amicable.[110] The importance of the London Temple as a safe depository was demonstrated in 1263 when the Lord Edward's theft of monies deposited there caused a riot of the citizens.[111]

Just as the orders came in conflict with the nobility over their privileges and land rights, they came into conflict with the merchant classes over their privileges and trading rights. Generous donations to the orders earlier in their history resulted in bitter conflicts during the course of the thirteenth century, exacerbated by the orders' ruthless exploitation of their privileges in order to meet their ever-increasing need for cash. In about 1270, the citizens of Provins complained to Thibaud, count of Champagne, that the Templars were charging toll for the weighing of wool, so that the abbeys which had traditionally supplied the townsmen with wool were taking it elsewhere.[112] A few years later, during the Hundred Roll enquiries in England, the burghers of Plumton and Dartsmouth in Devon complained of the Hospitallers' exemption from toll, which they claimed was 'in prejudice of the lord king', but which also damaged their own trade.[113] There was also great resentment among the burghers of Totnes and Grimsby at the privileges of the Hospitallers and Templars respectively, which enabled them to have the burghers summoned to answer cases in courts at the other end of the country, at immense expense and inconvenience to the burghers.[114]

Other evidence is sparse. It has been claimed that the *fabliaux*, humorous, sometimes scurrilous old French poems, offer an insight into the interests and concerns of the merchant classes and peasantry. In fact, as has recently been shown, they were written for the high nobility and recited in seigneurial courts, although they were also recited in burghers' houses, public places and in the houses of well-off villeins.[115] They appealed to all classes, and, like all literature of this period, followed certain conventions, so that they are not strictly realistic. However, it is striking that the military orders only make one, completely respectable, appearance in these tales. In Bernier's version of *La Housse Parti* (dated to the second half of the thirteenth century), the Temple is cited as the order into which a knight is most likely to retire in his old age.[116] In contrast, the Franciscans appear in two *fabliaux*, both times in a dubious role, while the parish priest appears regularly, usually as a would-be seducer, and married.[117]

(ii) Heretics. The Cathar and Waldensian heretics opposed the principle of a military order, believing that Christians should not use force against their enemies, nor to encourage non-Christians to convert. James of Vitry indicates that by *c.*1220 their arguments were having a considerable demoralizing effect upon the knight-brothers.[118]

There are no recorded instances, however, of antagonism between the military orders and the heretics. During the Albigensian crusade, the orders of the Hospital and Temple did not take up arms against the heretics, although representatives of the orders appeared on the side of the Church during the war, and the Temple occasionally lodged crusaders.[119] Both orders were regarded by the inquisitors as fully orthodox,[120] but, in the Treaty of Paris of 1229, they were regarded as neutral.[121]

(iii) Non-Catholic Christians, Jews, Muslims and pagans. The attitudes of these groups towards the military orders are particularly interesting because, although they were unaffected by many of the prejudices which influenced the attitudes of the brothers' co-religionists, they often concurred with their opinions.

There was some admiration for the military orders. Benjamin of Tudela, a Spanish Jew who visited Jerusalem *c.*1170, made particular mention of the Hospital and Temple, which greatly impressed him.[122] In the late twelfth century, Michael the Syrian, Jacobite Patriarch of Antioch from 1166 to 1199, praised the discipline and self-sacrifice of the Temple and Hospital, their charity to the poor, and their hospitality. He mentioned their military function, protection for pilgrims and the defence of the Holy Land against the Muslims, but also noted their tolerance of all Christians, whatever their creed. He was not, however, aware that there were two orders, thinking them one and the same. The thirteenth-century Armenian translator of his work realized that a difference existed, but apparently believed that the Hospital fought the Muslims and practised hospitality, while the Temple existed purely to acquire land; perhaps a reflection on the poor relations between the Temple and King Leo of Armenia, and the order's long struggle to recover the castle of Baghras.[123]

Michael's successor as Jacobite chronicler, Gregory Abû'l-Faraj, known as Bar Hebraeus, and his continuator regarded the military orders, both Templars and Hospitallers, as recklessly brave and brilliant warriors, but treacherous and too fond of gold.[124] His observations are strikingly similar to those of European writers. They are also endorsed by the Russian Orthodox chronicler of Novgorod, describing the Teutonic order; the brothers were skilled warriors, but treacherous, 'the accursed transgressors of right'.[125] Nevertheless, alliance with the Teutonic order offered tempting possibilities to a ruler wishing to consolidate his position and extend his power; in 1254 Prince Daniel made an alliance with the intention of winning some territory from the pagan Prussians, while the pagan Mindaugas of Lithuania used the brothers' influence to establish himself firmly as king of the Lithuanians, then broke his alliance with them.[126]

The Muslims were of the same general opinion. The military orders were terrible enemies, who should be given no quarter. Treachery against them was pardonable, for they themselves were treacherous. Their annihilation was a cause for great rejoicing. 'Imâd ad-Dîn al-Isfahânî, secretary of Saladin, regarded the military orders as the backbone of the Christian forces. Every rhetorical celebration which he wrote over the defeat of the Christians included a reference to the Templars and Hospitallers. 'What evils he cures in harming a Templar!'[127] The brothers were intractable enemies, the Templars 'demons', the Hospitallers cunning and deadly: even when the Muslims thought they had them cornered in their castle of Belvoir (Kaukab), the Hospitallers sallied out by night and murdered them in their beds.[128] Saladin always executed any Templars or Hospitallers whom he captured, he recorded.[129] This was standard practice among Muslim generals.[130] Abou 'L-Feda, who was born at Damascus in 1273 and was an eyewitness of some of the events he recorded, rejoiced over the capture of Margat, in 1285: 'In this memorable day were revenged the evils caused by the house of the Hospitallers, and the brightness of day replaced the shadows'. He happily admitted that in 1266 Sultan Beibars had massacred the Templar garrison of Saphet after they had surrendered on the understanding that their lives would be spared.[131]

Nevertheless, friendly relations did exist between the military orders and certain Muslim princes, although Muslim chroniclers, like their Christian counterparts, deplored any friendship with the enemy faith.[132]

(c) Chapter summary

Some images of the military orders were obviously not simply the result of prejudice, for they were held universally, by all who encountered them. The military orders were admired by Christians and non-Christians alike for their great courage in battle, and zeal for their faith, although by the mid thirteenth century in the more sophisticated circles of western Europe they were regarded as foolishly idealistic. The other face of their great courage, however, was their pride, the root of the intransigence which 'Imâd ad-Dîn both admired and feared. Both friend and foe agreed that the brothers could not always be trusted, an indication that they put the interests and policies of their order before fidelity to Christian or non-Christian allies. An unquestioning loyalty to their order was a common fault among members of religious orders.

The military orders were also included in the general complaints by the laity of spiritual decline in the Church in general and religious orders in particular. Just as the clergy distrusted them as knights, so the laity distrusted them as monks; their dual character brought dual criticism. Some moralists, such as Jacquemart Giélée and Hugh of Trimberg, singled out the failings of the military orders because they had formerly (they believed) been the best of all orders. But most writers overlooked them. The orders' privileges in land and trade were also criticized by noblemen and merchants, but they were far from being the only religious orders to be criticized on these grounds.

Surprisingly few of the laity criticized the orders for failing in their particular vocation: the defence of pilgrims and the Holy Land. The criticism from the disgruntled French crusaders was due more to disagreements within the crusader army than to the orders' failings, although it was no less damaging for that. In lay sources, it was more common for Europeans to be criticized for failing to assist the military orders in the Holy Land than for the military orders to take sole blame.

The most striking aspect of lay criticism of the military orders before 1291 is how little there was; and even this little was mostly confined to France, where the orders and their privileges were most entrenched. Taken in the context of criticism of the Church as a whole, it pales into insignificance.[133] Yet Jacquemart Giélée expressed a serious doubt. As God's warriors, fighting for the triumph of good over evil, the military orders should be faultless; and they clearly were not.

CHAPTER 5

THE REPRESENTATION OF THE MILITARY ORDERS IN LITERARY SOURCES AND LEGEND

We shall now turn from conventional historical analysis to consider the depiction of the military orders in twelfth and thirteenth century works of fiction. These include the vernacular epics and romances written for lay audiences, and the legends developed around the orders by the chroniclers, who wrote for the clergy and educated laity. These differ from the satires and political protests discussed in chapter four in their factual basis. Satires and political protests reflected and mocked contemporary reality, although in an exaggerated form. The material under discussion in this chapter reflected the world of the imagination. Epics and romances were usually set far back in history and were largely fiction, while the legends were based on recent events, but were exaggerated and adapted by chroniclers to suit their literary purpose.

It is unclear how far even contemporaries distinguished between literary fact and fiction. It has been argued that some audiences thought that anything in prose was true, especially if it was Latin prose.[1] Yet it is not clear that this was always the case.[2] Even if, as Jeanette Beer has argued, sophisticated audiences were aware of different literary conventions and could tell fact from fiction,[3] most audiences were far from being sophisticated.

The military orders were given different stereotyped images in different types of literature. In the legends, the Templars and Hospitallers were usually portrayed as greedy, jealous and treacherous, impeding the Christian cause for their own ends; although they were partially redeemed by their courage in battle, and even some renegades were shown as men of conscience and integrity. The brothers were depicted as being 'out of the ordinary' through their close connection with the magical, mystical Muslim world, whether as victims or victors. However, only rarely were they seen as being spiritually outstanding.

The writers of epics and romances also had little concern for the spiritual aspect of the military orders' vocation. They saw them as knights of Christ, men of great courage, integrity and piety; but the piety was taken for granted, never emphasized. The Templars in particular were seen as 'out of the ordinary', but what set them apart from other orders was their special association with lovers.

Many listening to these tales would have been familiar with both types of stereotype, and presumably found each perfectly acceptable within its context.

The greedy, jealous image bestowed on the orders by the chroniclers sprang from the nature of the genre. Histories tended to be pessimistic and moralizing, and any anecdotes more likely to criticize than to praise. The military orders were a natural subject for moralizing anecdotes, since their decline in reputation could be seen to epitomize the decline in society. Clerical criticism of the military orders has been discussed above; most chroniclers were clerics, and they expressed their criticisms of the military orders in the legends they developed.

Romances and epics also claimed to record historical events, but their primary purpose was entertainment, and their perspective was more optimistic than chronicle history, portraying even villains in the best possible light. In addition, they reflected the prejudices of their knightly audiences, regarding the military orders as allies of the laity, and distrusting the mainstream clergy.

I shall now examine the orders' images in these two types of writing in more detail.

(a) Legends and unlikely tales in chronicles

Most of these illustrated the accusations thrown at the military orders, especially by the clergy: that they were proud, greedy, treacherous and jealous, and that their vices undermined the Christian cause in the Holy Land. The chroniclers always restricted their scandal-mongering to these familiar accusations.

The most frequent accusation was of greed, which usually appeared in the form of the legend of the enchanted gold. This tells how a greedy fool was cheated out of his possessions by magicians, who paid him in base metal that had been enchanted to look like gold.[4] The story was first recorded in connection with events in the Holy Land by Gerhoh of Reichersberg (around 1160–2) and Michael the Syrian (before 1199). Both had heard that when the second crusade was besieging the Muslim city of Damascus in 1148, the Palestinian Franks had received gold from the defenders in return for raising the siege, but that this gold later turned out to be only copper.[5] Although some chroniclers accused the Templars of taking a bribe in order to raise the siege, they were not at this stage accused of taking enchanted gold.[6]

Roger, parson of Howden, Yorkshire, was the first to transfer the legend to the Templars, at the end of the twelfth century. He told it in connection with the siege of Harenc, in 1177.[7] Between 1209 and 1222, Otto of St Blasien, describing the German crusade of 1197–8, applied the legend to the Templars at the siege of Tibnin, in 1197.[8] Around 1210, Gervase, a monk of Canterbury, was retelling it in the context of the siege of Damascus in 1148, with the Templars replacing the Palestinian Franks as the guilty dupes.[9]

Obviously the story provided a useful explanation as to why mighty expeditions to the Holy Land failed to achieve anything. It was only applied specifically to the Templars after the order's image in Europe had become badly tarnished. The brothers had been heavily criticized at the third Lateran council, in 1179, for their abuses of their privileges; they had failed to prevent the loss of Jerusalem to Saladin in 1187, and had failed to win the city back; and their reputation was severely attacked in the work of William of Tyre, which was already known in England by 1192.[10]

After the fifth crusade the Hospitallers joined the Templars in the role of guilty dupes. Both appear in a version of the story set at the siege of Damascus of 1148, included in the 'abridged Ernoul' written up to 1227.[11] The inclusion of the Hospitallers appears long overdue; the order had been thoroughly militarized for around sixty years[12] and shared the Templars' responsibilities and failings in the defence and advancement of Christendom. The Hospitallers' military role had been made known throughout Europe in 1187, when the Hospital was mentioned in Pope Urban III's encyclical informing the prelates of the Church of the Christians' defeat by Saladin on 1 May 1187.[13] But the Hospitallers had not become prominent in crusaders' accounts until the fifth crusade (1217–1221). Their reputation had come under attack during this crusade, since, with the Templars and King John of Jerusalem, they were accused of some now unknown deed of treachery.[14] This made them suitable subjects for this legend.

After this the legend did not appear in any new chronicle until Albert Milioli, notary of Reggio, wrote his chronicle of the emperors, between 1281 and 1286. He told it of the Templars, Hospitallers and King Baldwin III of Jerusalem, again in the context of the siege of Damascus.[15] Obviously the legend had now become fixed around the siege of Damascus, which limited its usefulness for chroniclers. It went unnoticed by a number of chroniclers who might have been expected to repeat it, such as Roger of Wendover, Matthew Paris and Alberic of les Trois-Fontaines. Possibly such fanciful legends had become unfashionable. In any case, by the second half of the thirteenth century the military orders were no longer a favourite focus for legends.

Two other legends of greed, this time of the Templars alone, originated with William of Tyre. William used these tales to show that the order loved money more than winning the Muslims for Christ. The first told how Nasr ed-Din, a party to the murder of Caliph El-Dafer of Egypt in 1154, was captured by the Templars while fleeing Egypt, converted to Christianity but was nevertheless sold back to the Egyptians, who put him to death.[16] Abou 'L-Feda's history indicates that Nasr was not converted to Christianity during his captivity; had he been, the authorities in Cairo would certainly have publicized the fact when he was executed.[17] Walter Map, however, developed William's tale into a miniature epic, a version of the popular tale of the Muslim who wished to become a Christian and who embraced the faith as soon as he was captured by the Christians. What dishonour for the Templars, for having sold him to his enemies! Steadfast in the face of torture, he received a martyr's death.[18] Yet there was another version of events in circulation, in which the Templars were God's instruments of justice against the treacherous regicide Nasr, and their booty God's reward to them.[19]

In contrast, William is the only source for his second tale, which recounted how in 1173 the Templars thwarted the conversion of the Assassins, a Shi'ite sect which was a thorn in the side of local Christian and Muslim princes. They did this in order to safeguard the tribute they received from the Assassins.[20] The various chroniclers who repeated the tale followed William's judgement on the order,[21] with the exception of James of Vitry, bishop of Acre, who carefully refrained from stating that the murderer of the Assassins' envoy was a Templar.[22] Presumably he did not believe that the order was guilty.

Less damaging to the Templars' image was the story of John Gale, the Templars and Saladin's nephew. This was based firmly in fact: some time before 1179 a renegade Christian knight had engineered the capture of one of Saladin's nephews by the Templars of Saphet.[23] When first noted by Robert of Torigny, before 1186, the order's role epitomized its steadfastness in the face of adversity and fidelity to its rule: the master of the order, Eudes of St Amand, was shown refusing to be released in exchange for Saladin's nephew.[24] In a later version, perhaps in Ernoul's original chronicle written before 1197, the tale was told in full, with a distinctly pro-Muslim flavour: the renegade, John Gale, first betrayed his Christian lord and his faith and then his Muslim lord (Saladin) and his trust. The Templars were depicted as powerful and influential, but played a rather dubious role in capturing a helpless child. Saladin became the heartbroken uncle, desperate to obtain the release of his sister's son. The Templars' gains, far from being their just reward for prowess, look distinctly ill-gotten.[25]

The final version, included in the 'abridged Ernoul', was probably toned down for European tastes, as it was more favourable to the Templars. In assisting John Gale to betray and capture the young man who had assisted him during his exile, the order was merely shown as ruthless and greedy for gain, rather than downright heartless.[26]

With the accusations of greed went accusations of envy and treachery.[27] One legendary account of the orders' envy and its harmful effects appears in Matthew Paris' *Chronica Majora* and, half a century later and with variations in detail, in Bartholomew of Neocastro's *Historia Sicula*.[28] The Templars and Hospitallers appear as papal agents, plotting to bring about the death of Emperor Frederick II by exploiting their close contacts with the Muslims. Matthew rewrote his account three times, decided to erase it because it was offensive to the Templars, and finally admitted that it could not be true, because 'it is not credible that such wickedness should come from religious men'.[29] Nevertheless it was an excellent story, and fine propaganda against the pope.

The brothers' alleged treachery was also reflected in tales of renegades. In the real world, all the military orders experienced problems with brothers who left their order and fled to the Muslims, and in the orders' statutes this was a crime by which a brother would be expelled from the house forever.[30] In addition, a number of Christian laymen deserted to the Muslims.

However, the great majority of renegades known in Europe were Templars. There is no reason to doubt William of Tyre's tale of the Armenian prince Melier, erstwhile Templar;[31] but Roger of Howden's tale of Brother Robert of St Albans reads like a fairy tale. In return for a promise to win Jerusalem for Saladin, the hero is promised the Sultan's heiress and all his kingdom![32] Matthew Paris reported that the Christians lost Damietta (captured during the fifth crusade) through a Templar renegade, Brother Ferrand, 'strenuous in arms and well-considered in counsel'. He had deserted because a good horse was taken from him.[33] The chronicle written for Bernard the treasurer at Corbie Abbey has an account of a Spanish knight, a Templar renegade who had retained his Christian faith, who so impressed Coradin, sultan of Damascus, by his good service that he was made regent and guardian of the sultan's three sons on the sultan's death. This is apparently the 'Martin' referred to by Alberic of Trois Fontaines; Alberic calls him a Hospitaller, but his own evidence suggests that he was a Templar.[34]

Even as traitors, these Templars were depicted as men to be admired. Melier was a redoubtable warrior, while Brothers Robert, Ferrand and Martin were said to be wise counsellors who were honoured and influential among the Muslims. In fact, they were depicted as being more effective than any of the Muslims. By a curious irony, the men who should have been the best of Christ's knights became, in the chroniclers' imagination, the only men able to overcome the Christians.

Moving still further into the realms of fantasy, Ralph of Coggeshall, who was fond of unlikely tales of the supernatural, told a story of some mysterious visitors to the abbey of Coggeshall who were mistaken for

Templars and welcomed enthusiastically, but then vanished without trace. This event occurred sometime in the late twelfth century, and indicates that Templars were still welcome at Cistercian houses by this period, despite local disputes![35] Yet, although the military orders might be associated with the supernatural, they were not associated with spiritual matters, except indirectly in tales of miracles of the Blessed Virgin Mary, where the grateful knight joins a military order. In one tale of this type, Walter Map's tale of Aimery, the knight joined the order of the Temple: in another, told by Stephen of Bourbon about 1230, he joined the order of the Hospital.[36]

Such tales are not far from the folktales told of the Templars. Early in this century, the Abbé Guillotin de Corson recorded two from Brittany, one of which depicted the Templars as fearless knights of the highest reputation, who were more than they seemed; while the other saw them as malignant otherworldly spirits carrying off young ladies. Unfortunately such folktales are undateable, but probably date from long after the order's destruction.[37]

The Abbé did not, however, find any folktales of the Hospital. Before the fifth crusade, it seems, no legends were developed around the Hospital; and even after it, very few. The order of the Hospital was criticized alongside the order of the Temple for its privileges, and it was equally as oriental as the Temple, but these two factors alone were not enough to inspire legends. The deciding factor appears to have been its militarization; only as it became perceived in Europe as a fully military order did legends begin to be told about it. Yet, it still escaped the excitement and scandal of tales such as those of Brothers Robert of St Albans and Ferrand. Either its brothers did not involve themselves in matters which made good stories, or, more likely, chroniclers could not conceive that they would. The order remained partly hospitaller: charitable, respectable and a poor subject for scandalous stories.

Only one renegade was attributed to the Hospital, Brother Martin, and even he was probably a Templar in reality. Perhaps Alberic of Trois-Fontaines made an error; but at least he, unlike every other chronicler, was prepared to record that the Hospital, as well as the Temple, suffered from renegade brothers. By 1240, when Alberic was writing, the Hospital was thoroughly associated with the Temple; both were accused of treachery during the fifth crusade, both had suffered at the hands of the emperor Frederick II and had been in conflict with him, both were accused of treachery in connection with the French crusaders' defeat at Gaza in 1239, both were included in the legend of the enchanted gold. It was therefore conceivable that the Hospital also had renegade brothers. Yet this image never developed to the same extent as that of the Temple; perhaps because, after 1250, few writers still saw the military orders as suitable subjects for legends.

The Hospital did not even obtain legendary status for its hospitaller function. Only one story was told in this connection, and this was principally concerned with Saladin, a favourite subject for legends. According to the so-called 'Ministrel of Rheims', writing in 1260, Saladin stayed at the Hospital in Acre in disguise, in order to discover for himself whether the tales of the Hospital's great charity were true. So impressed was he that he made a large donation to the order on his return to his own country, and he and his mother were buried at Acre. A great lamp, the story says, hung over the tombs, paid for by the Hospitallers, in thanks for the great gifts that Saladin and his mother gave them.[38]

Another story associated the order with a sultan of Egypt, at the time of Louis IX's first crusade. Following Louis' release from captivity, a number of Christian captives were also released, among them the master of the Hospital, William of Châteauneuf. The annals of Winchester state that the master knighted the sultan of Egypt. This may have been popular belief, as an earlier legend stated that the Christian nobleman Humfrey of Toron, lord of Crac of Montreal in the kingdom of Jerusalem, had knighted the young Saladin.[39]

Chroniclers told no legends of the other military orders: the Teutonic order, the orders of St Lazarus or St Thomas or other small orders. None of these orders was much in the public eye in Europe, or caught public notice to the same degree as the Temple or Hospital. To be the subject of legends and anecdotes, an order had to capture the imagination of writers and to have a distinct image developed around it, which allowed it to be fitted into familiar legends. However, while chroniclers preferred to exploit a tarnished image which allowed them to scandalize their readers and to moralize on declining standards in society, the writers of epic and romance retained the military orders' original image as virtuous knights of Christ almost undamaged throughout the twelfth and thirteenth centuries.

(b) The military orders in epic and romance

Literary tradition assigned to the military orders a number of roles, which developed with time. Firstly, they appeared as monks, fulfilling the traditional roles of monks: providing a place of penance for wrongdoers, and a place of retirement from the world, either at the end of one's life, as a thankoffering to God, or for a man grieving at a personal loss. They also performed various charitable duties, such as guiding pilgrims, giving lodging, and burying the dead. Secondly, they appeared as knights of Christ, usually fighting at the hero's side against the enemies of Christendom, but in Wolfram von Eschenbach's Parzival preventing the impure hero from approaching the holy place, the Grâl (Grail) Castle. As a corollary of their role as knights they appeared as counsellors of kings and of the hero. However, although their spiritual virtues were always taken for granted as prerequisite for these roles, they were never stressed to the extent of making the military orders the spiritual guides of the Christian knight. The assistance which they gave the hero was worldly and physical rather than spiritual.

The earliest reference to a military order in an epic or romance appears in the epic *Raoul de Cambrai*, written between 1175 and 1200. This was a popular tale, to judge from the number of references to it in other twelfth and thirteenth century texts. The story is set in the ninth century AD, and describes the career of Bernier, squire of Raoul de Cambrai. After Raoul has burned down the convent where Bernier's mother was a nun, killing all the inmates, Bernier pursues and kills Raoul. Threatened with death by Raoul's uncle, Bernier offers to sail to Acre and serve with the Templars there in penance. The offer is rejected.[40]

The order appears in a similar role in *Orson de Beauvais*, written between 1180 and 1185, or early in the thirteenth century. This work was not well known, although it probably remained popular at Beauvais beyond the thirteenth century; a fifteenth-century prose romance refers to it. It was also known in Lorraine, where the only surviving manuscript was copied at the end of the thirteenth century. It is set in the eighth century, in the reign of either Charles Martel or Charlemagne. Here the Templars appear in a false account given by Hugh, count of Berri, of the fate of his companion, Orson, whom Hugh has in fact sold to the Muslims. Hugh claims that Orson, on pilgrimage to Jerusalem, confessed to him that he had planned to assassinate King Charles, and then entered the order of the Temple. The bishop of Beauvais in the 1180s was an enthusiastic crusader, which may account for the poet's interest in the real Jerusalem and the order of the Temple during a period when few works of fiction mentioned either.[41]

The same order appears in the same role in the immensely popular epics *La chevalerie d'Ogier de Danemarche* and *Renaut de Montauban*. Both are set in the eighth century, in the reign of Charlemagne. *Ogier* was written around the end of the twelfth century. *Renaut* also dates from the twelfth century, but it is unclear at which stage in the development of the story the Templars were introduced. In the oldest surviving manuscript, copied out in the mid thirteenth century, it is the Holy Sepulchre, not the Temple, which is cited as a place of penance. It is probable that the order of the Temple was introduced later in place of the Holy Sepulchre by a redactor who knew that it was right and proper for a noble knight accused of murder to offer to go overseas and serve at the Temple, as occurred in *Raoul* and *Ogier*. In *Ogier*, in fact, both the Hospital and Temple are mentioned at this point, the first mention of the order of the Hospital in epic literature.[42]

The same theme appeared again in *La fille du comte de Ponthieu*, a popular tale which linked the descent of Saladin with the counts of Ponthieu, in northern France. Here it is again the Temple which is to be the place of penance, and the hero is guilty of the murder of his own daughter; who is in fact alive, and fated to become the great-grandmother of Saladin.[43] This dates events to the late eleventh century, before the order of the Temple existed. It is unclear when this tale was written, but probably nearer 1250 than 1200, as it is in prose rather than verse.

However, in Jean Renart's *Roman de la Rose* or *Guillaume de Dole,* written around 1228 for the bishop of Beauvais, the theme was slightly altered. Here the crime was not murder, but a seneschal's attempts to block the path of true love.[44] There is no evidence that the work was known outside the court of the bishop of Beauvais, as only one manuscript survives, and it is not mentioned in other contemporary works. Yet it is interesting that Jean Renart saw the Temple, previously used by poets as a place of correction for murderers, as a suitable place of correction for men who had flouted the rules of love. This connection between the Temple and lovers was also emphasized by other writers, as we shall see below.

Three works written by Jean Renart survive, of which two, *L'Escoufle* and *Roman de la Rose,* mention the Templars. *L'Escoufle* was written between 1200 and 1202, and dedicated to Baldwin, count of Flanders and Hainaut, who had recently taken the cross, and who became Latin emperor of Constantinople in 1204. Like Jean Renart's later work, *L'Escoufle* survives in only one manuscript, and was apparently unknown outside the court of the poet's patron. Nevertheless its depiction of the military orders is important, because it reflects the literary image portrayed in other, better known works. The Temple appears as a place of retirement from the world, and the Templars as knights of Christ fighting the Muslims: both images reflecting the order's role in the real world.

In *L'Escoufle,* as the hero's father lies dying his doctors suggest that he join the Temple: 'for it would be a great shame if such a doughty man should die in his bed like a beast'.[45] The same theme appears in the biography of William Marshal, earl of Pembroke, written in the 1220s and based on fact, but adapted to the conventions of romance. The Marshal, however, had bequeathed his body to the Templars many years before his death in 1219.[46] The Marshal's biography was more widely read than *L'Escoufle,* at least by the English nobility: in the early fourteenth century the earl of Warwick owned a copy.[47] In the third French version of *Bueve de Hantone* (written after 1220), the hero's father-in-law enters the order of the Temple in his old age specifically to do penance for his sins. Bueve of Hampton was a popular hero, but this particular version of his career survives in only three manuscripts and three fragments.[48]

Various parts of the Crusade Cycle also depict knights entering the Temple as a place of retirement, for various motives. At the end of some manuscripts of the *Chanson de Jérusalem,* it is announced that Harpin of Bourges is to retire into the newly-formed order of the Temple 'to

serve'; no other motive is given.[49] In the third part of *Les Chétifs*, the
Christian Baldwin and Muslim Corbaran undertake to serve at the
Temple for a year as a thankoffering if they are preserved from their
present peril; the implication is that these are two of the first
Templars.[50] In the *Jérusalem continuations* of the late thirteenth or early
fourteenth centuries, Harpin of Bourges is shown as having entered the
order of the Temple, not simply in retirement but following the death of
his wife.[51] This last had by that time become a familiar theme: entrance
into a military order as a result of personal loss.

This theme first appeared in fiction in the work of the poet Gontier
de Soignies, writing in the early thirteenth century, before 1227/8.
Lamenting his failure in love, he declares that, in order to escape his
love-pangs and to avoid hearing love mentioned, he will leave society,
go overseas for God's sake and join the order of the Temple.[52]
However, the theme had already appeared in works of history: in the
'abridged Ernoul', and in the Genoese *Regni Iherosolymitani Brevis Historia*,
written at the beginning of the thirteenth century. According to these
sources, Gerard of Ridefort, master of the Temple 1185—1189, had
originally joined the order as a direct result of his failure to win the hand
of the heiress of Botron. However, a fuller version of Ernoul's chronicle
states that Gerard joined as a result of serious illness; presumably retirement in fear of death, as in the examples quoted above.[53]

The theme recurred in the immensely popular thirteenth-century poem
La Chastelaine de Vergi, written before 1288. This story ends with all but
one of the major characters dead of grief or violence; the lone survivor,
the duke, enters the order of the Temple, or, as in two manuscripts, the
order of the Hospital.[54] This is the only occasion where the Hospital
appears in this romantic role. The familiarity of the theme is underlined
in the romance *Sone de Nausay* (written during the second half of the thirteenth century). Here a noble young lady, Ydain, is informed by her
nurse, Sabine, that because she has refused Sone's love, he will go
overseas and give himself to the Temple, as if this were an act expected
from disappointed young lovers, tantamount to killing himself.[55]

The connection between the order of the Temple and love is most
marked in *Sone*, where the Templar master of Ireland, Margon, appears
as a lovers' go-between, arranging a meeting between his queen and the
fugitive Sone, and later bringing their child to Sone in Norway, where
he acts as the baby's godfather.[56]

Probably the military orders' knighthood prompted writers to link
them with romantic love. Possibly the Templars, as knights of the
Temple of Solomon, became linked in literary tradition with King
Solomon's reputation as a great lover, but there is no direct evidence for
such a connection.[57]

The Templars also appeared in other monastic roles, performing their charitable and hospitable duties. Their charitable function first appeared in literature after the fifth crusade, around 1225, in the French versions of the romance of Bueve of Hampton. In the second French version, a Templar guides a pilgrim to the land of 'Hermine', (Armenia) to find King Bueve: in the third French version, Templars greet the fugitive Bueve and direct him to Jerusalem, where he offers in the Temple of Solomon his warhorse and armour, in return for a pilgrim's garb. The patriarch gives him a meal, a mule and a hundred shillings (five pounds), while the Templars give him twenty pounds.[58] Again, in *La fille du comte de Ponthieu*, the Templars of Brindisi lend money to the destitute count and his entourage,[59] while in *Sone* the Templars of Ireland take in the fugitive Sone, his Norwegian sweetheart Odee, and his horse Morel, then assure their guests' safe escape from the country without the knowledge of the amorous queen.[60] In the Arthurian romance *Le roman de Laurin*, written in the 1250s or 1260s, the count of Provence lodges at a house of the Temple near the castle at St Outin.[61]

Burying the dead was an important act of charity, and one which the military orders performed in real life. In literature the role was only assigned to the Templars. Again, it first appeared after the fifth crusade, around 1225, in the third French version of *Bueve de Hantone*.[62] Here the brothers bury the hero's uncle, killed in battle by the Muslims. However, later instances were linked with love. The fictional *vida* (biography) of the twelfth-century troubadour Jaufré Rudel was written shortly before 1250. This tells how Jaufré takes the cross and crosses the sea in order to set eyes on the countess of Tripoli, whom he has loved without ever seeing her. Becoming ill on the voyage, he has one glimpse of her beauty before expiring in her arms. Heartbroken, she has him buried in the house of the Temple at Tripoli and becomes a nun.[63] Here the order becomes the eternal resting place for a lover, rather than a place of escape for his lifetime.

The most interesting appearance of the Templars in this role was in the Arthurian romance *Claris et Laris*. This may be dated from evidence in its introduction to the period 1261–1268; probably before 1263, as it refers to the Tatars as a threat to the Holy Land, but not the sultan of Egypt.[64] The poem survives in only one manuscript, and may not have been intended for a wide audience; its humour suggests that the author was writing only for his immediate circle of friends. His concern for the Holy Land and the war against pagans in eastern Europe, his sense of humour and his realism may all have been factors prompting him to place the Templars in the role of hosts and undertakers for wandering knights, a role usually assigned in Arthurian romance to hermits.

The Templars appear in connection with the adventures of the *Lai Hardi*, the bold, ugly knight, who has undertaken to avenge a young lady whose lover has been murdered. The Templars bury the dead man and lodge the *Lai Hardi* and the lady. After her lover has been avenged, the lady returns to his grave and falls dead. 'The Templars laid her in the grave alongside her lover and then wrote letters which explained her death; they were of fine enamelled gold'.[65]

This author was obviously familiar with the tradition linking the Templars with the tragedy of romantic love; this made them more suitable for this particular role than hermits, who were only interested in love for God. Significantly, the burial of this knight is the only aspect of the hermit's literary role which the author assigns to the Templars. Hermits also appeared in Arthurian romance as the spiritual advisers of wandering knights, a role which we might expect would naturally belong to the military orders, but which they never play. Even in *Parzival*, where the *Templeise* appear as chaste guardians of the Grail, they do not act as spiritual guides to knights seeking spiritual fulfilment; they act only on a worldly level.

The Templars first appear in a military role alongside Richard of Montvilliers in *L'Escoufle*.[66] They reappear, this time with the Hospitallers, in Gautier de Tournai's *Gille de Chyn*, written in the 1230s. This work, surviving in only one manuscript, was apparently commissioned by the monks of St Ghislain, Hainaut, to publicize the career of their noble patron, whose body lay buried in the abbey church. It is not known when Gilles de Chyn was in the Holy Land, but it was certainly before the militarization of the Hospital.[67]

One of the Templars' most striking appearances in this role was in the Anglo-Norman poem *Du bon William Longespee*, written probably at the request of William's family to commemorate his death at the battle of Mansourah in 1250. The master of the Temple is depicted as fighting with great skill and courage, wreaking much havoc on the Muslims before he himself is slain and his soul carried at once to God. The soul of a Templar who is slain assisting him is said to have been carried off by St Michael to Paradise, while another Templar, Brother Richard or Wymound of Ascalon, an English brother, is one of five companions who die fighting at William's side. The poet has high praise for Brother Richard, who is depicted encouraging William in the name of God and His Mother, and swearing never to desert him while he is alive; only after William's death does he finally fall, over his companion's body.[68] This poem enjoyed some success among the English nobility, as Guy, earl of Warwick, possessed a copy in the early fourteenth century.[69]

The Hospital makes no appearance in this poem, but both orders appear in *Esclarmonde*, written between 1250 and 1300. They are depicted as fighting valiantly, but, when the Muslims have been put to flight, the Templars pursue the hero, Hugh, who is chasing the fugitives, and forbid him to follow them any further. Although no criticism is expressed, the situation is reminiscent of events during the crusade of 1239, when the military orders were criticized by some French crusaders for hindering them from winning prestige in deeds of prowess against the Muslims.[70] *Esclarmonde* shows a departure from literary tradition and a recognition of contemporary reality. However, this is the only French epic or romantic work of our period in which this aspect of the orders' image appears.

We should also consider three German works which depicted the military orders in a military role, although one of these may belong to the fifteenth century. The earliest of the three is Ulrich von Etzenbach's *Wilhelm von Wenden*, based on the legend of St William of Parrit: the hero, a Muslim prince, wishes to become a Christian and sets off for Jerusalem to seek baptism, accompanied by his faithful wife. After arriving in Jerusalem and receiving baptism he joins the Christian army in fighting the Muslims, with the Teutonic knights, Hospitallers and Templars. Wilhelm is described alongside the Templars, wishing to share their prize of salvation. This is the only occasion in epic or romance where the Templars are held up as Christian knights whose example is to be emulated. However, they are presented as a model to the converted Muslim, representing all Christendom, rather than an example to the Christian knight who is seeking to advance in the spiritual life.[71]

Ulrich von Etzenbach was for a long period court poet of King Wenceslas II of Bohemia. He wrote this poem between 1287 and 1297. Although it survives in only two manuscripts, his work would have reached a considerable audience within the court alone. The kings of Bohemia in the second half of the thirteenth century were much involved in the crusade in Prussia, hence the appeal of a poem about the crusade against the Muslims in the Holy land. Yet, as the Hospitallers and Teutonic knights were more esteemed in Bohemia than the Templars, it is interesting that Ulrich singled out the Templars as the epitome of Christian knighthood for Wilhelm's emulation. Clearly, literary convention could be more important than a patron's personal preference.[72]

The long version of *Wolfdietrich*, written between 1280 and 1300, gives more prominence to the Teutonic order than any other epic or romance written before 1300. Arriving at Acre, the hero is met by the master of the Teutonic house, who greets him warmly. On hearing that the house has been under Muslim attack, Wolfdietrich declares that he will ride out and destroy the Muslim army with the assistance of forty of the brothers; this he does. At the end of his life, in retirement in the monastery of St George at Tischâl, he again rides out to repel a Muslim force, this time assisted by 'five hundred lords of the Temple', apparently a joking reference to his own monks.[73]

Wolfdietrich was a popular tale, surviving in four different versions. This was the last version to be composed, and survives in ten manuscripts. It indicates that, even when the Teutonic order became established in German literary tradition, the Templars retained a niche as outstanding knights of Christ. It is possible that this was due to the work of Wolfram von Eschenbach as much as to the actual reputation of the order in Germany.

The date of the last of these German works is disputed. *Orendal* has been dated to before 1170, after 1196, and 'the late middle ages'. Only one manuscript of the verse romance survives, dated to 1477, but two printed versions also exist, one in prose. The simplistic style, language and plot suggest that it dates from before 1170, but this date is incompatible with the appearance of the Templars, who were not well enough known in Germany by this date to be included in romances. Friedrich Wilhelm Wentzlaff-Eggebert dated *Orendal* to after 1196. He was of the opinion that it began as a genuine crusader romance, but was rewritten in the late middle ages into its present disjointed form.[74] The Templars appear as the loyal servants of Bride, queen of Jerusalem. They are noble men but lack spiritual awareness, ignoring the hero on his first arrival at the Holy Sepulchre, and refusing to accompany him against the Muslims on the grounds that they will not follow a captain who is not wearing armour. However, when Bride rides into the fray they hasten to assist her, and accept Orendal as their king as soon as they realize his identity, setting him honourably on the throne.[75] Again they appear in connection with a love affair, and again their role is secular rather than spiritual, but more so than in previous works. It is impossible to say whether the Templars appeared in the earlier version of the poem in the same dubious role that they play in the fifteenth-century version. It would be strange if they did, as all other German romances written before 1307 are favourable towards the order.[76]

Alongside their role as knights of Christ, the military orders perform an advisory role. This is usually in the Holy Land, but, in *Sone*, the Templar Margon acts as chief minister to Sone and is left in a position of authority when Sone is summoned to become emperor. Margon had previously been the trusted advisor of the queen of Ireland.[77] The Hospital and Temple also appear in positions of authority in the Holy Land, acting to choose a new king.[78] They perform a similar role in the first and third French versions of *Bueve de Hantone*.[79] Similarly, in *L'Escoufle*, the Templars appear with the patriarch and barons as part of the king's council.[80] Again, this role is realistic, but only in *Sone* does the orders' role approach the importance it held in reality.

Finally, we must consider the military orders' role in the Grail legend.

When Sone of Nausay sails away to Rome to be crowned emperor, he leaves behind him to rule Norway Margon the Templar and the abbot of the Grail castle, who has the care of Sone's heir. Perhaps the writer of *Sone* was familiar with the Templars as guardians of the Grail castle in Wolfram von Eschenbach's *Parzival*.[81]

Wolfram wrote for Hermann, landgrave of Thuringia, in the early thirteenth century, before 1210. He introduced *Templeise*, or Templars, into his romance of the Grail as guardians of the 'temple' where the Grail was kept.[82] These *Templeise* are not the same as the brothers of the military order, although they have some superficial similarities: they serve in penance for their sins, protect the holy domains, and remain chaste. But they do not live under a monastic rule, and may marry if they are sent away from the holy place to rule other lands. Their badge is a turtle dove, the symbol of chastity, not a cross. Although they are guardians of holiness and are allowed to gaze upon holy things barred from ordinary sinners, they do not act as spiritual advisers or guides to those seeking holiness; as usual in romances, this role is taken by a hermit. The Templars also appear in the so-called *Titurel* fragments, which recount events before those in *Parzival*: here their role is the same as in *Parzival*.[83]

Wolfram was probably influenced in his choice of Templars to guard his castle by the great interest which he and his patron had in the mysterious east, and his own sympathetic interest in the Muslims.[84] There is no evidence in his poem that he, a poor German knight, possessed any secret knowledge about the order of the Temple, which at that time still held very little property in Germany, and most of whose members were French; Wolfram's French was not fluent. Although Wolfram claims a Provençal source, 'Kyot', such claims were literary convention, just as Wolfram's contemporary Manessier claimed to have found the Latin text of his Graal story at Salisbury.[85]

Wolfram's selection of the name 'Templar' for the guardians of his *Grâl* only reveals that he believed the real order of the Temple to be a holy, dedicated, chaste order of knights; otherwise he would have gone to greater pains to distinguish his *Templeise* from the real order.

Wolfram's work had a beneficial influence on the literary image of the order of the Temple in other German romances. For instance, at the end of the thirteenth century, the author of *Reinfrid von Braunschweig* remarked apropos a turtle dove offered as a prize at a tournament: 'I think that this had come from the Grail, where, on many occasions, in battles and expeditions, the Templars were seen bearing the chaste turtle dove', and goes on to add that only the chaste could serve at the Grail.[86] As Wolfram's work enjoyed great popularity among German speakers, it is possible that it was instrumental in encouraging patronage towards the order of the Temple in the thirteenth century; but this can only be speculation.

Although the Templars do not appear in other Grail romances, there are some connections between the 'perfect knight' who wins the Grail, and the Templars and/or the military orders in general. Scholars have noted the parallel between the red cross on a white field which is borne

Figure 6. A fresco from the Templars' church of San Bevignate, Perugia: the Muslims (left) and Templars (right) join battle. Note the bearded figure of the Templar on the right, bearing the order's distinctive arms. (Phot. Francesco Tommasi.)

by Galaad in *La Queste del Saint Graal*, the thirty-three holy men clothed in white with a red cross on the breast, who meet Perlesvaus at the castle of the four horns in *Perlesvaus*, and the red cross on white which was borne by the Templars. However, this device was also borne by other military orders and confraternities, while the Hospitallers bore the same colours in reverse, a white cross on a red field.[87] Likewise, the flag of St George is a red cross on a white field. Thus the fact that a knight bears this symbol in a romance need not imply a connection with the Templars, but simply that he is a knight of Christ, the white symbolizing purity, the red martyrdom.

The *Queste del Saint Graal* does make a possible connection between the order of the Temple and the perfect knight by stating that Solomon knew of the coming of the perfect knight and prepared for it.[88] This suggests that the Templars, knights of Solomon's temple, were not perfect knights; Galaad, the knight to come, is the fulfilment and completion of knighthood. In this case, the new knighthood of the *Queste* would surpass and replace the old knighthood of the Templars: the new knighthood is based on a personal relationship between the knight and his God, without need for an order, and the perfect knight does not kill his enemies but spares them to repent.[89] Perhaps the author of the *Queste* considered that the military orders had failed to reform knighthood, and was setting up a new ideal to replace them: although it was an ideal which excluded all but those of the highest birth.[90]

The following points may be drawn from this survey.

Firstly, the orders' literary image. The problems which we face in analysing these texts, lack of information on authors, patrons and circulation of individual works, should not prevent us from drawing obvious conclusions. The image of the orders is consistent across all the texts we have discussed. Unlike that painted in the chroniclers' legends, this image was unextraordinary, often unexciting, and depicted the military orders in roles which they performed in reality, although standardized and romanticized, especially in *Parzival*. The knight-brothers took a supporting role, assisting the hero in his battles, giving him food and shelter, advising him, providing a suitable place of retirement. This role was usually minor: only in *Sone de Nausay* was it crucial. Spiritual guidance, where it was needed, was always in the hands of hermits. Although the military orders were considered fit places for penance or for retirement, they were never held up as an ideal of knighthood for Christian knights to copy.

The emphasis in the epics and romances is very much on the Christian knight making his own peace with God, without the intervention of a monastic order. Where a knightly hero joins a monastic order in order to make his peace with God, he meets numerous difficulties, and it is made clear that the knight was more pleasing to God as a knight than as a monk.[91] Patrons of romances obviously preferred the individual way of obedience, particularly the way of the hermit;[92] failing this, a knight could make his peace with God through living a godly life in the world.[93] Although the military order appears in literature as a suitable place to do penance, and a few knights are depicted entering a military order towards the end of their lives, their subsequent careers in the order are never a matter of interest, unlike those who become hermits. This is hardly surprising. It was only natural that knights, never renowned for their discipline or ability to work together, should prefer to hear of knights winning salvation by an individual path rather than in an order. Again, it was only natural that they should prefer to exalt knights who sacrificed everything for the love of a woman, the likes of Lancelot, Tristan and Palamedés, rather than knights who sacrificed everything, including their independence and freedom of action, for the far less tangible love of God.

Secondly, the military orders did not begin to appear in literary works until the last quarter of the twelfth century: *Raoul de Cambrai* was written after 1175. One possible reason for this is that the majority of fictional works were set in some dim and distant past, whereas the military orders were known to be recent foundations. Admittedly, the average knightly audience, like its modern counterpart, had only a vague idea of historical perspective. Yet individuals were unlikely to accept that the military orders had existed from time out of mind while they themselves could remember a time before they were founded. It is significant that such tales began to appear at the same time as the legends of the orders' ancient histories were becoming established; epic and legend reinforced each other.

Thirdly, and most importantly, of the three major military orders, it is the Templars who predominate in epics and romances, not only in French but also in German works. Of a total of twenty-eight works examined above, only nine mention the Hospital, and two the Teutonic order. This is the same kind of pattern that we found in examining chroniclers' legends and anecdotes.

Why was this? In the case of legends, it could be argued that more tales were told against the Templars because the Templars were more unpopular than other military orders: however, the evidence examined so far in this book has shown that this was not the case. What is more, not all the legends were wholly derogatory: many, such as the tales of renegades, indicated admiration for the order. On the other hand, there is no evidence that the order of the Temple appeared more often in epic and romance than other military orders because it was *more* popular. This was clearly not the case in Germany, for instance, where the Teutonic order was the most popular of the three major military orders; yet, in

German romances, the Temple usually received more attention than the Teutonic order.

The order of the Temple had obviously captured the imagination of chroniclers and poets alike to a far greater extent than the other military orders. This may have been partly because the order of the Temple was the first military order, but also because it was the only international military order which had not developed from being a hospital. Other military orders shared its exotic location, in the Holy Land, and its religious aura; but only the order of the Temple, with its wholly military vocation, could be regarded as untouched by the pious, respectable and colourless hand of conventional monasticism. Humbert de Romans stated that the Templars were particularly associated with knighthood,[94] and the evidence we have examined in this chapter depicts the order as consisting entirely of knights and their squires, men who were adventurous, amenable to love, a little scandalous. Such an image would have made it uniquely suited to play a role in legends, epics and romance. Although the order was known to be religious, this was overshadowed by its knighthood: the brothers were holy knights, rather than knightly monks. Thus, for example, although the Church was notoriously hostile to lovers, the Templars, as knights, could be expected to be friendly towards them.

If the military aspect of an order encouraged the development of legends around it, then we would expect the order of the Hospital to have acquired legends as it became progressively militarized and its military role was more and more in the public eye. This was indeed the case: from around 1220 the order appeared in the legend of the enchanted gold, Matthew Paris' tale of the assassination attempt on Frederick II, and a number of other legends, while its first appearance in epic came in the last decade of the twelfth century. However, there were never as many legends developed around it as there were around the Temple. Instead, after 1250 fewer legends were recorded of the military orders, and the orders made fewer appearances in literature: thirteen of the twenty-seven works in which they appeared before 1300 were written in the first half of the thirteenth century, but only nine in the second half of the century.

(c) Changes in literature after c.1250

By 1250, the heyday of the verse romance and epic was over. Old epics were still being read and copied, notably the Crusade Cycle, but few were being written.[95] Verse romances still enjoyed some popularity, and even the most eminent of patrons commissioned them; but the new works seem to have enjoyed a very limited circulation compared to older poems, surviving only in single manuscripts. When in 1312 Guy of Beauchamp, earl of Warwick, gave a part of his library to the abbey of Bordesley, virtually all the non-devotional texts were epics or verse romances: obviously his family had collected these avidly in the past, but now no longer wished to house them.[96]

The fashion was now for prose romances, which had first appeared in the early thirteenth century. Patrons seem to have seen them as 'truer' than verse. They were a completely different literary form, developing a highly formalized fantasy world of chivalry which was much further from contemporary realities than either epics or verse romances. Most of the appearances of the military orders in literature were in the more 'realistic' works; it is therefore not surprising that the writers of prose romances found no place for them. What is more, the concept of knighthood exalted in the most popular prose romances was quite different from that represented by the military orders. In the romances, audience attention was focused on the knight who served his lady faithfully, rather than the knight who served God: even where, as in *La Queste del Saint Graal*, the latter was shown to be superior to the former. Furthermore, in the extremely popular prose romance *Tristan*, written circa 1230, even the Christ-like Galaad, chaste and dedicated to God, was declared to be a knight inferior to the lover Tristan, dedicated to his mistress.[97] Whether or not knights accepted this spiritual standard, they certainly enjoyed reading about it.[98]

Yet the military orders themselves were also less suited to a role in romance and legend by 1250. Although their literary image was self-perpetuating, and largely independent from reality, scandalous or exciting tales about the orders would have less appeal when the orders themselves were no longer scandalous or exciting. They had become an established part of the *status quo* in Europe, far from their image of extraordinary, holy knights. Moreover, the crusaders' defeat at Mansourah in 1250 seems to have weakened the brothers' negative image in the chroniclers' legends. According to the account of the battle reported to Matthew Paris, the count of Artois had goaded the Templars and Hospitallers with the accusation that the Holy Land would have been won long ago if the military orders had not prevented it. The brothers had hotly denied this, and, to prove their integrity, had ridden into battle alongside the count. As they had predicted, the Christians were routed, and only two Templars, one Hospitaller and one villein escaped.[99] This had been a battle in the military orders' legendary style, against hopeless odds, fought for the glory of God. It was a terrible defeat, but something of a propaganda coup: very few derogatory legends were recorded after this date.

The disappearance of the military orders from epic and romance, as well as from the chronicles, was not, therefore, a result of their declining reputation. If this had been so, they would simply have appeared in increasingly dubious roles, betraying Christendom in epics and romances, and worse in the chronicles. Instead, they ceased to be attractive subjects for the imagination, and so were increasingly ignored by writers. Where their duties in government, for example, could prove useful to the plot, their role was as great as before, or more so, as in the case of the Templars in *Sone de Nausay*. When they did appear, there was little sign of a declining reputation.

(d) Fictional image and everyday image: the question of influence

We know too little of the writers, patrons and circulation of the works discussed to draw firm conclusions about the influence which the orders' image in these works would have had on their everyday image. Most of the works in which the military orders receive the best and most thorough treatment had only a small circulation, if the number of manuscripts surviving is a reliable guide to popularity: *L'Escoufle*, *Claris et Laris*, and *Sone de Nausay* survive only in single manuscripts. Others were better known: *Bueve de Hantone III* survives in three manuscripts and three fragments, while *Raoul de Cambrai*, *Ogier le Danois*, *Renaus de Montauban* and *La chastelaine de Vergi* all enjoyed a wide circulation, as did *Parzival*. Nevertheless, without specific references to the military orders' role in legend or romance by contemporaries, we cannot say with certainty that a particular role was accepted, taken up by the popular imagination and treated as the norm.

A few such instances occur. The reference to Wolfram von Eschenbach's *Templeise* in *Reinfrid von Braunschweig* indicates that, as a result of Wolfram's work, this author and his expected audience were familiar with the Templars as active, chaste knights, the guardians of holiness, although they may have regarded this only as a literary image, not an image of reality.[100]

Again, one of the knights with Robert, count of Artois, at Mansourah, was reported as complaining that the Templars and Hospitallers had 'wolf's skin', (that is, that they were wolves in sheep's clothing).[101] The accusation is reminiscent of a remark recorded by Ernoul: Gerard of Ridefort, master of the Temple, during the advance to Hattin, in July 1187, accused Count Raymond of Tripoli of giving advice mixed with wolf's hair.[102] The similarity suggests that the count's companion knew Ernoul's story. In any case, he and the count knew the persistent rumours that the military orders impeded Christian advance in the Holy Land, such as the tale of the enchanted gold and those told by William of Tyre and Matthew Paris.[103] Although the report goes on to refute these accusations, the implication is that they were well known in Europe.

How far did audiences believe what they heard? Walter Map advocated that they should ask the Templars themselves about the tales told of them, rather than believing all that they were told;[104] but he said it tongue in cheek, probably to divert criticism which would fall on him for repeating such tales. Many fictional writings claimed to be true; educated audiences would have been aware that such claims were only literary convention, but 'ordinary' people probably were not.[105] Crusade preachers obviously expected their audience to believe in Arthurian romances and Carolingian epics, as they quoted anecdotes from them to illustrate their sermons.[106] Matthew Paris records general confusion as to whether to believe accounts from the Holy Land or not.[107]

From the point of view of the military orders themselves, neither the Latin legends nor the vernacular epics and romances portrayed a desirable image, for both were inaccurate. The legends discouraged patronage by painting too black a picture. The epics and romances implicitly contrasted the high spiritual standards of the past with the worldliness of the present day, suggesting the military orders' standards had greatly declined.[108] Legendary tales of victories, when contrasted with the reality of the second half of the thirteenth century, would prompt contemporaries to ask why God had abandoned the military orders, and some to conclude that they must have become sinful. As a result, the military orders were forced to counter the legend and romance invented by outsiders by devising and fostering propaganda which reinforced and bolstered the image they wished to convey of themselves.

CHAPTER 6

THE MILITARY ORDERS' SELF-PERCEPTION AND PRESENTATION[1]

During the twelfth and thirteenth centuries, all religious orders were anxious to maintain a good public profile, in order to encourage alms-giving. Those who criticized the failings of monasticism were aware of this: John of Salisbury and Walter Map both suffered a heavy backlash from the monks they mocked.[2] As the number and variety of religious orders mushroomed in the twelfth and early thirteenth centuries, competition for alms forced orders to take particular care to protect their image. The military orders had the additional problem that their reputation was affected as much by events in the Latin east as by their own behaviour. They also needed to build up and maintain a distinctive and positive self-image in order to attract desirable recruits, and to foster morale and a sense of identity among the brothers, since their houses were scattered across most of the known world.

Outsiders expected the military orders to be concerned about their image; even Matthew Paris admitted that the military orders could not be guilty of the evil deeds of which they were accused, because this would harm their reputation, as well as their souls.[3] Indeed, the orders' rules contain many references to the need to protect the reputation of the house among outsiders. Hospitallers or Templars travelling should take care not to cause offence by their behaviour.[4] The Templar rule specified that brothers who left the order must return their white mantles within two nights: 'because the bad brothers who leave the house and take the habit with them wear it in the taverns and brothels and places of ill repute and pawn them and sell them to criminals and persons who bring the house into disrepute . . .'[5]

The orders took care to ensure that internal scandals were kept secret from outsiders.[6] In particular, by the mid thirteenth century, the rules of all three orders contained regulations forbidding the brothers to make public the chapter proceedings of the order, or to allow outsiders to see copies of the rule.[7] If the rule were kept secret, brothers could not be accused of failing to keep it; the prohibition on publicizing chapter proceedings was to protect the reputation of individual brothers who were accused of, or confessed, faults during chapter meetings. The Hospital first introduced a judgement to prevent brothers from revealing chapter proceedings shortly after a complaint from Pope Gregory IX (in March 1238) that he had heard that the brothers were guilty of several gross abuses.[8] Perhaps the order was anxious to prevent the pope from hearing of such things in future.

Where scandals became known, the orders attempted to minimize the damage to their image. When three Templars at Antioch murdered some Christian merchants, the order had them whipped through Antioch, Tripoli, Tyre and Acre, in order to restore public confidence in the order's discipline.[9] In 1274, during a bitter dispute between the Templars and Hospitallers in Aragon, the master of the Temple, Brother William of Beaujeu, wrote to the Templars urging them to make peace with the Hospitallers because of the need to avoid scandal and offence to others.[10] As the evidence discussed in chapters two to four has shown, such measures were only partially successful in protecting the orders' reputation.

Clearly, the military orders recognized the need to protect and promote their reputation; it is less clear how they went about doing so. As no evidence survives of their procedures for forming policy, it is not possible to trace the processes by which they decided upon or changed the presentation of their image. There was probably no systematic formation of policy. The image which each order projected would have been based on the initiatives of the master and leading brothers, and the custom of the order; as traditions built up, the brothers' self-perception became fixed.

Policy-making has to be deduced from its results. An examination of the evidence reveals various means by which the military orders influenced their own image. Although the material is scattered, taken together it produces a coherent picture of the military orders constantly working to maintain and improve their image in Europe, if necessary at the expense of their rival military orders.

The following means could be used by the military orders to influence their image for the better:

(a) most directly, through representatives at royal and papal courts;
(b) through reports of their military activities and the state of the Holy Land;
(c) through other information put out by the orders, visual, oral, and written.

Through these means, the military orders stressed their military activity and successes, both in the Holy Land and elsewhere, and promoted the brothers' piety and holiness. These two processes went hand in hand, as the brothers' holiness was considered to be essential to their success against the Muslims.

In order to improve their spiritual image further, the brothers also promoted the ancient and venerable character of their orders and of their vocation, through the development of historical legends, and emphasized their dual role as charitable institutions and military forces.

Some of these aspects of self-presentation have been thoroughly discussed by other historians, and I do not intend to consider these in detail.

(a) Representatives at royal and papal courts

By the mid thirteenth century the three major military orders had permanent representatives at the papal court. The master of the Hospital, for instance, had set up a full-time representative of the order, Brother Marquisius, in 1231.[11] Members of the orders acting as personal servants of individual popes could also promote their order's interests. Pope Alexander IV specifically stated that his notary, master John of Capua, a brother of the Teutonic order, frequently beseeched him to favour his order.[12] As it was common for the dual posts of papal chamberlain to be filled by a Templar and Hospitaller, it is likely that this form of influence was much used by these orders.

The orders also had permanent representatives at royal courts, often acting in some official capacity such as royal almoner or treasurer, but sometimes simply as a brother of the order. Henry II of England granted lodging for one knight of the Temple at his court: this was confirmed by his sons and successors Richard and John.[13] In 1216 Emperor Frederick II granted to the Teutonic order that the master for the time being and one companion could be provided for in the household of the Imperial court for six months, while two knights of the order, with three mounts each, would be provided for on a continual basis.[14] There were numerous brothers of the military orders holding influential posts in royal courts throughout Europe during the twelfth and thirteenth centuries, as we discussed in chapter two. Our concern here is not the political importance of such royal servants, but how far their orders were able to take advantage of their position to promote their own interests and image.

Officials of the orders in the Holy Land and others certainly expected them to be able to promote their orders. For instance, in 1267 the patriarch of Jerusalem wrote to Amaury of la Roche, then preceptor of the Temple in France, instructing him on the terms he should negotiate with the pope and kings of France and Sicily for the relief of the Holy

Land.[15] He evidently expected Amaury to have the interests of the Holy Land foremost in his mind. Certainly Amaury did win a concession for his order in the Holy Land from Pope Urban IV,[16] but during Louis IX's Tunisian crusade his efforts were directed more towards the interests of King Charles of Sicily than of his order. His insistence that the crusaders await Charles' arrival before attacking Tunis prevented the crusade from achieving anything.[17]

The case of Amaury of la Roche was typical. Monarchs and popes usually expected brothers of the order to put the interests of their order after the interests of their royal or papal master. Although in theory the brothers were not subject to any man on earth other than the pope, in practice the brothers acted as the loyal liege men of the reigning king. In fact, they had no choice but to do so.

Even where the military orders were successful in winning the confidence of princes, this confidence did not necessarily translate into effective aid of the sort the orders were seeking. The orders spent considerable time and money keeping rulers such as Louis VII of France, Henry II and Edward I of England, informed of events in the Holy Land; but with little return, as these rulers were preoccupied by more pressing needs at home.[18] Hence the orders required other means of promoting their cause in Europe.

(b) Reports of military activities[19]

The military orders were responsible for a large proportion of the continual stream of information which was sent from the Holy Land to Europe throughout the twelfth and thirteenth centuries. It was intended to publicize the deeds of the Palestinian Franks, to stress their plight and their need for aid; but also to celebrate their victories, in order to reassure patrons that good use was being made of their alms, and that God was still showing them His approval.

Such news reports were deliberately designed to mould western Christendom's image of the Latin east, and were intended for wide circulation, even where they were addressed to an individual. A letter sent in 1239 by Amaury, count of Montfort, to his wife, describing the defeat of the French crusaders at Gaza in that year, was sent by her to Richard, earl of Cornwall, her brother-in-law.[20] The earl presumably showed it to his friend Matthew Paris, as the latter copied it into his *Chronica Majora*.[21] Matthew collected a vast store of such material, probably forwarded to him by his wide circle of friends and acquaintances.[22] Other chroniclers obtained similar material: the chronicle of Melrose contains a letter of 1219 from Hermann of Salza, master of the Teutonic order, to Leo, cardinal of Holy Cross in Jerusalem,[23] while the

Burton annals include a letter from Thomas Berard, then master of the Temple, to the master of the Temple in England, of 1261.[24]

Through such regular reports to Europe, the military orders strove to remain 'in the public eye'. They not only drew attention to their campaigns, but also to their constant efforts to provide long-term defence for the holy places, by building castles. The order of the Temple in particular was at pains to publicize the immense resources it was pouring into the building and maintenance of fortresses. For instance, between 1261 and 1266 a Palestinian Frank wrote a description of the Templars' rebuilding of their fortress of Saphet.[25] His purpose was to publicize the great gains which the order had won for Christendom by refortifying this strategic site. Although the treatise only survives in two manuscripts, the order's publicity campaign appears to have been successful in attracting European attention to the fortress. When the castle fell to the Muslims in 1266, the disaster received extensive coverage in the European chronicles;[26] although the master of the Hospital, Hugh Revel, remarked that it had fallen remarkably quickly considering that the Temple had boasted so much about it.[27]

In the same way, in 1218 the order of the Temple found a publicist for its new fortress of Castle Pilgrim. Oliver *Scholasticus* gave a detailed account of the construction of the castle in a letter of late August or September 1218, to the archbishop and clergy of Cologne, which he repeated in his *Historia Damiatina*.[28] His account was used by a number of other German and English chroniclers, some in great detail,[29] and others more briefly,[30] thus further publicizing the Templars' achievement.

The Teutonic order also publicized its castle-building. Early in 1229 the master of the order, Hermann of Salza, writing to Pope Gregory IX on the truce made between the emperor and the sultan of Egypt, mentioned 'Montfort, our new castle which we have begun to fortify in the mountains this year'.[31] In July 1230 the pope wrote urging all Christians to make donations towards the cost of building this castle, 'from which the Christians in the area are known to receive great advantage'.[32]

The importance of the fortification and garrisoning of castles is underlined by the Templars' decision, early in 1291, to seek permission from Pope Nicholas IV to acquire and restore the ruined fortress of *Castavilla*, for the protection of pilgrims.[33] Permission was granted on 3 May 1291, just before the loss of Acre. As it is unlikely that the order possessed the resources for such an undertaking, this can hardly have been more than a public relations manoeuvre, designed to reassure the papacy and patrons in Europe that the order was still active in guarding the pilgrim routes, the function for which it was originally established.

For the military orders must always be seen to be doing something, in order to reassure such as Matthew Paris that their great undertakings did justify the immense sums of money which they took from Christendom.[34] Those military orders which lacked the resources to attract general attention remained poor, so poor in the case of the order of St Thomas of Acre that by the 1260s the brothers in Acre were negotiating terms of incorporation into the order of the Temple.[35] The order of St Lazarus fared only slightly better; whereas the order of St Thomas was unable to attract notice from chroniclers outside England, the brothers of St Lazarus occasionally won a mention in European chronicles, when the brothers had acted excessively rashly or suffered exceptional losses in the field.[36] Nevertheless, there was only slight awareness in Europe that this was a military order. There are few references to its military function in charters; where these can be dated they date from after 1250. Albert, count of Gleichen, gave a gift in 1283 to 'the religious men of the order of St Lazarus of the knighthood of Christ of Jerusalem',[37] and there are a few references in the cartulary of the order's major English house at Burton Lazars, and in the royal letters patent.[38]

Even the Teutonic order was unable to attract much attention from European writers for its deeds in the Holy Land, and where it did appear it played only a minor part. It did not achieve fame until the loss of Acre. In that the orders of the Temple and Hospital had already won the limelight in the Holy Land, the move to Prussia was essential for the order's survival. Here at least westerners were aware that the order was winning victories, even if, like the Flemish friar William of Rubruck, they were rather vague as to what those victories might be.[39]

It was dangerous to rely solely on the publication of military successes to win the confidence and alms of Christendom. During periods of upheaval in Europe, reports of military successes went largely unpublicized. When the contents of a letter circulated orally, it could become corrupted, thereby failing to achieve its original purpose.

Again, publicity could fall on hostile ears. Matthew Paris commented dourly that many Christians could not believe the good reports from the Holy Land in 1244, because they distrusted the Templars and Hospitallers. In 1250 he reported that when rumours of success turned out to be false, some people were so disillusioned that they refused to believe any subsequent reports, even those which were true.[40] During periods of military reversals, Europeans tended to believe that God was sending these defeats on the Latin east as a punishment for sin, and were therefore reluctant to send aid. The search for success by expanding operations into the eastern European frontier could reduce the orders' prestige in the eyes of patrons who considered such a move to be a betrayal of the Holy Land. The military orders had, therefore, to use other methods to emphasize their sanctity, less vulnerable to fortune.

(c) Other information emanating from the orders

We shall now consider information contributing towards the image of the military orders, which was, or appears to have been, disseminated by the military orders themselves, through channels other than the direct methods of communication discussed above.

This information promoted the orders' spirituality rather than their military prowess, although of course their success in battle was seen to depend on the quality of their spirituality. It was broadcast generally rather than to a specific audience, and much of it was probably aimed originally at the orders' members, only gradually reaching outsiders. Sometimes it is impossible to say where information originated, as it is recorded by outsiders but is consistent with material known to have originated with the orders.

One well-known example of this kind of information is the commemorative inscription for Peter of Vieillebride, master of the Hospital 1239–42, which the Hospitallers erected at Acre in such a position that it would be seen by crusaders and pilgrims arriving from Europe. This proclaimed the success of the late master's policy of alliance with Egypt.[41] Less well-known is a commemorative inscription for one Brother Hugh of Quiliugo, marshal of the Temple, date unknown, describing the brother in terms reminiscent of St Bernard's *De Laude Novae Militiae* ('fearsome to his enemies, humble with his companions') as all literate persons who passed would realize.[42] But most image-forming was more subtle.

Another method was by visual aids, particularly through the images displayed on the orders' official seal. The obverse of the earliest seal known for the master of the Temple, dating from 1158 and the mastership of Bertrand of Blanchefort, shows two knights riding one horse. Matthew Paris, who was familiar with this image, declared that it harked back to the early days of the order, when the knights were so poor they could only afford one horse between two brothers.[43] The reverse of the leaden seal of the master of the Hospital in the twelfth and thirteenth-century seal showed a man lying on a mattress or bier, symbol of the pilgrim hospital in Jerusalem.[44] Anyone doing business with the orders was repeatedly reminded of these foundations of their existence.

Another kind of visual aid was in architecture. Michael Gervers has pointed out that the Templars and Hospitallers embellished their houses in London (and elsewhere) with round churches reminiscent of the Church of the Holy Sepulchre in order to impress visually upon English society their direct connection with Jerusalem.[45]

Even the internal decor of the orders' chapels could be used to reinforce the brothers' self-image. The frescoes in the Templars' chapel of S. Bevignate at Perugia are a fine example: depicting the life of the brothers

Figure 7. Matthew Paris' sketch of the Templars' seal, from the *Historia Anglorum*, BM Royal MS 14 C vii f.42v.

in the Holy Land, defying the devil and fighting the Muslims.[46]

Other methods of presentation were oral and literary: tales celebrating the brothers' piety (which were at first recorded orally, and later in writing); edifying literature written specifically for the brothers, such as lives of saints; legends of the orders' distant past; and association of the orders with the cults of popular saints. Not every military order used all of these methods. The Hospital promoted its founders as saints, while the Temple apparently did not. There is also evidence that the Hospital in particular played on its dual charitable—military role in order to present itself to potential donors in the best possible light at any one time.

(i) Tales celebrating the brothers' piety. Some edifying and miraculous tales of the Templars were recorded by James of Vitry in his two sermons to

a military order while he was bishop of Acre (between 1216 and 1228). These were the tale of 'lord bread-and-water', the Templar who fasted too much and was unable to sit his horse in battle; a story of the courage of the master of the Temple in the face of defeat at the siege of Ascalon in 1153; an anecdote of a Templar who bid his horse Morel (Blackie) carry him to Paradise as they rode into battle; and the tale of 'Templars' leap', where a Templar escaped from the Saracens by sending his horse leaping from the cliff road into the sea. The tale of 'lord bread-and-water' was later retold by the Dominican Stephen of Bourbon.[47] These tales probably originated within the order and were originally intended to encourage and edify the brothers. James claimed that his tale of the capture of Ascalon was recorded 'in ancient history', (although it appears in no other surviving work) and that the last was told to him by the Templar who made the miraculous leap.[48]

Another Templar anecdote was recorded by Caesar of Heisterbach, a Cistercian monk who, like James of Vitry, was a preacher of the fifth crusade. In his *Dialogus Miraculorum*, written between 1219 and 1223, he told a story of Templar steadfastness at prayer. Surprised by a Saracen attack while they are at prayer, a group of Templars are ordered by their master to remain praying. Meanwhile, the Saracens are defeated by an army of angels.[49] As Caesar was friendly with at least one member of the order of the Temple, perhaps he had heard the story from the brothers.[50] The *Dialogus* was one of the most influential treatises of its kind during the Middle Ages, so this particular illustration of the Templars' piety would have become well known.[51]

The Teutonic order recorded such improving tales in histories, aimed initially at the brothers of the order, but also at patrons. At the end of the thirteenth century, the *Livländische Reimchronik* was written to record the piety and prowess of the Teutonic brothers during their early years in Livonia,[52] while in the 1320s Peter of Dusberg, a priest in the order, compiled a collection of such accounts from the brothers' early days in Prussia. Presumably these tales had been passed down orally among the brothers.

The Templars and Hospitallers did not produce such contemporary histories during the period from 1128 to 1291. It was suggested by William Stubbs in 1864 that the author of the *Itinerarium peregrinorum et gesta regis Ricardi*, a chronicle of the third crusade, was a Templar. But, while some early chapters in the chronicle, describing the battle at Nazareth on 1 May 1187 and the battle of Hattin on 4 July 1187,[53] are told from a Templar viewpoint and therefore probably came from a Templar newsletter to Europe, this is not the case with the rest of the chronicle. On the contrary, the deeds of the Templars are omitted; there is no mention of the Templar role in the defence of Tyre in the winter of 1187–8, or of their heroic defence of their tower at Tortosa in 1188.[54]

It seems that the Templars and Hospitallers generally preferred not to put resources into producing their own histories of recent events, although in the 1280s the Hospitallers of Acre had copies of the *Histoire d'Outremer* copied for the brothers' use.[55] Instead, they relied on newsletters and oral tradition to preserve their deeds for posterity.

The Hospital does not appear to have collected or recounted miracle stories of the brothers during the twelfth or thirteenth centuries. Two edifying stories which survive may or may not have come from the order: a tale told by Stephen of Bourbon concerning a young man who joined the Hospitallers after his life was saved by the Blessed Virgin Mary, and an account in the 'Ministrel of Rheims' history of how the house of the Hospital at Acre acted as host to Saladin, disguised as a sick pilgrim.[56] The lack of such stories concerning the Hospitallers is particularly interesting in view of the evidence discussed in chapter five. Possibly such material has not survived, but it seems likely that the Hospitallers' self-image did not lend itself to modern miracles and flights of spiritual fancy.

(ii) Edifying literature produced for the brothers. Other material generated by the orders for their own members took the form of vernacular lives of biblical and other saints, lives of the Fathers, and edifying allegories. Again, the surviving material of this type was produced for the Templars and for the Teutonic order, not for the Hospitallers.

The bulk of the surviving material produced by the order of the Temple was written by an anonymous clerk for Brother Henry of Arcy, commander of Temple Bruer, Lincolnshire, from 1161 to 1174. This consisted of a 'Lives of the Fathers'; a short version of the tale of the converted prostitute Thais; an account of the coming of Antichrist; and an account of the descent of St Paul into Hell, which reflects popular piety and superstition rather than deep theological truths.[57] All these works were very monastic in tone, extolling chastity, prayer, fasting and the solitary life. No mention at all was made of military activities. This must reflect the lifestyle which the brothers followed in a provincial commandery such as Temple Bruer. Around the same time, between 1150 and 1175, and again in England, a translation of the Old Testament book of Judges into French was undertaken by an anonymous clerk at the request of the two leading Templars in England, Stephen of Hastings and Osto of St Omer. Unlike the other works, this is largely devoted to warfare, but the translator's principal concern was to emphasize the importance of holding to the faith, virtues such as chastity, and the disasters which befell God's people when they ignored these principles.[58] A copy of this was made for the Templars at Acre, as part of an Old Testament codex.[59]

The material produced for the Teutonic order, from the end of the thirteenth century, was very similar in content. There were works on the life of the Blessed Virgin Mary, the order's patroness, and of St Martina, the legend of the Holy Cross, the Fathers of the Church, and the Biblical heroines Judith and Esther. (There was a preference for female subjects.) Another work, the *Sunden Widerstreit*, was more military in tone, being an allegorical depiction of virtue fighting against vice. Interestingly, there was nothing written during this period on the military saints, George, Sebastian or Michael.[60]

Literature produced for the Hospital had a different emphasis. It contained some material of an edifying nature, but the main concern was to show the brothers that they were continuing a long and holy tradition. As in the case of the order of the Temple, the Hospital's earliest vernacular literature was produced for the English members of the order. This was the Anglo-Norman translation of the rule, the so-called *Hospitallers' Riwle*, written between 1181 and 1185, which also recounted the foundation of the order.

(iii) Tales of the distant past. In a world full of uncertainties, it was common for religious institutions to seek security in claiming an ancient history, perhaps back to apostolic origins or even earlier.[61] A long history made an institution respectable in the eyes of outsiders. In the twelfth century, the image of the Hospital and Temple suffered simply because they were 'modern' orders, founded within the last century. Walter Map in particular made much of this failing.[62] It was therefore very much in their interests to convince Christendom that they were in fact orders of ancient foundation, or at least with a long ancestry. The Hospital seems to have gone to great lengths to develop the legend of its past. The evidence for the Temple is vaguer, but there are indications that it claimed venerable ancestors in Old Testament times.

Third-party evidence shows that the legend of the Hospital's past was already in wide circulation before the Anglo-Norman rule was written. Gerhoh of Reichersberg refers to the Hospital's claim to have existed since the time of the Apostles in his *De investigatione Antichristi*, written in 1160–62.[63]

According to the Anglo-Norman rule, the order was founded by Bishop Melchiazar and King Antiochus in Jerusalem, at the time of the first Roman emperor. In fact, Antiochus ruled in the second century BC, while the first Roman emperor, Caesar Augustus, did not assume power until the late first century BC. It was claimed that Judas Maccabaeus had been a patron of the Hospital, that John the Baptist's parents had served the poor there, that Christ visited the Hospital with his disciples and spoke some of His most famous words there, that this was the house where He had appeared to the disciples after His resurrection, and that this was the house where the first Christians had met together; St Stephen, the first martyr, had been master there.[64] None of this had any Biblical foundation. However, if we consider how many events in the Bible, and how many of Christ's sermons, were reported as having taken place in the Temple, it seems likely that this pseudo-history was developed at least in part in competition with the order of the Temple.

A decade after the Anglo-Norman rule was written, Pope Celestine III showed no doubts as to the legend's truth, stating categorically that Christ sanctified the Hospital by His presence during His time on earth.[65] This was repeated by Innocent IV in 1254.[66] In 1274, Rudolf, king of the Romans (Holy Roman emperor-elect) stated in a general confirmation charter for the order that 'it is known to have flourished from antiquity'.[67]

In the first half of the thirteenth century the legend was included at length in two letters of accreditation for the Hospitallers' almscollectors in Franconia, in central Germany. A different version appeared in a general letter of accreditation for the order's almscollectors in Europe. The date of this letter is disputed, but Delaville le Roulx ascribed it to Master Hugh Revel, and dated it between 1262 and 1267. The master informed his readers that Pope Urban II 'in whose time Jerusalem was captured', and his successors had set up a confraternity for the order, in which he had promised to all who gave alms a share in the prayers and alms which had been given 'in the Hospital from the time of the Holy Apostles, who set up the Holy Hospital in the early Church, and of St Stephen the protomartyr, who after their division obtained the priorate of the place, and which are made forever'.[68]

This material was carefully selected at a time of crisis. The confraternity had, in fact, been set up by Innocent II, pope from 1130 to 1143, whose papacy was marred by schism. Urban II, and the reminder of the capture of Jerusalem by the first crusade, were far more auspicious. Previously claiming to have originated in the time of the Old Testament, the Hospital was now made a creation of the apostles, and, notably, of the first martyr. The suggestion was made to potential donors that the Hospital shared these men's sanctity, willingness to face martyrdom, and the hope of recapturing Jerusalem. As Brother William of San Stefano, a member of the order, remarked late in the thirteenth century: 'I reckon that seekers (of alms) invented these things in order to get more...'[69]

The order of the Temple had no such clear-cut pseudo-history. The available material had already been fully exploited by the canons of the *Templum Domini*, or Lord's Temple, which stood opposite the 'Temple of Solomon' (the al-Aqsa mosque). The Templars, and outsiders, seem instead to have picked up Biblical references and popular myths which suggested a long lineage for the order. This is indicated, for example, by the interpolations in the order's translation of the Book of Judges.

Presumably to hold his listeners' attention, the translator inserted some material not in his original, which had special application to the Templars. For example, after a description of the lands taken by various tribes of Israel, following Judges chapter 1 verse 21, the translator added that the lineage of Levi was chosen to serve God in the Temple. This was an anachronism: the Temple had not yet been built, and the tribe of Levi served before the Ark of the Lord. At chapter 8 verse 27 the translator gave a description of an ephod: 'a sort of vestment which the provost had then for serving in the Temple, in the time of the Old Testament'. Here two of the scribes making later copies of the translation realized that this was an error and replaced 'Temple' with 'Tabernacle'.[70] However, the translator seems to have believed that the Temple had always existed, and that God's true worshippers (here the Israelites) had served in it ever since they came into the Holy Land. There was an obvious parallel between the Levites serving in the old Temple and the Templars serving in the modern one.

We might have expected the Templars to claim a special relationship with King Solomon, as the order was based in the so-called Temple of Solomon. 'The Temple of Solomon' was often, but by no means always, cited in donations to the order. However, there is only the vaguest hint that Solomon was connected with the foundation of the order. The romance La Queste del Saint Graal, probably written between 1220 and 1230, indicates that King Solomon was linked with an ideal of knighthood, as he is shown rejoicing that his final descendant (Galaad) will be a knight better than Joshua.[71] However, this reference may simply be a reflection of the fact that Solomon was a greatly respected figure at this time, regarded as an ideal of kingship and wisdom.

A clearer indication occurs in the late twelfth century Libellus de expugnatione terrae sanctae per Saladinum, in the account of the battle at Nazareth on 1 May 1187. Gerard of Ridefort, master of the Temple, is shown addressing his brothers before the engagement: 'Remember your fathers the Maccabees, whose duty of fighting for the Church, the Law, for the inheritance of the Crucified One, you have already been carrying out for a long time'. He goes on to remind them that their 'fathers' overcame the enemy not by force of numbers but by faith and justice and observing God's mandates.[72] Probably the author of the Libellus invented this speech, but it is unlikely that he would have attributed these words to the master unless they were the sort of language which the order actually used. If the order claimed to be a descendant of the Maccabees, with Judas Maccabaeus as a past or first master, then the Hospital's eagerness to claim Judas as a past patron may be explained by the rivalry between the two orders. However, Judas Maccabaeus was revered throughout Christendom, not by the military orders alone. In the romance *Lancelot*, written around 1215 to 1225,[73] Judas is claimed as one of the first knights; all knights are called to be God's knights, and in this respect Judas Maccabaeus was indeed the forefather of the Templars, but also of the rest of knighthood.

The order could certainly claim, and with more justification than the Hospital, that many incidents during Christ's ministry had taken place in the Temple; and it could also benefit from contemporary fascination with the Temple,[74] and the legends built up around it, particularly those connected with its patroness, the Blessed Virgin Mary. The *Chanson de Jérusalem* refers to a legend that the Annunciation took place in the Temple of Solomon: a 'fact' recorded nowhere in the New Testament.[75] It is not known, however, whether the order actively exploited these connections.

It is clear that the order made some effort to influence the pilgrim traffic in Jerusalem in its own interests. A pilgrim guide of around 1170 described the traditional site of the Sheep Pool, and then added: 'but the Templars show you another pool and say that that is the site of the Sheep Pool'.[76]

Evidently the order of the Temple was not concerned to develop and record an ancient history for itself, as the order of the Hospital did. Nevertheless, the order, or at any rate individual brothers, seem to have made a connection between knights of God who defended the Holy Land in the past, such as the Israelites in the times of the Judges, the Maccabees, and themselves. Some may have believed their order to be the direct descendant of the Maccabees; the order of St Lazarus certainly made that claim later in its history.[77]

Whatever the military orders might claim, however, contemporary chroniclers generally placed the establishment of the Hospital in the eleventh century and of the Temple in the early twelfth. In this respect, the orders' 'propaganda' failed. On the other hand, the fact that the Templars and Hospitallers appear in a number of romances and epics set in the distant past indicates that the knightly classes were prepared to believe these legends; although apparently most listeners had no idea of historical perspective.

While the Teutonic order did not claim ancient foundation, it did claim that Frederick of Staufen, Duke of Swabia, was involved in its foundation, and also claimed to be a descendant of the German hospital in Jerusalem, which was destroyed by Saladin in 1187.[78] The order's claim to be a continuation of the Jerusalem hospital was supported by Frederick of Swabia's nephew, the emperor Frederick II.[79] Chroniclers, however, were not convinced: opinions differed over when the order began, but the majority considered that it was founded in the early years of the thirteenth century.[80] The views on the order expressed in the second half of the thirteenth century by the Dominican friar Humbert of Romans (taken from James of Vitry) show that this could be a good thing.[81] By the time that Humbert wrote, a modern order was regarded as virtuous and faithful to its first calling, unlike older orders, which had become corrupt.

The order of St Thomas of Acre also claimed royal foundation, in this case by Richard I of England. It had in fact been founded by the chaplain of Ralph of Diceto, dean of St Paul's, although Richard may have assisted with the original endowment. Whether the legend was true or false, it was believed, enabling the order to claim the protection and patronage of Henry III and Edward I, without which it would not have survived.[82]

The orders not only claimed special relationships with ancient Biblical characters and modern royalty; they also claimed spiritual reinforcements in the form of saints and relics.

(iv) Association with the cults of popular saints. We have already noted that the literature produced for the military orders did not emphasize their military role, and that authors writing for the Templars and Teutonic order tended to concentrate on female saints. This was also the case with the saints whom the military orders chose as patrons. Admittedly, the Teutonic order had some connection with St George: a donation of 1252 by Henry, margrave of Meissen and Osterland, was given to the Teutonic order in honour of the holy martyr George.[83] Yet this was not exploited as much as its connections with the Blessed Virgin Mary or St Elizabeth of Marburg. References to St George in connection with the order of the Temple are equally sparse. The account in the *Itinerarium peregrinorum* of the death of the Templar Brother Jacquelin of Mailly on 1 May 1187 states that the Muslims mistook him for St George; and an Italian cleric on the fifth crusade recorded the Templars calling on St George to assist them against the Muslims who had broken into the crusaders' camp on the 31 July 1219.[84] I have not found any such allusions for the Hospitallers, who, naturally, laid greatest stress on their principal patron, St John the Baptist.

All the military orders claimed the Blessed Virgin Mary as a patroness. This was normal for religious orders. The Teutonic order and the order of the Temple claimed her as their special patroness.

The Teutonic order's claim to have a special relationship with God's Mother has been much discussed.[85] The cult dated from quite early in the order's history: the full title of the order, 'the Hospital of St Mary of the Teutons in Jerusalem', became fixed around 1220.[86] The *Livländische Reimchronik*, written at the end of the thirteenth century, describes

the Teutonic brothers in the mid thirteenth century fighting under
Mary's banner, to the last man if need be;[87] Peter of Dusberg described
how, during the 1270s, at a battle at Christburg during the Prussians'
'second apostasy', the Prussians were defeated on seeing Mary bearing
the order's banner into battle, at which sight their strength melted
away.[88] The order's dedication to Mary became one of its best known
features, and seems to have bolstered its image. Humbert of Romans,
drawing up his model sermon for the order in the second half of the thirteenth century, recommended that the brothers be urged not to offend
their 'great patroness' through unclean actions or pride.[89] Almsgivers
would probably expect it to maintain high standards of spirituality
because of Mary's patronage.

The relationship of the Templars to the Blessed Virgin is less well
known. The relationship may have been due to Cistercian influence, as
the Cistercians also had Mary as their patroness; or it may simply have
been because Mary's cult was rapidly gaining popularity during the
order's early years. Donors to the order first began to cite Mary in the
early 1130s.[90] Some donors referred to the order as Mary's special
order: in 1137, one Ermengaud de Son dedicated a gift to 'the
knighthood of the Blessed Mary which is in Jerusalem'.[91] Many of the
order's churches and chapels were dedicated to Mary, including the
order's house at Richerenches, where a number of donors referred to 'the
house of the Blessed Mary' rather than to the Temple.[92] However, the
precedence of Mary seems to have varied from one area to another, as
the cartulary of Provins makes no mention of her.

There were also a number of legends connecting Mary with the order
of the Temple. As mentioned above, the Annunciation was said to have
taken place in the Temple of Solomon. A pilgrims' guide of the thirteenth century states that a stone on which Mary had rested was outside
the Templars' fortress of Castle Pilgrim.[93] The Templars also publicized
the miracle of the icon of Our Lady of Saidnaia, which exuded milk from
its 'breasts'.[94] The brothers' devotion to Mary was emphasized during
the trial of the order by an anonymous sympathizer who wrote in their
defence to the doctors and scholars of the University of Paris.[95]

Both the Templars and the Teutonic order claimed special relationships
with other female saints. The Templars possessed the relics of a St
Euphemia at Castle Pilgrim.[96] There are a number of St Euphemias,
including some native to Palestine, but the brothers claimed that this was
the illustrious St Euphemia of Chalcedon, miraculously translated to
Palestine from Constantinople. We may surmise that the relics probably
came as booty from the fourth crusade, but the *Acta Sanctorum* makes no
mention of relics of this saint ever having been in Palestine.[97] In any
case, the relics impressed the pilgrims.

The Teutonic brothers possessed the head of St Barbara at Culm, which they had carried off from the Pomeranians in a raid on the castle of Sartowitz in the 1240s. The brothers claimed that the saint had deliberately abandoned her former resting place in order to be in their midst, witnessing to their great spirituality.[98] They also possessed the body of St Elizabeth at the hospital of St Francis of Marburg, which she had founded. The saint had bequeathed her hospital to the Hospitallers, but Pope Gregory IX, on the request of her brothers-in-law, had given it to the Teutonic order.[99] The order claimed that oil flowed miraculously from her tomb, and they distributed this oil to religious men for the establishment of basilicas in her honour.[100]

The order of the Temple was, likewise, involved in the promotion of local cults. At Perugia, in Italy, the order was one of the parties involved in an unsuccessful attempt to secure the canonization of the local anchorite S. Bevignate during the 1260s and 1270s.[101] In 1289 Nicholas IV reported that many miracles were taking place at the order's church at Silva, Rodez diocese, which was dedicated to the Blessed Virgin Mary.[102]

Like all religious institutions, the military orders collected every sort of relic, in order to attract pilgrims and, therefore, alms. The possession of such relics also reflected favourably on their sanctity; as in the case of St Barbara, who wished her head to be in the keeping of holy men. The Teutonic order in Prussia possessed a portion of the Lord's Cross, which Pope Gregory IX urged the crusaders in 1233 to visit and adore.[103] A pilgrim's guide to Jerusalem of around 1170 mentions the 'very holy relics' kept at the Hospital's church of St John the Baptist. Another guide, from early in the century, states that one of these was 'the stone water pot in which the Lord made the water into wine'.[104]

Relic-collecting even led to competition within each order. In 1281 Nicholas le Lorgne, the master of the Hospital, commanded the prior of St Gilles, Brother William of Villaret, to give up some relics which he had illegally acquired from the brother who was taking them to the priory of Auvergne.[105] Obviously the prior had felt that his house needed additional tourist attractions.

With all this in mind, we should expect the military orders to have used every possible means to convince potential almsgivers of their sanctity and worthiness to receive donations. The most obvious method of doing this was for an order to ensure the canonization or beatification of its founders or leading members. By the end of the twelfth century, this required papal approval, and a stringent investigation into the 'saint's' credentials. Nevertheless, other 'modern' orders, such as the Cistercians, and the Friars Preacher and Minor, had such saints, and we would expect the military orders to set out to obtain papal approval for cults based on their most outstanding martyrs, thereby demonstrating divine approval for their vocation.

However, there is little evidence that they did so. The Teutonic order, and the lesser military orders, boast no saints at all. The *Acta Sanctorum* ascribes only one saint to the order of the Temple, John of Montfort: and, on investigation, he proves not to have been a Templar at all, but count of Montfort, a companion of Louis IX on his first crusade.[106] The Hospital promoted the cults of its first two masters, the Blessed Gerard and the Blessed Raymond of le Puy. There was a cult of the Blessed Gerard at Manosque, in the Languedoc, from the 1280s.[107] However, the sanctity of the Blessed Gerard rested on the traditional virtues of piety, charity to the poor, and courage in the face of the Muslim threat.[108] The basis of Raymond's sanctity is less clear; William of Tyre says only that he was a religious man, who feared God.[109]

It is interesting that only the Hospital was prepared to promote its leading founders as saints in true monastic style. Perhaps the order of the Temple and the Teutonic order ignored this because they were further from the monastic tradition, or perhaps they were less successful, so that the results of their efforts have not come down to us.

It is also possible that the senior brothers among the military orders preferred not to encourage cults around individual brothers. Perhaps it was not desirable in a military order that one member be honoured above the rest. Knights were already aggressive individualists, and one of the great concerns of the Templars' rule, for instance, was to ensure that they fought together as a unit instead of charging as they pleased. All brothers were potential martyrs, all the deceased were remembered in the daily service. Brothers should not be encouraged to strive for distinction, as this would undermine the discipline of the order.

Two other Hospitallers were canonized during this period, both from Italy: St Ubaldesca of Pisa (died 1206)[110] and St Hugh of Genoa (died 1230).[111] Their lives are well-documented, and they were canonized soon after their deaths. However, although their sanctity was important at a local level, in their own cities, it did nothing to promote the military religious life. Instead, they were famed for their humility, piety and good works.

Other saints have been attributed to the Hospitallers during this period, but there is considerable doubt as to whether most of them existed. Jonathan Riley-Smith gives a complete list: as well as the four already discussed, he notes St Flore, St Nicasius of Palermo, the Blessed Gerard Mecati, and the Blessed Gerhard the German.[112] Interestingly, although St Flore was French, the last three were Italians.

St Flore in fact lived outside this period, as she was born in 1300 and died in 1347.[113]

There is no contemporary evidence for the other three, and even no official life for St Nicasius of Palermo[114] and the Blessed Gerhard the German. Huillard-Bréholles dismissed the principal evidence for the

existence of St Nicasius as *'falsum, imo falsissimum'*,[115] and this saint does
not even appear in the *Acta Sanctorum*. The evidence for the Blessed
Gerhard the German is so vague that the writers of the *Acta* were
inclined to think that he had been a Templar.[116] Gerard Mecati, better
known as Gerard of Villamagna, may have existed, but the evidence for
his supposed membership of the order of the Hospital is very unsatisfac-
tory.[117]

Yet, whether these saints existed or were honoured during our period
or not, the fact remains that none of them was principally honoured as
martyrs in battle. Nicasius was said to have died as a martyr at
Hattin,[118] on 4 July 1187, but his special claim to piety was his patient
suffering of swollen glands in his neck. Gerard Mecati was said to have
gone on the third crusade, but his only notable achievement was to be
captured by the Muslims. Roger of les Moulins, master of the Hospital,
and Brother Henry of the Hospital died bravely in battle against the
Muslims on 1 May 1187, but no cult developed around them.[119] The
body of Brother Jacquelin of Mailly, of the Temple, who died in the
same battle, attracted some local devotion, but no lasting cult.[120]

Perhaps this was partly because cults develop around locations, and the
location of battles tended to be in dangerous territory; the body might
even be lost. In the Italian cities, where most of the Hospitaller saints
were created, there was an obvious focus for the cult in the saint's burial
place. There was also an incentive, in the form of fierce civic pride which
needed local saints to bolster a city's self-esteem. Yet it also appears that
the Italians were not impressed by military virtues, for the traditions
around their Hospitaller saints say little of their military careers.[121]
Religious men and women attracted attention for traditional monastic
virtues of prayer, fasting, humility, charity. Apparently, popular Italian
piety did not believe that laying down one's life for Christ in battle was
of equal merit to living a life of self-denial and charity. This is the same
attitude that we noted in chapter five: although the military orders
caught the imagination of the writers and audiences of epic and romance,
they were never considered to be of equal merit to hermits.

How far were the military orders aware of this perception, and did
they react to overcome it? The evidence is that the Hospital and Temple
did react, but that the Hospital went further to meet popular opinion,
and was more successful.

(v) Appealing to the orders' dual role. Charters and official documents issued
by the military orders, or under their influence, indicate that the order
of the Hospital exploited its dual hospitable—military role, tailoring its
self-image to its circumstances and correspondents.

An early example of this occurred in the 1170s. The order of the

Hospital had become undeniably militarized, having taken part in the Egyptian campaigns of King Amalric I during the 1160s. But this development had brought complaints from within and without the order, and in 1169 the then master, Gilbert of Assailly, had resigned. Jobert, master from 1172 to 1177, wrote to Henry, archbishop of Reims, asking for a place for his order within the diocese of Reims, and describing the order's work. He made much of the order's hospitable duties, but no mention of its military activity.[122]

A later example appears in two donations to the Hospital in August 1240, made by Andrew III, lord of Vitré, and Geoffrey IV, lord of Preuilly, pilgrims in the Holy Land. These were clearly based on a standard form of donation charter used by the Hospital, and praised the works of 'piety and mercy' done daily in the house, but made no mention of its military operations. This is interesting in view of the orders' implication in the crusaders' defeat at Gaza in the previous year. Perhaps the Hospital wished to be seen for the time being as a simple order which fulfilled the works of charity, rather than in the somewhat tarnished role of a powerful military order.[123]

The tendency becomes most striking by the mid thirteenth century. When Hugh Revel, master of the Hospital, wrote to Ferraud of Barres, the prior of St Gilles, in 1268 to ask for the help of the brothers in Europe, he spoke as if the order was purely military in purpose, its properties given to it for the help of the Holy Land, with no mention of Christ's poor.[124] Yet, in an open letter to accredit the order's almscollectors in Europe, the master had made no reference at all to the order's military work, writing as if the order was a hospital only, and stressing its alleged connection with the Apostles.[125]

Most interesting is a bull of Nicholas IV, of 15 March 1291. He had previously banned all unlicensed almscollecting for the Holy Land, in order to prevent fraud. He now granted the Hospital leave to collect alms, because the brothers had informed him that they were not collecting for the Holy Land but for the poor and sick.[126] The timing of this statement by the order, so soon before the loss of Acre, when the coming catastrophe must have been clear to those governing the order, strongly suggests that the Hospital was actively exploiting its dual role in order to maintain its position in public opinion.

The Teutonic order shared the Hospital's dual role, but it does not appear to have exploited it. The bulk of donations were given simply to 'the Teutonic house', emphasizing neither hospitality nor knighthood. This suggests that, to most donors, its national identity was the most important thing about the order.

Although the Templars were involved in attending to the needs of pilgrims and almsgiving, they very seldom drew attention to this. In theological theory, the brother's role of protecting pilgrims in the Holy

Land and self-sacrifice on the battlefield on behalf of Christendom was charity in itself.[127] In practice, however, not all contemporaries took this view. John of Würzburg, visiting Jerusalem around 1170, certainly did not: he was much more impressed by the Hospital's combined role than the predominantly military operations of the Templars.[128] The traditional forms of charity seem also to have impressed the Italian townspeople more than military activity. Hence we might expect that in times of crisis and defeat the brothers would have emulated the Hospital in reminding public opinion in Europe that they performed more conventional charitable tasks as well as fighting. Yet, they did so only once during our period.

This occurred in 1274, on the occasion of the second council of Lyons. The orders of the Temple and Hospital compiled a memorandum setting out the arguments which the master of the Temple and the senior brothers of both orders who were attending the council were to put to the Roman cardinals, in support of the orders' continuing exemption from episcopal jurisdiction. (The memorandum indicates that the orders believed that their exemption was threatened, although this was not borne out by events.) One of the arguments proposed was that, if exemption was lost, the orders' work on behalf of pilgrims, the poor, and orphans would suffer.[129]

Note that it was at this same council that the first proposal was made to unify the military orders. In the same way, in the early fourteenth century Jacques de Molay, then master of the Temple, appealed to the order's dual role in the face of a proposed merger of the military orders.[130] It appears that the order of the Temple only drew attention to its more conventional, hospitable work when its very existence was under threat.

This would indicate that the order of the Temple felt that its position in the eyes of Christendom was sufficiently secure without resorting to ingenious arguments to shore up its reputation. The prominence given to the order of the Temple over the other military orders in epics and romances, and in accounts of the loss of Acre, shows that this view was to some extent justified. However, by the late thirteenth century, the order could not afford to be complacent, both in the face of events in the east and in Europe, and of fierce rivalry from other orders.

(d) Rivalry between the military orders

There is some evidence that the military orders sometimes tried to boost their own image by defaming their rivals. We noted in chapter four that the orders' quarrels made a considerable impact on contemporaries.[131] Although the military orders' official policy was that they remain on friendly terms, records of settlements made between them demonstrate that rivalry was deep-seated and bitter.[132]

Joshua Prawer deduced that in the early 1240s the Hospitallers and Templars carried on a concerted propaganda campaign against each other, over the question of whether the Palestinian Franks should ally with the sultan of Damascus, as the Temple preferred, or the sultan of Egypt, as the Hospital preferred.[133] Walter Kuhn suggested that, during the 1250s, the order of the Temple in Germany assisted the Polish princes who were attempting to launch a crusade in Prussia in competition with the Teutonic order.[134] But this is highly speculative.

More certain evidence of denigration appears in the letter of Hugh Revel, master of the Hospital, to the prior of St Gilles in 1268. He mentioned the recent loss of three Templar castles and remarked how quickly they had fallen, and then contrasted this with the loss of one Hospitaller castle, which had held out much longer than expected against the Muslim siege. The implication seems clear: the Templars were incompetent in holding their strong fortresses, whereas the Hospitallers could achieve wonders even with their weaker fortresses.[135] In similar style, in 1289 the Flemish satirist Jacquemart Giélée, in his poem *Renart le Nouvel*, showed a Hospitaller denigrating the order of the Temple in order to win support for his own cause.[136]

Yet, such negative policies tended to backfire on the orders themselves. As Pope Gregory IX pointed out to the Templars and Hospitallers in a letter of 1235, their rivalry damaged their reputation and the Holy Land.[137] What was more, because the orders were so frequently in conflict, inter-order criticism was unlikely to convince outsiders. Matthew Paris, for one, considered that no one should believe anything that the Templars and Hospitallers said, because of their rivalry.[138]

(e) The success of these measures

We may conclude this survey by asking how far the military orders were successful in their self-presentation.

To a large extent, they failed. The ceaseless flow of information from the east to Europe, the orders' constant emphasis on their poverty and the justice of their cause, never persuaded enough influential patrons and potential crusaders in Europe to act on their behalf. They were unable to carry out their primary role of protecting pilgrims to the Holy Land, and the land itself was lost. They failed to achieve the highest reputation for sanctity at the popular level, in that few of their members were recognized as saints, and none was so recognized for his self-sacrifice on the battlefield. This may also be reflected in the fact that very few of their brothers were created bishops or archbishops, in stark contrast to other 'modern' orders, notably the friars and Cistercians. However, it may be that the military orders preferred not to have their members created bishops, because of their continual manpower shortage.

Yet they were to some extent successful. The Hospital convinced many that its history stretched back to apostolic times. The three great military orders, but particularly the order of the Temple, appear as holy knights or knight—monks in a number of epics and romances. To this degree they penetrated the thought-world of their times. They convinced the papacy of the necessity of their exempt status, which was never, despite numerous threats, rescinded. Although they were criticized alongside the other religious orders, they were never the most severely criticized. Finally, although they failed in their vocation in the Holy Land, they escaped from the loss of Acre with their reputations largely intact, and Christendom still looking to them to spearhead attempts to recover the Holy Land.

CHAPTER 7

THE IMPLICATION OF THE MILITARY ORDERS IN THE LOSS OF ACRE, MAY 1291

After May 1291 attitudes towards the military orders were irrevocably altered by the devastating news of the loss of Acre to the sultan of Egypt. Acre was the last stronghold of Latin Christendom in the Holy Land, and, when it was lost to the Muslims, the military orders lost their true purpose for existence. They had developed to protect pilgrims on the pilgrim routes in the Holy Land; these routes were now under Muslim control. They had been enlisted to help defend the frontiers of Christendom against the Muslims; in this they had failed.

Although the loss of Acre did not mark the end of European interest in the Holy Land, and many campaigns were planned for its recovery,[1] with hindsight we can see that it marks the end of an era. Although the event can hardly have come as a surprise, chroniclers recording the disaster expressed great grief, and some tried to find a scapegoat or scapegoats. As the military orders had been the best-known defenders of the Christians in the Holy Land, it was inevitable that some blame for the loss of Acre should fall on them. Soon after the loss of the city, John of Villiers, master of the Hospital, wrote to William of Villaret, prior of St Gilles, describing the recent events. His tone is that of a man who feels guilt at being alive, and who knows that his audience will blame him for saving his own life when his duty was to die at his post (as the master of the Temple had done). He escaped, he wrote, only after he had done all that he could to defend the city; he had been mortally wounded, and was carried into a ship by his servants. Otherwise, the reader feels, he would have stayed until the end.[2]

This impression is reinforced by one of the earliest third-party accounts of the loss of the city, by the chronicler of St Peter's abbey at Erfurt. This account was written before news of the evacuation of Sidon and Castle Pilgrim had reached the writer; probably in the summer of 1291. It states that the Templars, and all those who had taken refuge in their house after the city fell to the Saracens, realizing that they had no hope of being rescued, conferred, prayed, committed their souls to Christ and

then rushed out on the Saracens and fought valiantly to the last man. In
default of better information on the fate of the last defenders of the city,
this was obviously felt to be a fitting end for the knight—brothers; the
order itself was destroyed with Acre.[3] The accounts of some other
chroniclers give the same impression.[4]

Master Thaddeo of Naples gave a different account in his moralizing
history of the fall of Acre. He praised the master of the Temple, William
of Beaujeu, and the marshal of the Hospital, Matthew of Claremont, who
had given their lives in the defence of the city, declaring them martyrs;
but castigated the rest of their brothers for escaping rather than dying.
In contrast, he had great praise for the Teutonic brothers, who 'in the
boldness of the mind of faith persisted in their intention of dying for
Christ. . .' and 'were taken up to the joys of eternal refreshment'.[5]

In the light of such reports, Pope Nicholas IV's proposal that the
military orders be unified seemed a reasonable means of providing for the
remaining brothers in Europe. Nicholas' stated reason for making his
proposal was that the disputes between the military orders had
contributed towards the downfall of Acre.[6] This opinion was shared by
the anonymous writer of the best known account of the loss of Acre, the
De excidio urbis Acconis.[7] But around fifteen years later, James of Molay,
then master of the Temple, accused Nicholas of calling the Church councils and making this proposal only in order to make it appear that he was
doing something to deal with the situation, and to deflect blame for the
loss of the city from himself.[8] Certainly, it is likely that those contemporary chroniclers who blamed the loss of the city on the military orders'
quarrels were inspired by the pope's remarks.[9]

Surprisingly, in view of the orders' past history of being accused of
treachery, their integrity was left unquestioned in the direct wake of the
loss of Acre. Only a letter sent to Europe by the king of Armenia, which
purported to have been sent to him by the victorious sultan of Egypt,
accused the Templars of acting treacherously, and rejoiced that all three
orders had been utterly destroyed. Although the letter was recorded both
by Bartholomew Cotton at Norwich and in the episcopal register of
Winchester,[10] such accusations by the hated enemy are more likely to
have vindicated the military orders' reputation than blackened it. Thaddeo of Naples denounced those Templars and Hospitallers who had
escaped alive as dishonoured cowards, but did not accuse them of
treachery.[11]

However, the De excidio urbis Acconis accused the Templars of being late
in coming to the defence of the city and ineffectual when they appeared,
in striking contrast to the Hospitallers. In particular, the prowess of
Brother Matthew of Claremont, the marshal of the Hospital, was
described at considerable length with much rhetoric and stirring
speech.[12] This account, written soon after the loss of the city, was the

most popular account of the disaster, surviving in a large number of Latin and French manuscripts, and was copied into many chronicles.[13] It must have done a great deal to redress the balance of European opinion in the Hospitallers' favour, after they had suffered the humiliating publicity defeat of failing to be annihilated in their last stand, even retaining their master alive. This account demonstrated that, although the master and many brothers had escaped, the courage and martyrdom of Brother Matthew had more than proven the order's virtue. By brushing over the deeds of William of Beaujeu, and belittling the Templars' efforts at defending their house when the city was lost (they are shown as ineffectual and principally concerned to save their treasure) this account effectively removed the order of the Temple from the limelight and gave all the glory for the defence of the city to the Hospital.

The significance of this version of events was even greater than appears at first sight, for, as Jacquemart Giélée shows, the Templars claimed to be solely responsible for the defence of the Holy Land, even claiming that, if they were to withdraw, there would be nothing to stop the Muslims overrunning the Holy Land and Europe as well.[14] Thaddeo of Naples endorses Giélée's description of the Templars' claims and extends it, showing that the master of the Temple was particularly responsible for the safety of Acre. The Saracens knew, he says, that as long as William lived, their evil could have no effect on the Christians.[15] Rutebuef had also made this clear in his poem *Nouvelle complaint d'Outremer*. Bar Hebraeus' continuator called William of Beaujeu the Franks' 'Governor, the great count', and showed that if he had not been killed, the city would not have fallen. Towards the middle of the fourteenth century, the Italian chronicler Giovanni Villani would repeat this belief in even stronger terms: William of Beaujeu had been 'capitano generale della guerra, e della guardia della Terra'.[16] Thus the Templars' failure to defend the city was a greater disaster for them than for any other order or group.

This final failure, more than any other, cast doubts on the order's worthiness to protect the Holy Places. Ricoldo of Monte Cruce made an observation on the master's death which will bear further consideration. If William of Beaujeu had not died, he wrote, the city could have been held; but he was shot by a Saracen, pierced by an arrow between stomach and liver, 'like a second Ahab'. The reference is to the Old Testament, the first book of Kings, chapter 22, verses 34–5, and appears innocent enough; but Ricoldo was a Friar Preacher, and knew his Bible better than most. The reference to Ahab may be considered curiously appropriate in view of William of Beaujeu's royal connections, his international reputation, his great worldly influence, his alliances with Muslims. For Ahab, king of Israel, was also a man of great international reputation; the king of Judah was subject to him; he built an ivory palace and many cities; and he had an alliance with the pagan monarch of Sidon, whose daughter, Jezebel, he married. Yet Ahab is perhaps the most memorably unworthy king of the Old Testament: 'Never was a man who sold himself to do what is wrong in the Lord's eyes as Ahab did'. Ricoldo appears to be saying that, just as Ahab, king of Israel, was unworthy to rule the kingdom of Israel, so William of Beaujeu, master of the Temple, was unworthy to hold the city of Acre; and likewise his order.[17]

CONCLUSION

We have examined various images of the military orders expressed by individuals between 1128 and 1291, attempting to identify these individuals and to establish patterns of opinions expressed over time and across Christendom. We have seen that there was considerable criticism of the military orders: of their canonical basis as religious orders, of their defence of the Holy Land and of their other activities; but that this criticism is no more significant than criticism of other religious orders or of the Church as a whole.

The principal criticisms levelled at the military orders between 1128 and 1291 were that they were proud, envious, greedy, hated their fellow military orders or used violence against each other, treacherous, that they were in alliance with the Muslims, slothful or cowardly, rash, impeded the conversion of non-Christians, and did not use their extensive assets effectively in support of the Holy Land. It is worth asking how far these criticisms were justified.

The brothers were certainly proud. Pride was a normal characteristic of knights, for whom it was a legitimate self-confidence in their own abilities. But monks also had a considerable pride in their own profession; hence knight—monks would be doubly proud. Again, clerical criticism of the orders' vocation probably aroused a defiant and self-protecting aloofness among the brothers.

Charges of envy cannot be easily substantiated. The accusations of avarice, however, appear fully justified.

Like the Cistercians, the orders were always willing to acquire land or other possessions. According to the story of the enchanted gold, they were prepared to betray their Christian comrades to this end. Certainly one attempt to bribe Templars was successful, when Brother Hugh of Stockton and other Templars of the English house released some criminals from their house at Bisham in exchange for a silver goblet.[1] The consuls of Muhlhausen suspected the Teutonic brothers of claiming parishes which had not been granted to them,[2] while in 1288 the Hospitallers and Templars in the kingdom of Sicily were accused of taking over monasteries and buying others which belonged by right to the Roman Church.[3] Jacquemart Giélée's Templar states that his order must keep increasing its possessions, in order to defend the Holy Church.[4]

Many legal cases arose out of such acquisitiveness. Before 1292, Christine of Esperston was evicted from her own house by Brother Brian of Jay, preceptor of the Templars' house at Temple, Midlothian, in Scotland.[5] In 1282 the Hospital in France lost a case against one Enguerrand of Fieffes, knight, who maintained that a loan of two hundred pounds which the order was claiming from him was in fact cash which they had paid him for a sale.[6] Such cases must have damaged the orders' reputation. Although they were far from being unique among religious orders in their involvement in such disputes, they gained a particular reputation for legal manoeuvring which caused considerable annoyance to lay opponents.[7]

The accusations of greed may also have reflected hostility to the orders as moneylenders. However, no specific complaints were ever made against these operations, except John of Joinville's annoyance at the Templars' bureaucracy.[8]

The orders' mutual quarrels certainly made a deep impression on contemporaries,[9] such that they had a reputation for constant quarrelling, although in fact they often co-operated.[10] Not only did the officials of the orders make frequent attempts to bring peace between the brothers, but local houses, or brothers within them, made gifts to each other on various occasions.[11] But it was easy to blame the Holy Land's troubles on such an obvious cause.

The military orders were often accused of treachery or deceit. Sometimes this was due to simple misunderstanding, such as the Peterborough chronicler's complaints that Hugh of Payns had lied in 1128 when he had collected money and men in England for 'a great war' between the Christians and the heathens.[12]

Another reason for suspicion was the many well-publicized cases of renegades occurring during the orders' history. Yet a 'renegade' could be no more than the commanding officer of a fortress besieged by the Saracens, forced to come to terms in order to save as much as he could for his order. Some accusations of treachery were simply attempts by disappointed crusaders to blame someone other than themselves for their defeat. The remarks attributed by Matthew Paris to the Templars and Hospitallers at the battle of Mansourah sum up the orders' natural defence against such accusations; why should they have joined a religious order if they were then to strive to overturn the Church and lose their souls?[13]

It is hardly surprising that the brothers were accused of being in alliance with the Muslims, as Gérald de Montréal, secretary of Brother

William de Beaujeu, master of the Temple, in 1285, recorded that the master was in close contact with a Saracen emir.[14] At the beginning of the thirteenth century, Leo, king of Armenia, had complained to Innocent III that the Templars were allied with the sultan of Aleppo against him.[15] Otto of St Blasien, writing between 1209 and 1222, accused all the Palestinian Franks, including the Templars and Hospitallers, of being friendly with the Muslims and so impeding the Germans' crusade of 1197–8.[16] Later critics such as Pope Gregory IX, Emperor Frederick II and Count Robert of Artois complained that the alliances of the Templars, or the Templars and Hospitallers, with the Muslims of Damascus or Cairo, were harming the Christian cause in the Holy Land.[17] Similar accusations were made against the Swordbrothers in Livonia, and the Hospitallers in the Latin empire of Constantinople.[18] But chroniclers also depicted the brothers as the Muslims' dupes.[19]

Accusations that the orders were not sufficiently enthusiastic about their vocation, of sloth or cowardice, usually stemmed from Europeans' failure to comprehend the actual situation in the Holy Land; for instance, the refusal of the Templars and Hospitallers during the third crusade to support campaigns to gain land and fortresses which could not be defended after the crusaders had gone home.[20] Nevertheless, even William of Tyre, who was fully aware of the problems, believed that they did not do enough to defend the Holy Land.[21] Certainly the rumours that the Templars were unwilling to besiege Ascalon in 1153 because they would lose a rich source of plunder were probably well founded.[22]

With this accusation we should expect to find the criticism that the orders were fond of easy living, *luxure*, which included a lack of chastity. The nearest thing to such an accusation is the remark of the writer of *Sur les états du monde*, in the first half of the thirteenth century, that the Hospitallers had no use for hired women as long as they had their horses, which were famed for their quality.[23] Jacquemart Giélée also implies such an accusation by placing both the Hospital and Temple under the control of *renars*. There were many complaints that the orders were wealthy,[24] and the orders themselves were at pains to point out to new recruits that life in the orders was not as comfortable as their image might have led them to believe;[25] but direct accusations of *luxure* were reserved for Cluniacs and the bishops.[26]

There were very few direct criticisms of the orders' use of violence; the overwhelming bulk of Christendom approved of it.[27] Yet accusations that the brothers were rash or failed to keep discipline may indicate opposition to the use of violence. Such accusations appeared sporadically, especially in connection with defeats; for instance, expressed by the Benedictine satirist Nigel of Longchamps shortly after the defeat of the Christian forces by Saladin in June 1179, and by Matthew Paris as a cause of the defeat of the Templars at Darbsak in 1237. This was a particularly significant criticism, as initially the Temple's discipline had greatly impressed onlookers.[28]

Accusations that the brothers impeded the conversion of non-Christians were more common, originating in William of Tyre's popular tales. They also appeared in connection with the activities of the Sword-brothers and the Teutonic order in Livonia and Prussia.[29] There is no reason to doubt these accusations. The Teutonic brothers were quoted as declaring that they held more power as lords of pagans than as lords of Christians.[30] Slaves were a valuable commodity, and if they were baptized their exploitation was limited, and the way opened for their manumission. In 1262, the Hospitallers' general chapter issued statutes forbidding slaves to be baptized without the master's special permission.[31] Although some onlookers considered that the orders should be encouraging conversions, the orders were more concerned to guard their economic interests so as to press on more effectively with their military and hospitaller activities.

Europeans did not believe that the military orders needed to guard their assets so jealously; they thought that they were rich, and that their constant cries of poverty were the result of using their assets inefficiently. Matthew Paris first recorded this complaint, but it was such a natural reaction to the orders' extensive exemptions from episcopal authority that it had probably been voiced for many years, at least since the Third Lateran Council, and possibly since the orders first started to acquire extensive properties in the west. The complaint arose in 1274 at the second council of Lyons and at the Church councils held in February 1292, as a result of the loss of Acre. The Church councils blamed the orders' quarrels for their inefficiency, and recommended that they be unified.[32]

The orders' defence was that they had far greater expenses than any monarch of western Europe, and very little income from their western possessions, for various reasons.[33] Certainly, the orders' bureaucracy was inefficient, but it was limited by contemporary communications and financial management. Nevertheless, the European complaints were understandable; they saw the orders' vast estates, privileges and exemptions, and were unable to understand how the orders could fail to make ends meet, unless they were riddled with corruption, or avaricious, or deceitful. Through the medium of letters alone, the military orders could not convince Europeans of the true crisis in the east.

What of the accusations made against the order of the Temple in 1307? We have seen that some of the accusations were certainly true. All the military orders kept their chapter meetings secret.[34] In view of the orders' record for legal wrangling, the brothers probably did not reckon it a sin to acquire property by illegal means, nor to procure profit for the order in any possible way, nor to commit perjury in order to do this.

There is no evidence, however, that the order had not made charitable gifts, and it certainly lodged bishops and kings on their travels. There is no evidence of any abuses in the admission of new brothers during our period. Nor were the brothers ever accused of errors in their beliefs, although as most of the brothers were uneducated men they were probably guilty of errors of ignorance.

The two most outrageous charges, sodomy and idolatry, never appeared among criticisms of the order before 1291. Pope Gregory IX once accused the Hospital of having heretics among its ranks, and warned the brothers to reform themselves; which they apparently did, as the problem was never mentioned again.[35] The orders' rules contained strict penalties for the sins of heresy or sodomy, but any cases which occurred did not attract public attention.[36] Walter Map, Matthew Paris and Jacquemart Giélée would certainly have mentioned sins of this type, had they known of them. In contrast, John of Salisbury and Walter Map had made accusations of homosexuality against Cistercians and Cluniacs.[37] Probably the military orders were thought to be too manly to resort to such practices, as they practised the virile profession of arms; keeping the brothers away from women was a far greater problem.[38] It is clear that the charges brought in the trial were no more than conventional accusations made against political opponents.[39]

While most of the criticism aimed at the military orders during the period 1128–1291 was justified or at least had a reasonable basis, it was balanced by praise. Although the orders' critics might call for reform, there were no calls for abolition. Criticism was aimed at all the military orders in general, although the Temple and the Hospital (in that order) received most attention from critics, simply because they were most in the public eye. And it was insignificant in comparison with the criticism aimed by both secular and regular clergy and the laity against corruption and lack of spirituality within the Church as a whole. Much of the criticism aimed at the military orders was simply part of this greater discontent at the state of Christendom, and must be considered in that context; it did not indicate vast discontent with the military orders in particular.

Yet, any criticism of the military orders was significant, in that they were the defenders of the Holy Land and all Christendom, 'the defenders of the Holy Church', as Jacquemart Giélée's Templar put it.[40] Their early popularity, the praises and gifts heaped upon them, reflected this. Even in the late thirteenth century, Jacquemart Giélée's treatment of them indicates that they were seen to represent the highest standards of the Church, the last bastion of virtue. Hugh of Trimberg drew attention to the 'high Templar order' as representing what had been best in all

Figure 8. The masters of the Temple (left) and Hospital (right) do homage to
Renart the fox, from Jacquemart Giélée's *Renart le nouvel*, BN MS Fr. 372 f.59.
(Phot. Bibl. Nat. Paris.)

religious orders, while Archbishop John Peckham mentioned the Temple
alongside the Grandmontines as an order which had formerly been of the
highest virtue.[41] Thus their fall from virtue was the most disastrous fall
of the whole Church.

Moreover, unlike other religious orders, the military orders had a
specific vocation in which they could be seen to succeed or to fail: the
care of pilgrims in the Holy Land and the defence of Christendom.
Failure was taken as a sign of God's displeasure, and therefore of sin.

The military orders were, therefore, particularly vulnerable to criticism, and none more so than the order of the Temple. This was not so much because it lacked the dual function of the Hospital and Teutonic order, but because, as we discussed in chapter five, it had caught public imagination to a greater degree than the other military orders, and was therefore more in the public eye. Moreover, as the first military order, it was considered to be principally responsible for the protection of the Holy Land.

Yet its weakness did not necessitate its destruction. In 1291 the order of the Temple and the other international military orders were well-established religious orders, indispensable to pope and kings, widely respected for their wealth and power, if not always their virtues. Christendom looked to them to spearhead the recapture of the Holy Land, after undergoing a few fundamental, necessary reforms to render them more efficient.[42] The orders were not so corrupt that they could not be saved. The concept of the military order remained unquestioned, and abolition unthinkable; at least, no one appears to have thought of it.

NOTES

Introduction

1. At the time of writing, there was no good general history of the Templars or the Teutonic knights in English. For the Hospitallers, see J. Riley-Smith, *The knights of St John in Jerusalem and Cyprus, c.1050–1310* (London, 1967). Alan Forey has written numerous articles on various aspects of the military orders: see the bibliography. Malcolm Barber is working on a general history of the Templars. The best general work on the Templars available at the time of writing is Marie Luise Bulst-Thiele's biography of the masters of the order, *Sacrae domus militiae Templi Hierosolymitani magistri: Untersuchungen zur Geschichte des Templerordens 1118/9–1314* (Göttingen, 1974). On the Teutonic order, H. Boockmann, *Der Deutsche Orden: Zwölf Kapitel aus seiner Geschichte* (Munich, 1982) is useful. A. Forey's *The military orders: from the twelfth to the early fourteenth centuries*. New studies in medieval history (Basingstoke, 1992) appeared while this book was at the press.
2. *Willelmi Tyrensis archiepiscopi Chronicon; Guillaume de Tyr, Chronique*, ed. R. B. C. Huygens, 2 vols., Corpus Christianorum — continuatio medievalis, 63 (Turnholt, 1986) (henceforth 'William of Tyre') Bk. 12, ch. 7 pp. 553–4; *Chronique d'Ernoul et de Bernard le trésorier*, ed. L. de Mas Latrie, SHF (Paris, 1871) (henceforth 'Ernoul') pp. 7–8.
3. These were Simon, a monk of St Bertin of Sith, Flanders (writing 1135–40), 'Gesta abbatum Sancti Bertini Sithensium', ed. O. Holder Egger, *MGHS* 13 p. 649; Anselm, bishop of Havelburg, an Augustinian canon (writing to Pope Eugenius III in 1145) 'Dialogus', *PL* 188, col. 1156; and Otto, bishop of Freising (writing between 1143 and 1158), 'Chronicon', ed. R. Wilmans, *MGHS* 20 pp. 252–3.
4. William of Tyre, p. 554, Bk. 12, ch. 7; *La Règle du Temple*, ed. H. de Curzon, SHF (Paris, 1886) para. 3 (translated as: H. de Curzon, ed., *The French text of the rule of order of Knights Templar*, trans. J. M. Upton-Ward, (Woodbridge, 1992)).
5. *CGH*, no. 130: Pope Innocent II.
6. A. Forey, 'The militarisation of the Hospital of St John', *Studia monastica* 26 (1984) 75–89, especially 82.
7. J. Riley-Smith, 'The Templars and the Teutonic knights in Cilician Armenia', in T. S. R. Boase, ed., *The Cilician kingdom of Armenia*, (Edinburgh, 1978)

pp. 93–4; S. S. Rovik, 'The Templars in the Holy Land during the XIIth century', unpublished Ph.D. thesis (Oxford, 1986) pp. 187–9.

8. See A. Forey, 'The military orders and the Spanish reconquest in the twelfth and thirteenth centuries', *Traditio*, 40 (1984) 198–9.

9. See *ibid.*, 200–1, for dates.

10. The best study of these orders in English is in E. Christiansen, *The northern crusades: the Baltic and the Catholic frontier 1100–1525* (London, 1980) pp. 76–8, 95–8. A more detailed account is given by W. Kuhn, 'Ritterorden als Grenzhüter des Abendlandes gegen das östliche Heidentum' *Ostdeutsche Wissenschaft* 6 (1959) 12–16, 26–42.

11. U. Arnold, 'Entstehung und Frühzeit des Deutschen Ordens, zu Gründung und innerer Struktur des Deutschen Hospitals von Akkon und des Ritterordens in der ersten Hälfte des 13 Jahrhunderts', in J. Fleckenstein and M. Hellmann, eds., *Die Geistlichen Ritterorden Europas*, Vorträge und Forschungen, 26 (Sigmaringen, 1980) pp. 81–98, especially pp. 96–7.

12. Kuhn, 'Ritterorden', 16–22; Boockmann, *Deutsche Orden*, pp. 68–9.

13. *HDFS* 2, pp. 549–52.

14. Peter of Dusburg, *Chronik des Preussenlandes*, ed. K. Scholz and D. Wojtecki (Darmstadt, 1984) p. 336, para. 221. For the conquest of Prussia, see Christiansen, *Northern Crusades*, pp. 100–4; Boockmann, *Deutsche Orden*, pp. 69, 80–114.

15. See P. M. Tumler, *Der Deutsche Orden in Werden, Wachsen und Wirken bis 1400* (Montreal and Vienna, 1955) pp. 178–181.

16. See my article, 'Templar attitudes towards women', *Medieval history* 1, 3 (1991) 74–80.

17. *RHGF* 18, p. 526, the emperor Henry to Pope Innocent III; also in *PL* 215 col. 708, year 8 no. 131.

18. See E. Delaruelle, 'Templiers et Hospitaliers en Languedoc pendant la croisade contre les Albigeois', *Cahiers de Fanjeaux, 4: Paix de Dieu et guerre sainte en Languedoc au XIIIe siècle* (1969) pp. 327–330.

19. *CGH*, nos. 3279, 3308 (vol.4).

20. See A. Forey, 'The military order of St Thomas of Acre', *English historical review*, 92 (1977) 481–503.

21. N. Housley, *The Italian crusades. The papal–Angevin alliance and the crusades against Christian lay powers, 1254–1343* (Oxford, 1982) pp. 151–6, 158–9, 162–70, 252–3, 257; E. Siberry, *Criticism of crusading, 1095–1274* (Oxford, 1985) pp. 217–220.

22. H. E. Mayer, *The crusades*, trans. J. Gillingham, 2nd edition (Oxford, 1988) pp. 320–1, note 143.

23. M. Barber, *The trial of the Templars* (Cambridge, 1978) pp. 248–52.

24. J. Prawer, 'Military orders and crusader politics in the second half of the XIIIth century', in Fleckenstein and Hellmann, eds., *Geistlichen Ritterorden*, pp. 217–229; M. Melville, *La vie des Templiers* (Paris, 1951) pp. 165–6; P. Partner, *The murdered magicians: the Templars and their myth* (Oxford, 1982) pp. 24–6, 31–2.

25. J. M. Upton-Ward, 'Attitudes towards the Templars (*c.*1119–1312)', unpublished M.A. thesis, University of Reading, 1986. I am grateful to Mrs. Upton-Ward for permission to read her thesis.

26. E.g., A. Forey, *The Templars in the* Corona de Aragon, (London, 1973) *passim*; 'The military orders and the Spanish reconquest in the twelfth and thirteenth centuries', *Traditio*, 40 (1984) 198–234; R. I. Burns, *The crusader kingdom of Valencia: reconstruction on a thirteenth-century frontier*, 2 vols. (Cambridge, Mass., 1967) 1 pp. 173–196.

27. Cf. Mayer, *The crusades*, p. 278.

28. See D. A. Trotter, *Medieval French literature and the crusades, 1100–1300* (Geneva, 1987) pp. 20ff., esp. p. 27.

Chapter one

1. Implied by Bernard of Clairvaux in his 'Liber ad milites Templi de laude novae militiae', in *Opera*, ed. J. Leclerq and H. M. Rochais, 8 vols. (Rome, 1957–77) 3 pp. 214–5, 217, 220–2; and by Hugh 'Peccator', published by J. Leclerq, 'Un document sur les débuts des Templiers', *Revue de l'histoire ecclesiastique*, 52 (1957) 86–9, esp. 86 paras. 1, 2.

2. E.g., by John of Salisbury, Gerhoh of Reichersberg, William of Tyre, Walter Map and the bishops at the third Lateran council. See chapter three.

3. John of Würzburg, 'Descriptio Terrae Sanctae', in *PL* 155, col. 1087; 'Annales Herbipolenses', ed. G. H. Pertz, *MGHS* 16 p. 7; see also John of Salisbury, *Historia pontificalis*, ed. M. Chibnall (London and Edinburgh, 1956) p. 57.

4. For example, 'Un poème contemporain sur Saladin', ed. G. Paris, *ROL* 1 (1893) 439–40; *Libellus de expugnatione Terrae Sanctae per Saladinum*, in Ralph of Coggeshall, *Chronicon Anglicanum*, ed. J. Stevenson, RS 66 (London, 1875) pp. 211–6, 225, 237, 239; *Itinerarium peregrinorum et gesta regis Ricardi*, in W. Stubbs, ed., *Chronicles and memorials of the reign of Richard I*, 2 vols., RS 38 (London, 1864–5) 1 pp. 6–8, 16–17; Ambroise, *Estoire de guerre sainte: histoire en vers de la troisième croisade*, ed. G. Paris (Paris, 1897) lines 2489–2506; 'Ein zeitgenössisches Gedicht auf die Belagerung Accons', ed. H. Prutz, *Forschungen zur Deutschen Geschichte*, 21 (1881) 457–94, lines 125–6, 145–156.

5. E.g., Ambroise, lines 3021–33; 'Zeitgenössisches Gedicht', lines 767–786, 1125–8.

6. See chapter five.

7. Roger of Howden, *Chronica*, ed. W. Stubbs, 4 vols., RS 51 (London, 1868–71) 4 pp. 76–77; Guiot of Provins, 'La Bible', in *Les oeuvres de Guiot de Provins, poète lyrique et satirique*, ed. J. Orr (Manchester, 1915) lines 1745–1782, 1789–1818; Innocent III, 'Liber registorum sive epistolarum', 3 vols., *PL* 214–216, 215 cols. 1217–8, Bk. 10 no. 121, 216 cols. 591–4, Bk. 15 no. 69, col. 688, Bk. 15 no. 162.

8. Ernoul, pp. 462–5. For the authorship of this chronicle see M. R. Morgan, *The chronicle of Ernoul and the continuations of William of Tyre* (Oxford, 1973).

9. Philip of Novara, 'Memoirs', in *Les Gestes des Chyprois, recueil de chroniques françaises écrites en orient en XIII et XIV siècles*, ed. G. Raynaud, SOL (Paris, 1887, reprinted Osnabrück, 1968) pp. 28–9, para. 102, p. 49, para. 137, p. 50, para. 138.

10. Philip Mousket, 'Historia regum Francorum', extr. ed. A. Tobler, *MGHS* 26, pp. 819–820, lines 31015ff., 31158ff; see also p. 718 for his origins. He was probably from Tournai, of good but non-knightly family.

11. 'Continuatio Cuonradi praepositi Urspergensis', ed. O. Abel and L. Weiland, *MGHS* 23, pp. 381, 383.

12. Bernart Sicart de Marvejols, 'Ab greu cossire', in M. Raynouard, ed., *Choix des poésies originales des troubadours*, 6 vols. (Paris, 1816–21) 4, p. 192, stanza 3.

13. The Templars were praised for their courage in the panegyric 'du bon William Longespee', in A. Jubinal, ed., *Nouveau recueil de contes, dits, fabliaux et autres pièces inédits des XIIIe, XIVe et XVe siècles*, 2 vols., (Paris, 1839–42) 2 pp. 339–353; *Annales Cestrienses, or the chronicle of the abbey of St Werburg at Chester*, ed. R. C. Christie, Lancashire and Cheshire Record Society, 14 (1886) p. 66. The Templars and Hospitallers were praised for their prudence by Matthew Paris, *CM* 5 pp. 147–154; the Templars were praised for prudence in 'La continuation de Guillaume de Tyr, de 1228 à 1261, dit du manuscrit de Rothelin', in *RHC Occ* 2, pp. 604–6.

14. Gilbert of Tournai, 'Collectio de scandalis ecclesiae', ed. A. Stroick, *Archivum Franciscanum historicum*, 24 (1931) 56–7, para. 17.

15. Bruno, bishop of Olmütz, 'Bericht am Papst Gregor X', in C. Höfler, 'Analecten zur Geschichte Deutschlands und Italiens', part 1, *Abhandlungen der philosophisch–historischen Klasse der Königlich Bayerischen Akademie der Wissenschaften*, series 3, 4 part 3 (1846) pp. 18–28; Humbert of Romans, 'Opus tripartium', in *Fasciculus rerum expetendarum et fugiendarum*, 2, Appendix, ed. E. Brown, 2 vols. (London, 1690) pp. 185–228.

16. In *Councils and synods with other documents relating to the English Church*, ed. D. Whitelock, F. M. Powicke et al., 2 vols. in 4 (Oxford, 1964–81) 2, 2 ed. F. M. Powicke and C. R. Cheney, p. 815.

17. James I, King of Aragon, *Chronicle*, trans. J. Forster, 2 vols. (London, 1883) pp. 647–650, chapters 532–534.

18. For a useful introduction, see J. Burton, 'Reform or revolution? Monastic movements of the eleventh and twelfth centuries', *Medieval History* 1, 2, 23–36. On monasticism generally see C. H. Lawrence, *Medieval monasticism: forms of religious life in western Europe in the middle ages* (London and New York, 1984).

19. In recent years, Jean Flori has carried out extensive research into contemporary attitudes towards the concept of knighthood and how these developed. See the bibliography.

20. J. Flori, *L'essor de la chevalerie, XIe–XIIe siècles* (Geneva, 1986) pp. 182ff., 186; see also, on the theory of three orders, G. Duby, *The three orders: feudal society imagined*, trans. A. Goldhammer (Chicago, 1980).

21. See Flori, *Essor*, pp. 218–9, 274; M. Keen, *Chivalry* (New Haven and London, 1984) pp. 44–63.

22. E.g., *Li romanz du Reis Yder*, ed. A. Adams (Cambridge, 1982) lines 3662–3727 (written in the early thirteenth century).

23. See *Le moniage Guillaume: les deux rédactions en vers du moniage Guillaume, chansons de geste du XIIe siècle*, ed. W. Cloetta, 2 vols., SATF (Paris, 1906–11); and *Le moniage Rainouart 1: publié d'après les manuscrits de l'Arsenal et de*

Boulogne, ed. G. A. Bertin, SATF (Paris, 1973) (both written in the late twelfth century).

24. *La mort de roi Artu, roman du XIIIe siècle*, ed. J. Frappier, TLF 58 (Geneva and Paris, 1964) pp. 258—9, para. 200, p. 263 para. 204 (examples of knights becoming hermits); p. 225 para. 176 (Gawain).

25. See *Renaut de Montalban*, ed. J. Thomas, TLF 371 (Geneva, 1989); cf. *Butler's Lives of the saints*, edited, revised and supplemented by H. Thurston and D. Attwater, 4 vols. (London, 1956) 1 pp. 48—9, 7th Jan: 'St Reinold'.

26. See Partner, *Murdered magicians*, pp. 39—40.

Chapter two

1. R. Hiestand, ed., *Papsturkunden für Templer und Johanniter*, (Göttingen, 1972) (henceforth 'Hiestand') nos. 8, 9, 11, 20, 26, 28, 32, 33, 44, 46, 49, 146; *PL* 188 col. 1537; C. R. Cheney and M. G. Cheney, eds., *The letters of Innocent III (1198—1216) concerning England and Wales. A calendar with an appendix of texts* (Oxford, 1967) no. 192; *Les registres de Clement IV*, ed. E. Jordan, BEFAR (Paris, 1893—1945) no. 1764. Judas Maccabaeus, the liberator of the Jews from the rule of pagan kings in the second century BC, was regarded during our period as the epitome of the knight of God.

2. E. Strehlke, ed., *Tabulae Ordinis Theutonici ex tabularii regii Berolinensis codice potissimum*, new edition with preface by H. E. Mayer (Jerusalem, 1975) (henceforth 'Strehlke') Honorius III: p. 290 no. 321, p. 333 no. 403, Gregory IX: pp. 56—7 no. 72. Cf. *ibid.*, p. 329 no.389: Honorius III compares the Teutonic knights to Mattathias, Judas Maccabaeus' father.

3. *CGH* nos. 1536 (as Strehlke, no. 389) 2928, 3153.

4. Templars as *athletae Christi*: Hiestand, nos. 38, 64, (*Paci et Quieti*, reissued nos. 65, 70, 82, 85, 91, 99, 100, 119, 137) *PL* 200, col. 774 no. 856; *Foedera, Conventiones, Litterae et cuiuscumque generis acta publica. . .* ed. T. Rymer and R. Sanderson, enlarged and amended by A. Clark and F. Holbrooke, 4 vols. in 7 parts, Record Commission (London 1816—69) 1, 1 p. 333 (*Paci et Quieti*). Hospitallers as *athletae Christi*: *CGH* nos. 290, 3997; in *Paci et Quieti*, *CGH* nos. 429, 1064, 1564, 1625, 1644, 1681, 1723, 1873, 1909, 2128, 2309, 2318, 2333, 2374, 2415, 2447, 2501, 2579, 2619, 2620, 2891, 2954, 3155, 3257, 3258 (last issued by Clement IV in 1267). Teutonic brothers as *athletae Christi*: Strehlke, no. 358: in *Paci et Quieti: ibid.*, nos. 379, 391, 392, 426, 433, 448, 454, 457, 503. All three orders: *Les registres de Nicolas IV*, ed. E. Langlois, 1 vol. in 2, BEFAR (Paris, 1905) nos. 4204—6, *CGH* no. 4147, Strehlke nos. 665—6. Temple and Hospital: *MGHES* 1 no. 80, p. 60.

5. Teutonic order: Clement IV in Strehlke, no. 647. Temple: *Reg. Nic. IV* no. 4098. Hospital: *Les registres de Nicolas III*, ed. J. Gay, BEFAR (Paris, 1938) no. 188, *CGH* no. 3677.

6. A. Luchaire, ed., *Études sur les actes de Louis VII*, (Paris, 1885) pp. 174—5, nos. 236, 239; J. Tardif, ed., *Monuments historiques* (Paris, 1866) pp. 267—8, no. 504.

7. *CGH* nos. 1590—1, 1602—3.

8. *CGH* nos. 955, 3303.
9. *Acta imperii adhuc inedita: acta imperii inde ab Henrico I ad Henricum VI usque adhuc inedita*, ed. K. F. Stumpf-Brentano, 2 vols. (Innsbruck, 1865–81) 1 p. 739 no. 528, p. 711 no. 510.
10. *HDFS* 2 pp. 157–9, 160–3, 163–5.
11. E.g., *Les registres de Gregoire IX*, ed. L. Auvray, 4 vols., BEFAR (Paris, 1896––1955) no. 4129; *Reg. Nich. III*, no. 167.
12. *Itinerarium*, p. 26; Gerard of Wales, *Opera*, ed. J. S. Brewer *et al.*, 8 vols., RS 21 (London, 1861–91) 8 p. 191; see also H. E. Mayer, 'Henry II of England and the Holy Land', *English historical review*, 97 (1982) 724–5.
13. *CGH*, no. 405.
14. *Records of the Templars in England in the twelfth century: the inquest of 1185 with illustrative charters and documents*, ed. B. A. Lees (London, 1935) (henceforth cited as 'Lees') pp. xxxix–xl; for the donations, see: *Regesta regum Anglo-Normannorum, 1066–1154*, 3 (1135–1154) ed. H. A. Cronne, R. H. C. Davis (Oxford, 1968) pp. 310–315, nos. 843–866 *passim*.
15. Rymer's *Foedera*, 1, 1 pp. 40, 49; *Rotuli Chartarum in Turri Londinensi asservati*, ed. T. D. Hardy (London, 1837) 1, 1 (1199–1216) pp. 67b–8; *Calendar of the Charter Rolls preserved in the Public Record Office*, vol.1ff., 1226ff. (London, 1903ff.) 1 (1227–1257) p. 200; S. Lloyd, *English society and the crusade, 1216–1307* (Oxford, 1988) p. 240, note; Forey, 'St Thomas of Acre', 481–2, 494.
16. Although both orders received gifts throughout the whole of Henry's reign, the Templars received a number of bucks at Pentecost each year for their annual chapter (first recorded in *Close Rolls of the reign of Henry III preserved in the Public Record Office*, 1227ff. (London, 1902ff.) (1231–1234) p. 90 (26 July 1232) and between 1235 and 1246 they also received a gift of wine for consumption at the chapter (first recorded *ibid.*, (1234–1237) p. 94; last *ibid.*, (1242–1247) p. 422). They also received an annual payment of fifty marks to maintain a knight in the Holy Land, unpaid after 1259 probably because of the king's financial difficulties: (*Calendar of the Liberate Rolls preserved in the Public Record Office: Henry III*, 6 vols. (London, 1916–64) 4, (1251–1260) pp. 53–4, 173, 482). Some of these gifts were due to the generosity of Henry's predecessors, but some would have been due to Henry's friendship with Brother Geoffrey the Templar, his almoner from 1229 to 1240 and keeper of the royal wardrobe from 1236 to 1240 (see A. Sandys, 'The financial and administrative importance of the London Temple in the thirteenth century', in A. G. Little and F. M. Powicke, eds., *Essays in medieval history presented to Thomas Frederick Tout* (Manchester, 1925) p. 150). In addition, in 1231 Henry III and his queen, Eleanor of Provence, bequeathed their bodies to the order of the Temple (*Charter Rolls*, 1 pp. 135, 210–1; *Monasticon Anglicanum*, ed. W. Dugdale, new edn. ed. J. Caley, H. Ellis and B. Bandinel, 6 vols. in 8 (London, 1817–30) 6, 2 p. 818 nos. 1, 2); but after 1245 Henry bequeathed his body to Westminster Abbey, his own foundation: cf. Matthew Paris, *Flores Historiarum*, ed. H. R. Luard, 3 vols. RS 95 (London, 1890) 3 p. 28. After around 1250, the Hospital received more individual gifts than the Temple: e.g. *Close Rolls*, (1251–1253) pp. 30, 152, (1256–1259) pp. 92, 217, 240, 372–3, (1259–1261) pp. 416–7, (1261–1264) pp. 79, 82, 83, 360, (1264–1268) p. 274, (1268–1272) p. 361; *CGH*

no. 3427. Under Edward I, the Hospital attained the importance that the Temple had held under King John and Henry III: Riley-Smith, *Knights*, p. 312; *Calendar of the Close Rolls preserved in the Public Record Office. Edward I.* (London, 1900ff.) (1271–1279) p. 32; special concessions to the Hospital: *ibid.*, p. 378; *Calendar of the Patent Rolls preserved in the Public Record Office*, 1216ff. (London, 1901ff.) (1281–1292) p. 113.

17. For references by Frederick II to his grandfather, father and uncle, or his ancestors in general, having founded and patronized the order, see: *HDFS* 1 p. 288, 2 pp. 224, 282, 3 pp. 154–5, 497, 4 p. 393. For his sons and grandson, see: *Regesta Imperii 5: Die Regesten des Kaiserreichs unter Philipp, Otto IV, Friedrich II, Heinrich (VII), Conrad IV, Heinrich Raspe, Wilhelm und Richard, 1198-1272*, ed. J. F. Böhmer, J. Ficker *et al.*, 4 vols. (Innsbruck, Cologne and Vienna, 1881–1983) 1 no. 4542 (Conrad IV: refers to his father's gifts) no. 4715 (Manfred: states that his great-grandfather, Frederick I, founded the house, and that his grandfather, Henry VI, and father, Frederick II, fostered it) no. 4774 (Conradin: reference to an alleged gift by his grandfather, Frederick II, and his father, Conrad IV).

18. See below, chapter six, pp. 115–6.

19. E.g., *PL* 200, cols. 1024ff. (bull of Pope Alexander III for the order of St James of Santiago); Hiestand, no. 89 (the same, for the order of Mountjoy); Innocent III, *PL* 216 col. 509, year 14 no. 149 (Swordbrothers of Livonia); *Reg. Greg. IX*, nos. 241–2 (Dobrin order of Prussia); A. Forey, 'The military orders and holy war against Christians in the thirteenth century', *English historical review* 104 (1989) 6–9 (on orders founded to combat heresy).

20. Forey, 'Military orders and holy war', 10–13, *CGH* nos. 3279, 3308, Bartholomew of Neocastro, 'Historia Sicula', ed. G. Paladino, *RIS NS* 13,3 p. 7.

21. Forey, *Corona*, pp. 15–24.

22. Kuhn, 'Ritterorden als Grenzhüter', 52–9.

23. Boockmann, *Deutsche Orden*, pp. 68–9, 72–92.

24. See N. Housley, 'Politics and heresy in Italy: anti-heretical crusades, orders and confraternities, 1200–1500', *Journal of ecclesiastical history*, 33 (1982) 195–196; Delaruelle, 'Templiers et Hospitaliers en Languedoc', 315–334; Forey, 'Military orders and holy war', 2–4, 6–9, 14–15.

25. *Crusaders as conquerors: the chronicle of the Morea, translated from the Greek*, ed. H. E. Lurier (New York and London, 1964) pp. 127, 130, 148–51. For the Teutonic order as defenders of the Morea against the Greeks, see also Strehlke, no. 131.

26. *CGH* no. 181 (1143); Forey, *Corona*, p. 377 (1208); *CGH* no. 1742 (1221), and no. 1603 (1218).

27. 'Ex chronico Turonensi auctore anonymo, S. Martini Turon. canonico', in *RHGF* 18, p. 304; cf. Philip's will in *Recueil des actes de Philippe Auguste, roi de France*, ed. H.-Fr. Delaborde, C. Petit-Dutaillis *et al.*, 4 vols. (Paris, 1916--79) 4 pp. 468–472, no. 1796.

28. *Les registres d'Innocent IV*, ed. E. Berger, 4 vols., BEFAR (Paris, 1884–1921) no. 7641; Alexander IV in Strehlke, no. 610.

29. See, for example, J. Riley-Smith, *Knights*, pp. 376–7, 379–80.

30. Matthew 16, verse 19.

31. See C. Morris, *Papal monarchy. The western church from 1050 to 1250* (Oxford, 1989) pp. 98—101, 107—8, 128—132, 205—19, 568—577.
32. *CGH* nos. 113 (1135), 122 (1137), 130 (1139—43).
33. Bulst-Thiele, *Sacrae domus*, p. 34.
34. Gerald of Wales, 4 p. 205.
35. The references are given by M. L. Bulst-Thiele, 'Templer in königlichen und päpstlichen Diensten', in P. Classen and P. Scheibert, eds., *Festschrift Percy Ernst Schramm*, 2 vols. (Wiesbaden, 1964) p. 301.
36. Walter Map, *De nugis curialium*, ed. M. R. James, C. N. L. Brooke and R. A. B. Mynors (Oxford, 1983) p. 70.
37. *Reg. Clem. IV*, no. 836.
38. See J. Richard, *The Latin kingdom of Jerusalem*, trans. J. Shirley, 2 vols. (Amsterdam, 1979) 1 pp. 264—5, 266, 286.
39. Mayer, 'Henry II', 721—739.
40. See Bulst-Thiele, *Sacrae domus*, p. 260; 'Estoire de Eracles empereur et de la conqueste de la Terre d'Outremer', in *RHC Occ.* 2 p. 475; Richard, *Latin kingdom*, 2 pp. 413—7.
41. Riley-Smith, 'Cilician Armenia', pp. 111ff.
42. *Codex diplomaticus et epistolaris regni Bohemiae*, ed. G. Friedrich *et al.,* 5 vols. in 7 (Prague, 1904—1981) 4 no. 209; *MGHES* 3 p. 692 no. 670; and see Christensen, *Northern crusades*, p. 102.
43. See Tumler, *Deutsche Orden*, pp. 33—42.
44. Rymer's *Foedera*, 1 p. 144.
45. For instance, the Hospitallers had custody of the royal castle of Marlborough for a time: *Roll of divers accounts for the early years of the reign of Henry III...* ed. F. A. Cazel, Publications of the Pipe Roll society, 82 (new series, 44) (London, 1982) p. 46 (1218—19); the Temple and Hospital made loans of £200 each in 1223—4: *ibid.*, p. 51; the Hospital made a loan of 620 marks in 1216—7: *Rotuli litterarum clausarum in turri Londinensi asservati*, ed. T. D. Hardy, 1 (London, 1833) p. 456; in July 1224 the king borrowed 300 marks each from the Temple and Hospital, 'in his great necessity': *Patent rolls*, (1216—1225) pp. 453, 455, in 1225 he borrowed another 100 marks from the Hospital: *ibid.* p. 529; and £100 in 1224—5: *Divers accounts*, p. 57. A mark was two thirds of a pound.
46. Strehlke, no. 560; *Les registres d'Urbain IV*, ed. J. Guiraud, *et al.*, 5 vols. BEFAR (Paris, 1899—1958) no. 213.
47. *Reg. Urb. IV*, nos. 1244, 1786, 2487; Bulst-Thiele, 'Templer', pp. 303, 304; *CGH* nos. 3094, 3789.
48. *MGHES* 1 pp. 334—5, no. 415, nos. IV, VIII, XVII.
49. *Reg. Urb. IV*, no. 880, 1 nos. 59, 126; Bulst-Thiele, 'Templer', p. 303.
50. *CGH*, nos. 3536, 3648, 3770, 3778.
51. For examples, see Bulst-Thiele, 'Templer', pp. 301—4. Note that in fact Brother Durand, a Templar, p. 301, was probably Brother Durand or Thurand, a Hospitaller: see *MGHC* 2 p. 42, no. 33; Thomas Wykes in *Annales monastici*, ed. H. R. Luard, 5 vols., RS 36 (London, 1864—9) 4 p. 56. See also *Reg. Greg. IX,* nos. 3696, 3846, 3852, 4455; *Reg. Inn. IV*, nos. 5288, 5300; *CGH*, nos. 2897, 3789.
52. *Reg. Nic. IV*, no. 7283.

53. *MGHES* 1 p. 90, no. 124.
54. A few examples: *MGHC* 2 pp. 206–9, nos. 168, 169 (Brother Hermann of
     Salza, master of the Teutonic order, for Frederick II); *MGHC* 3 p. 64 no.
     76 (Brother Berengiar, prior of the Hospital in Germany, for Rudolf I);
     *Recueil des actes de Henri II, roi d'Angleterre et duc de Normandie, concernant les
     provinces françaises et les affaires de France*, ed. L. Delisle and E. Berger,
     Introduction (Paris, 1906) and 3 vols. (Paris, 1916–1927) 1 pp. 407–8 no.
     262 (Brother Ernold and Brother Philip, Hospitaller, guiding Henry II's
     envoys on a secret mission to the pope); Brother Garin, Hospitaller, vice-
     chancellor of France and bishop of Senlis, is described by the Anonymous
     of Béthune in *RHGF* 24, pp. 764, 768; see also Bulst-Thiele, 'Templer',
     passim.
55. E.g., Bulst-Thiele, 'Templer', *passim*; H. Johnstone, 'Poor relief in the royal
     households of thirteenth century England', *Speculum* 4 (1929) 163; Sandys,
     'Financial importance', pp. 147–162; L. Delisle, 'Mémoire sur les opérations
     financières des Templiers', *Mémoires de l'Institut National de France, Académie
     des Inscriptions et Belles-Lettres*, 33, 2 (1889) pp. 40–73; Forey, *Corona*, pp.
     344–46; A. Macquarrie, *Scotland and the crusades, 1095–1560* (Edinburgh,
     1985) pp. 15–16, 50.
56. E.g., the Teutonic brothers in the Holy Roman Empire *c.* 1240: *Albert von
     Beham und Regesten Innocenz IV*, ed. C. Höfler, BLVS 16b (Stuttgart, 1847)
     p. 14; D. Wojtecki, 'Der Deutsche Orden unter Friedrich II', in J. Flecken-
     stein, ed., *Probleme um Friedrich II*, Vorträge und Forschungen, 16 (Sigmar-
     ingen, 1974) pp. 219–23; Hugh of Forcalquier, master of the Hospital in
     Aragon under James I: James I, *Chronicle*, pp. 183–8, 191, 221, 267–9, 297,
     301–6, 317 etc.
57. E.g., *Reg. Inn. IV*, no. 4957.
58. *Reg. Inn. IV*, nos. 2973, 3006, 4667, 4711, 8320.
59. *Reg. Clem. IV*, nos. 217, 811, 1451, and cf. no. 134.
60. *Reg. Nic. IV*, nos. 617, 618, 1142–1152, 2136 (etc.), 4204–6.
61. See, for example, Brother Geoffrey Fulcher of the Temple in *RHGF* 16 pp.
     38–9 no. 124; and Brother Nicholas le Lorgne in Champollion–Figeac, ed.,
     *Lettres de rois, reines et autres personnages des cours de France et d'Angleterre depuis
     Louis VII jusqu'à Henri IV*, 1 (Paris, 1839) pp. 338–9, no. 253.
62. See, for instance, Flori, 'Chevalerie et liturgie. Remise des armes et
     vocabulaire «chevaleresque» dans les sources liturgiques du XIe et XIVe
     siècle', *Le moyen âge*, 84 (1978) 275–277; Flori, *Essor*, pp. 182f., 186f.
63. P. Partner, *The lands of St Peter – the papal state in the middle ages and the early
     renaissance* (London, 1972) pp. 165–6; Morris, *Papal monarchy*, pp. 143–153.
64. I. S. Robinson, 'Gregory VII and the soldiers of Christ', *History*, 58 (1973)
     169–192; Forey, 'The emergence of the military order in the twelfth
     century', *Journal of ecclesiastical history* 36 (1985) 183–9.
65. See F. H. Russell, *The just war in the middle ages* (Cambridge, 1975) pp. 294–
     5; Forey, 'Emergence', 189–194.
66. Bernard of Clairvaux, 'Liber ad milites Templi', pp. 217, 223.
67. For instance, *PL* 200 cols. 228–9, no. 162, col. 1333, no. 158; *Die Register
     Innocenz' III*, ed. O. Hageneder and A. Haidacher, 2 vols. in 4 (Graz-
     Cologne, 1964–8, and Rome-Vienna, 1979–83) 1 no. 379, 2 no. 54; *Regesta*

Honorii Papae III, ed. P. Pressutti, 3 vols. (Rome, 1888—95, reprinted Hildesheim/New York, 1978) nos. 1971, 5794; *CGH*, no 1977.

68. Forey, 'Militarisation', 79; Riley-Smith, *Knights*, pp. 60—1.
69. *CGH* nos. 391*ter*, 527; Riley-Smith, *Knights*, p. 76.
70. Forey, 'Militarisation', 75—89; chroniclers hardly ever mention the deeds of the Hospitallers in battle before 1187, Lambert Waterlos being the exception: 'Annales Cameracenses', ed. G. H. Pertz, *MGHS* 16, p. 547; see Riley-Smith, *Knights*, p. 86, note 1.
71. See, for example, *La chanson de Roland*, ed. F. Whitehead (Oxford, 1946) lines 1605—7, 1876—81 (date disputed, but probably early twelfth century: p. xiii); *Le couronnement de Louis: chanson de geste du XII siècle*, ed. E. Langlois, CFMA 22 (Paris, 1984) lines 1692—99 (written around 1130); *Moniage Guillaume*, II lines 510—521, 637—646, 669—676, 1039—41 (before 1180); *Moniage Rainouart 1, passim*, especially lines 3169—3202, 3279—93, 3375—96, 3837—3905, 4943—74, 5491—97 (written between 1190 and 1200: p. lxxvii).
72. Michael Schüpferling suggested that the order's house in Metz, Lorraine, dated from St Bernard's visit to the city in 1133. He connected the order's acquisitions of land in Bavaria and Brunswick to the pilgrimages to the Holy Land of Duke Welf of Bavaria (1168) and Duke Henry the Lion of Saxony (1173) respectively: M. Schüpferling, *Der Tempelherren-Orden in Deutschland. Dissertation zur Erlangung der Doktorwürde von der philos. Fakultät der Universitat Freiburg in der Schweiz* (Bamberg, 1915) pp. 14—15, 69—70, 87—88.
73. *CGH* no. 270; *Acta imperii*, 1 p. 739, no. 528: the confirmation for the Temple may have been a result of the papal-imperial conference in Verona in November 1184.
74. *Reg. Hon III*, no. 5912; *CGH*, no. 1218.
75. *CGH*, nos. 278, 401.
76. See Schüpferling, p. 163; Bulst-Thiele, *Sacrae domus*, p. 211 note 4.
77. Flori, *Essor*, pp. 231, 253—7, 257—63, 266—7, 329f.
78. *Register Innocenz' III*, 1 p. 823, no. 564 (570).
79. *Reg. Greg. IX*, no. 1708, (1234); *ibid.*, no. 2944 (1236).
80. An informant of Roger of Wendover was certainly confused: compare Roger of Wendover, *Flores historiarum*, ed. H. R. Hewlett, 3 vols., RS 84 (London, 1886—9) 3 p. 108; *CM*, 3 p. 318, and note; and *HDFS* 4 p. 515, which indicates that the delegates were not Templars but Teutonic knights.
81. Strehlke, nos. 299—300, pp. 269—70.
82. *MGHES* 1 pp. 134—5, no. 192.
83. *Reg. Greg. IX*, no. 491.
84. *Ibid.*, no. 3005.
85. *MGHES* 1 pp. 345—6, nos. 427—8; *Reg. Greg. IX*, nos. 544, 545; *CGH*, nos. 1975—6.
86. *MGHES* 1 p. 645, no. 749.
87. *Reg. Greg. IX*, nos. 4917, 3878, 4918; see also 6070, 6971; Strehlke, nos. 131—3, 139.
88. *CGH* nos. 154, 2247, 2230; cf. Riley-Smith, *Knights*, pp. 173—5.
89. *Preußisches Urkundenbuch*, ed. A. Philipps *et al.*, 6 vols. (Königsberg, Aalen and Marburg, 1882—1986) 1, 1 pp. 100—2, no. 134; E. Kennan, 'Innocent

III, Gregory IX and political crusades: a study in the disintegration of papal power', in G. F. Lytle, ed., *Reform and authority in the medieval and reformation church* (Washington D.C., 1981) pp. 31—2.

90. *HDFS* 3 p. 74.
91. *MGHES* 1 p. 340 no. 428.
92. *HDFS* 5 p. 708; *CM* 3 pp. 177—9; Bartholomew of Neocastro, pp. 116—7.
93. Roger of Howden, *Chronica*, ed. W. Stubbs, 4 vols., RS 51 (London, 1868—71) 1 p. 218; Lees, pp. lii and note, 273.
94. *CGH*, no. 4007.
95. *HDFS* 4 pp. 227—9.
96. *HDFS* 5 pp. 252—3.
97. William of Tyre, p. 955, Bk. 20 ch. 30.
98. 'Eracles', pp. 474—5, Bk. 34 chs. 28—9.
99. *Reg. Hon. III*, no. 5913.
100. *CGH*, nos. 1590—1, 1602—3, 1803.
101. Strehlke, p. 156, no. 158.
102. Strehlke, p. 158 no. 166.
103. *Reg. Greg. IX*, no. 2917 (*CGH* no. 2135); *CGH* nos. 2896, 2920.
104. *CGH,* no. 2182.
105. S. Raban, *Mortmain legislation and the English church, 1279-1500,* (Cambridge, 1982) pp. 21—3; P. A. Brand, 'Control of mortmain alienation in England, 1200—1300', in J. H. Baker, ed., *Legal records and the historian,* (London, 1978) pp. 29—40.
106. *CM* 5 p. 339.
107. *MGHC* 3 p. 29 no. 28.
108. Philip II: *Actes de Philippe Auguste,* 4 pp. 403—5, no. 1736; Louis VIII: *Layettes du trésor des chartes,* ed. A. Teulet *et al.*, 5 vols. (Paris, 1863—1909) 2 pp. 117, 319, nos. 1914, 2453, 3 p. 116, no. 3917; Louis IX: L. Delisle, ed., *Cartulaire Normand de Philippe-Auguste, Louis VIII, Saint Louis et Philippe le Hardi* (Caen, 1882, reprinted Geneva, 1978) nos. 601, 797; *CGH* no. 3303; further restrictions: *Layettes,* 4 pp. 387—8, no. 5583; *Les Olim ou registres des arrêts rendus par la cour du roi,* ed. le comte Beugnot, 4 vols. (Paris, 1839—48) 1 pp. 647, 929, 2 pp. 193, 248—9; *Actes du Parlement de Paris,* ed. E. Boutaric, 2 vols. (Paris, 1863—7, reprinted Hildesheim/New York, 1975) 1 no. 2025; *CGH* nos. 2900, 2968, 3011, 3411, 3416, 3418, 3479, 4072, 4100.
109. *Actes de Philippe Auguste,* 4 pp. 471—2, no. 1792; *Layettes,* 4 pp. 419—21, no. 5638 (Louis IX); *Spicilegium sive collectio veterum aliquot scriptorum qui in Galliae bibliothecis delituerant,* ed. L. d'Achery and L. F. T. de la Bavre, 3 vols. (new edition, Paris, 1723) 3 pp. 691—2 (Philip III).
110. *Councils and synods,* 2, 2 p. 815.
111. *Cod. dip. Boh.* 4 no. 209.
112. *CGH* no. 2685.
113. *Register Innocenz' III,* 1 no. 450, *CGH* no. 1050.
114. *PL* 215 cols. 1217—8, Book 10 no. 121.
115. Roger of Howden, *Chronica*, 4 pp. 76—7. For Roger's career see D. Corner, 'The *Gesta regis Henrici secundi* and *Chronica* of Roger, parson of Howden', *Bulletin of the Institute of Historical Research,* 56 (1983) 126—144.

116. Gerald of Wales, 4 p. 54, 6 p. 44; Matthew Paris, *Flores*, 2 pp. 116–7.
117. E. Winkelmann, ed., *Acta inedita seculi XIII: Urkunden und Briefe zur Geschichte des Kaiserreichs und des Königreichs Sicilien in den Jahren 1198 bis 1273* (Innsbruck, 1880) 1 p. 370 no. 437.
118. James I, *Chronicle*, pp. 646–53.
119. *Monumenta Corbeiensia*, ed. P. Jaffé, Bibliotheca rerum Germanicarum, 1 (Berlin, 1864) pp. 225–6, no. 144.
120. *MGHL* p. 262.
121. E.g. *Reg. Greg. IX* nos. 3932–4.
122. *Reg. Greg. IX*, no. 4129, cf. no. 544.
123. *CGH* no. 2186.
124. *CGH* no. 3581.
125. *Reg. Nich. III*, no. 167 (*CGH* no. 3674).
126. *Reg. Greg. IX*, no. 3116 (*CGH* no. 2139).
127. Gerhoh of Reichersberg, 'De investigatione Antichristi', ed. E. Sackur, *MGH Libelli de Lite Imperatorum et Pontificum*, 3 (Hanover, 1897) pp. 378, 379, 384–5, 391; William of Tyre, 2 p. 820, Bk. 18 ch.7; Walter Map, p. 70; Roger Bacon, *Opus Maius*, ed. J. H. Bridges, 3 vols. (Oxford, 1877–1900, reprinted Frankfurt, 1964) 3 p. 122, part 3 ch.13. See also *CM* 5 p. 97 on the Temple and Hospital at the papal court in 1250.
128. *Reg. Urb. IV*, nos. 760, 765; *CGH*, nos. 3221, 3228.
129. *CGH*, no. 3279.
130. See *CGH* no. 3308 (vol.4).
131. *CGH* no. 3285, and see also no. 3308 (vol. 4).
132. Bartholomew of Neocastro, p. 7.
133. R. Filangieri, ed., *I Registri della cancelleria Angioina*, vols. 1ff. (Naples, 1950ff.) 2 pp. 65–6, no. 234, 7 pp. 274–5, no. 29, 8 p. 110, no. 105.
134. Temple: *CM* 4 p. 302; Hospital: *CGH* no. 2186; Teutonic order: *Preuß. UB*, 1, 1 pp. 100–2, no. 134.

Chapter three

1. In *Lettres des premiers Chartreux*, I, Sources Chrétiennes no. 88 (Paris, 1962) pp. 154–60.
2. *PL* 196, cols. 1616–7, letter 18.
3. Luke 16, verse 26.
4. They refer to the three orders, of prayers, defenders and workers. Le Marquis d'Albon, ed., *Cartulaire général de l'ordre du Temple, 1119?–1150*, (Paris, 1913) no. 31; cf. Duby, *Three orders, passim*; *Règle*, pp. 11–12, paras. 1–2.
5. Simon of St Bertin, p. 649.
6. Bernard of Clairvaux, 'Liber ad milites Templi', pp. 214, 215, 220–222.
7. Orderic Vitalis, *The ecclesiastical history*, ed. M. Chibnall, 6 vols. (Oxford, 1969–80) 6 p. 310, Bk. 12 ch. 29.
8. Otto of Freising, pp. 252–3.
9. 'Ex Ricardi Pictaviensis chronica', ed. G. Waitz, *MGHS* 26 p. 80.
10. *PL* 188, col. 1156.

11. Bernard of Clairvaux, 'Liber ad milites Templi', pp. 214–5, 217, 220–2.
12. Matthew 10, verse 10.
13. Hugh 'Peccator', in Leclerq, ed., 'Un document', esp. 86, paras. 1, 2; and C. Schlafert, ed., 'Lettre inédite de Hugues de Saint-Victor aux chevaliers du Temple', *Revue d'ascetique et de mystique'*, 34 (1958) 275–299.
14. *The letters of Peter the Venerable*, ed. G. Constable, 2 vols. (Cambridge, Mass., 1967) 1 pp. 407–413, nos. 172–3, esp. no. 173 p. 411.
15. See B. Z. Kedar, *Crusade and mission: European approaches towards the Muslims*, (Princeton, 1984) pp. 111–2.
16. 'Annales Herbipolenses', pp. 3–7, esp. p. 7; for this author's opposition to the second crusade, see G. Constable, 'The second crusade as seen by contemporaries', *Traditio* 9 (1953) 268–9.
17. Ralph Niger, *De re militari et triplici via peregrinationis ierosolimitane*, ed. L. Schmugge (Berlin, 1977) p. 194, Bk. 3 ch. 85.
18. See Kedar, *Crusade and mission*, pp. 65–72, 159–161.
19. Isaac of l'Étoile, sermon 48, *PL* 194, col. 1854; see Kedar, *Crusade and mission*, pp. 104–6.
20. Roger Bacon, 3 pp. 121–2; see Kedar, *Crusade and mission*, pp. 177–9.
21. Roger Bacon, 3 pp. 121–2.
22. *Reg. Hon. III*, no. 3786.
23. *Preuß UB*, 1, 1 pp. 100–2, no. 134.
24. *Preuß UB*, 1, 2 pp. 56–7, 60–2, no. 62, 65.
25. See Kuhn, 'Ritterorden als Grenzhüter', 49–51.
26. In 1266, when Roger was writing, a general chapter of the Franciscans was held at Paris, where he was in prison. It is possible that he obtained his information from brothers from eastern Europe attending the chapter.
27. Ramon Lull, 'Blanquerna', in *Obras literarias*, ed. M. Batllori and M. Caldentey (Madrid, 1948) Bk. 4, ch. 80, paras. 7, 11, pp. 407–8, 410.
28. Walter Map, pp. xxii, 60–62; see Kedar, *Crusade and mission*, pp. 106–8, 111.
29. James of Vitry, 'Sermones vulgares', in J. B. Pitra, ed., *Analecta novissima spicilegii Solesmensis: altera continuatio 2, Tusculana* (Paris, 1888) sermon 38, p. 419.
30. Thomas Aquinas, *Summa theologica*, 2a2ae. 188, 3: Blackfriars edn vol 47 (London, 1973) pp. 188–92.
31. John of Salisbury, *Policraticus*, ed. C. C. J. Webb, 2 vols., (Oxford, 1909) 2, pp. 198–9, Bk. 7, ch. 21, 695a.
32. Nigel of Longchamps, *Speculum stultorum*, ed. J. H. Mozley and R. R. Raymo (Berkeley and Los Angeles, 1960) pp. 76–7, lines 2051–2068.
33. Guiot of Provins, lines 1709–88, esp. line 1709, 1789–1818, and pp. xi–xvii.
34. Alexander Minorita, *Expositio in Apocalypsim*, ed. A. Wachtel, *MGH* Die Deutschen Geschichtsquellen des Mittelalters 500–1500, Quellen zur Geistesgeschichte des Mittelalters 1 (Weimar, 1955) pp. 401–3. Eight manuscripts survive, three of which date from the thirteenth century, and three more have been lost (pp. xii–xxi).

35. Roger of Howden, *Chronica*, 2 p. 354 (Temple); the anonymous pilgrim 5, 2 in *Anonymous pilgrims I–VIII (11th and 12th centuries)* trans. A. Stewart, PPTS 6 (London, 1894) pp. 29—30 (Temple); Nigel of Longchamps, p. 77 lines 2069—76 (Hospital); John of Joinville, *La vie de Saint Louis: le témoinage de Jehan, seigneur de Joinville. Texte du XIVe siècle*, ed. N. L. Corbett (Quebec, 1977) p. 189, paras. 507—8 (Hospital).

36. Cf. the comments of Hugh 'Peccator', 87—9, paras. 2—5, on the Temple; and John Peckham, archbishop of Canterbury, on the Hospital in 1284: *Registrum epistolarum fratris Johannis Peckham, archiepiscopi Cantuariensis*, ed. C. T. Martin, 3 vols. RS 77 (London, 1882—5) 3 p. 860, no. 617.

37. James of Vitry, sermon 37, pp. 410—11; this indicates that this was a problem with all religious orders.

38. Cf. *The Hospitallers' riwle, (miraculis et regula Hospitalis Sancti Johannis Jerusolimitani)* ed. K. V. Sinclair, Anglo-Norman texts 42 (Oxford, 1984) lines 587—92.

39. Cf. Morris, *Papal monarchy*, pp. 257, 280—1.

40. E.g., John of Salisbury, *Policraticus*, 2 pp. 190—201, Bk. 7 ch. 21; Walter Map, pp. 70—2.

41. E.g., John of Salisbury, *Policraticus*, 2 pp. 199—200, Bk. 7 ch. 21, 695d; Walter Map, pp. 72—112; *Councils and synods, 2*, 1 pp. 83—4; C. V. Graves, 'The economic activities of the Cistercians in medieval England, 1128—1307'. *Analecta sacri ordinis Cisterciensis* 13 (1957) 45—55.

42. *CGH* no. 560.

43. For the main privileges of the military orders, see Hiestand, nos. 3, 8 (Temple); *CGH* nos. 30, 113, 122, 130 (Hospital); Strehlke, nos. 330, 305, 306, etc. (Teutonic order); Riley-Smith, *Knights*, pp. 377—88.

44. 'Annales Herbipolenses', p. 7; John of Salisbury, *Historia*, p. 57 (written 1164). The 'Casus monasterii Petrihusensis', ed. O. Abel and L. Weiland, *MGHS* 20 p. 674 (written before 1156: p. 622) blames 'knights of God', which could mean crusaders or Templars.

45. William of Tyre, 2 p. 988, Bk. 21 ch. 25 (26), and 1 p. 555, Bk. 12 ch. 7, 2 pp. 812—4, 817—23, Bk. 18 chs. 3, 6—8.

46. *CM* 3 pp. 177—8.

47. *Councils and synods*, 1, 2 pp. 1068—9 section 14.

48. J. D. Mansi, ed., *Sacrorum conciliorum nova et amplissima collectio*, 55 vols. (Florence, Venice, Paris, Arnhem and Leipzig, 1759—1962) 22 cols. 1047—50.

49. *CGH* nos. 2281bis, 3887, 4029.

50. *CGH* nos. 2805, 2863.

51. Bruno of Olmütz, 23—6.

52. E.g., Bishop of Hebron: Strehlke, nos. 101, 102, 104, 126; *CGH* nos. 3120, 3202, 3203, 3515; Bishop of Acre: Strehlke, no. 112, *CGH* nos. 1718, 1911, 2200, 2199, 2865; Bishop of Tortosa: *CGH* nos. 2553, 2613, 3093, 3278, 3282, 3307; *Reg. Inn. IV*, nos. 5129, 5861; *Reg. Urb. IV*, nos. 1709, 1710.

53. *CGH*, nos. 4051, 4052, 4096, 4146, 4160; *Reg. Nic. IV*, nos. 1306, 2739, 4098, 4974, 4975.

54. E.g., *Register Innocenz' III*, 1 no. 450; *PL* 215 cols. 1217—8, year 10 no. 121; *MGHES* 1 p. 645 no. 749; *Reg. Clem. IV* no. 836.

55. P. Amargier, ed., 'La défense du Temple devant le concile de Lyons en 1274', in *1274: L'année charnière: mutations et continuités*, Colloques internationaux du Centre national de la recherche scientifique (Paris, 1977) p. 497, no. 7.

56. Council of Canterbury: *Councils and Synods*, 2, 2 pp. 1107–8, 1112, 1113; Lyons: Bartholomew Cotton, *Historia Anglicana*, ed. H. R. Luard, RS 16 (London, 1859) p. 213; Arles: *ibid.*, p. 215; Rheims: John Thilrode, 'Chronicon', ed. J. Heller, *MGHS* 25 p. 581; Sens: *ibid.*, p. 582; Salzbury: Eberhard, archdeacon of Ratisbon, 'Annales', ed. P. Jaffé, *MGHS* 17 p. 594.

57. Gerhoh of Reichersberg, p. 384, ch. 67. For dating, see Siberry, *Criticism*, p. 200 n. 57.

58. 'Annales Herbipolenses', p. 7.

59. William of Tyre, 1 p. 555, Bk. 12 ch. 7, 2 p. 813, Bk. 18 ch. 3, p. 1002, Bk. 21 ch. 28 (29); Walter Map, p. 62.

60. Guiot of Provins, lines 1745–1788; James of Vitry, sermon 37, pp. 406–8; *CM* 3 p. 177, 4 pp. 168, 302; Ramon Lull, 'Blanquerna', Bk. 4 ch. 80 para 7, p. 408.

61. *Fontes Egmundenses*, ed. O. Oppermann, (Utrecht, 1933) p. 161; also in MGHS 16 p. 459; P. Riant, *Expéditions et pèlerinages des Scandinaves en Terre Sainte au temps des croisades*, 2 vols., (Paris, 1865–9) 1 p. 258ff.

62. William of Tyre, 2, pp. 798–9. Bk. 17 ch. 7.

63. *Ibid.*, pp. 822–3, Bk. 18 ch. 9, pp. 953–5, Bk. 20 chs. 29–30; and see below, chapter five, p. 83.

64. Walter Map, pp. 62–6.

65. Alberic of Trois Fontaines, 'Chronicon', ed. P. Scheffer-Boichorst, *MGHS* 23, pp. 846, 859; Kedar, *Crusade and mission*, p. 82.

66. Thomas Tusci, 'Gesta imperatorum et pontificum', ed. E. Ehrenfeuchter, *MGHS* 22, p. 507.

67. 'Annales Herbipolenses', p. 7 (written soon after the second crusade); Ralph of Coggeshall, p. 12 (written in the early thirteenth century).

68. See below, chapter five, pp. 81–2.

69. 'Menkonis Chronicon', ed. L. Weiland, *MGHS* 23, pp. 557–8 (referring to the Temple, Hospital and Teutonic knights); Odo, bishop of Tusculanum, in *Spicilegium* 3 p. 625 (referring to the Temple and Hospital).

70. John of Columna, 'Mare historiarum', *RHGF* 23, p. 119; William of Nangis, 'Gesta Ludovici', *RHGF* 20 pp. 366–8; 'Chroniques de Saint-Denis', *RHGF* 21 p. 114.

71. *CM* 4 p. 291.

72. See the hatred of the Greeks expressed by Odo of Deuil, *De profectione Ludovici VII in orientem*, ed. V. G. Berry (New York, 1948) pp. 66–88, 98; *Itinerarium* pp. 45–6; the hatred of the Palestinian Franks expressed by Gerhoh of Reichersberg, p. 377; and the mysterious Orient described by William of Tyre, 2 pp. 887–9, Bk. 19 chs. 18–19; *The legend of Duke Ernst*, trans. J. W. Thomas and C. Dussère (Lincoln (Neb.) and London, 1979) *passim*; Chrétien de Troyes, *Cligès*, ed. A. Micha, CFMA 84 (Paris, 1982) pp. vi–viii and lines 5488ff.

73. John of Würzburg, cols. 1087, 1082; Otto of St Blasien, 'Continuatio Sanblasiana', ed. R. Wilmans, *MGHS* 20, pp. 318, 327.

74. 'Maius Chronicon Lemovicense', *RHGF* 21, pp. 773—4. His account is belied by the eye-witness account of Fidenzio of Padua, 'Liber recuperationis Terre Sancte', in P. G. Golubovich, ed., *Bibliotheca bio-bibliografia della Terra Sancta e dell'oriente Francescano*, 2 (Quaracchi, 1913) pp. 24—5.

75. William of Tyre, 2, p. 661, Bk. 14 ch. 22, p. 776 (castle of Gibelin given to the Hospital), Bk. 17 ch. 12 (castle of Gaza given to the Temple), p. 831, Bk. 18 ch. 14 (praise of Bertrand of Blancafort, master of the Temple), p. 1032, Bk. 22 ch. 17 (16) (criticism of fighting clerks).

76. See, e.g., P. W. Edbury and J. G. Rowe, *William of Tyre: historian of the Latin east* (Cambridge, 1988) pp. 17—22.

77. William of Tyre, 2, pp. 812—822, Bk. 18 chs. 3—8.

78. *Ibid.*, 1, p. 555, Bk. 12, ch. 7, and, for example, 2, p. 879, Bk. 19 ch. 11, p. 955, Bk. 20 ch. 30.

79. R. H. C. Davis, 'William of Tyre', in D. Baker, ed., *Relations between east and west in the Middle Ages* (Edinburgh, 1987) pp. 65—70; Edbury and Rowe, *William of Tyre*, pp. 25, 159—66.

80. E.g., William does not mention the Templars' victory of 1157 described in *RHGF* 15 p. 682, nor the Muslims' fear and respect of the orders: Riley-Smith, *Knights*, pp. 75—6; nor describe Brother Geoffrey Fulcher's role in making a truce with Egypt, although he was an experienced diplomat: William of Tyre, 2, p. 887, Bk. 19 ch. 18; Bulst-Thiele, 'Templer', pp. 290—1.

81. Davis, 'William of Tyre', pp. 71—5; Edbury and Rowe, *William of Tyre*, p. 4.

82. R. Vaughan, *Matthew Paris*, (Cambridge, 1958) pp. 59—60, 152—4.

83. Vaughan, *Matthew Paris*, pp. 13—17, 181.

84. E.g., *CM* 3 pp. 177—9, 4 p. 291, 5 pp. 745—6; *Flores*, 2 pp. 194—5, 250, 264, 272; *Historia Anglorum, sive. . . Historia Minor, item Abbreviatio chronicorum Angliae*, ed. F. Madden, 3 vols., RS 44 (London, 1866—9) 2 pp. 312—5, 368 and note, 472, 477, 3 pp. 259, 270 (as 2 p. 368).

85. E.g., *CM* 3 pp. 404—6, 4 p. 291; *Flores*, 2 p. 264, *Historia Anglorum*, 2 p. 472.

86. *CM* 4 p. 168.

87. *CM* 3 p. 490; *Historia Anglorum* 2 p. 410; *Abbreviatio* 3 p. 277.

88. *CM* 5 p. 196; also p. 745; *Flores* 2 p. 272; *Historia Anglorum* 3 p. 95; *Abbreviatio* 3 p. 317.

89. E.g., *CM* 5 pp. 655, 3 pp. 404—6, 5 pp. 147—154.

90. *CM* 3 p. 406, 4 pp. 44, 643.

91. *CM* 3 p. 629 and note, 5, p. 150; *Historia Anglorum*, 2 p. 312 note 4, 3 p. 259.

92. 'Annales Colonienses maximi', ed. K. Pertz, *MGHS* 17, pp. 832, 833—5, 846, 845.

93. 'Continuatio Cuonradi', pp. 381, 383.

94. Bruno of Olmütz, pp. 23—6. For further criticism of the friars, see *CM* 3 pp. 287—8, 332—4, 4 pp. 9, 256, 279—80, 291—4, 511—7, 5 pp. 73—4, 194-5, 546, 744; 'Dunstable annals', in *Annales monastici*, 3 pp. 213, 336—7.

95. Gilbert of Tournai, 40—62, especially 56—7, paras. 17.

96. Humbert of Romans, 'De eruditione praedicatorum', in M. de la Bigne, ed., *Maxima bibliotheca veterum patrum et antiquorum scriptorum ecclesiasticorum*, 27 vols. (Lyons, 1677) 25 pp. 472—474; cf. James of Vitry, 'Historia

Orientalis', in J. Bongars, ed., *Gesta Dei per Francos*, 2 vols. in 3 (Hanover, 1611) 1, 2 pp. 1082—1085. James' Sermon 37, p. 405, and Humbert, p. 473, both apply Zechariah 9 verse 8 to the Templars.

97. James of Vitry, 'Historia Orientalis', pp. 1082—3; William of Tyre, 1 p. 817, Bk. 18 ch. 6.

98. Roger Bacon, 1 pp. xxi—xxxiii, 3 pp. 121—2.

99. Cf. M. R. Morgan, 'The Rothelin continuation of William of Tyre', in B. Z. Kedar, H. E. Mayer and R. C. Smail, eds., *Outremer: studies in the history of the crusading kingdom of Jerusalem presented to Joshua Prawer* (Jerusalem, 1982) pp. 254—257.

100. *Chronica Buriensis, the chronicle of Bury St Edmunds 1212-1301*, ed. A. Gransden (London and Edinburgh, 1964) pp. xvii, 46—7, 82; cf. A. Gransden, *Historical writing in England c. 550-1307* (London, 1974) pp. 396—9.

101. James of Vitry, Sermon 37, pp. 405—414.

102. *Lettres de Jacques de Vitry (1160/1170—1240) évêque de Saint-Jean d'Acre*, ed. R. B. C. Huygens (Leiden, 1960) pp. 99—100, III lines 41—48; pp. 115, 121, V lines 69—75, 251—2, p. 124, VI lines 34—5, 47—52.

103. *Historia Orientalis*, p. 1085.

104. Fidenzio of Padua, pp. 24—5, 15.

105. J. C. M. Laurent, ed., *Peregrinatores medii aevi quattuor*, 2nd edition (Leipzig, 1873) pp. 31, 34, 83, 88—9. For the loss of Saphet, see also 'Eracles', pp. 454—5; Primat, 'Chronique', trans. Jean du Vignay, *RHGF* 23 p. 83; Abou 'L-Feda, 'Annals', *RHC Or* 1 p. 151.

106. *PL* 155 cols. 1085, 1087.

107. *Theodoricus: Libellus de Locis Sanctis*, ed. M. L. and W. Bulst (Heidelberg, 1976) pp. 21, 26—7, 35—37, 43—4, 46, 49.

108. *Anonymous pilgrims*, pp. 29—30.

109. Odo of Deuil, pp. 124, 134.

110. 'Gesta Obsidionis Damiatae', Johannes de Tulbia, 'de domino Johanne Rege Ierusalem', 'Liber duelli Christiani in obsidione Damiatae exacti', in R. Röhricht, ed., *Quinti Belli Sacri Scriptores minores* SOL (Geneva, 1879) pp. 99—100, 130—1, 157, also pp. 80, 103, 121, 132, 135, 145, 159, 161—2; *CGH* no. 1633.

111. *Die Schriften des Kölner Domscholasters, Späteren Bischofs von Paderborn und Kardinalbischofs von S. Sabina, Oliverus*, ed. H. Hoogeveg, BLVS 202 (Tübingen, 1894) 'Historia regum Terrae Sanctae', pp. 118, 119, 126, 129, 142—3, cf. pp. 120, 134; 'Historia Damiatina', pp. 180, 194—5, 209—11, 214—5, 217, 223—4, 234, 244—5, 254—6, 271, 273; cf. 279, para. 84.

112. Roger of Wendover, 2 pp. 202—4, 206—7, 228—51; *CM* 3 pp. 35—42, 44—56.

113. 'Annales Colonienses maximi', pp. 832—36; 'Gesta crucigerorum Rhenanorum', in *Quinti Belli*, p. 36ff.; 'Annales S. Rudberti Salisburgensis', ed. D. Wattenbach, *MGHS* 9 pp. 780—1; 'Cronica S. Petri Erfordiensis moderna', ed. O. Holder-Egger, *MGHS* 30 pp. 385—9; 'Historia Damiatina', in *Gesta Dei*, 1, 2 pp. 1125ff.

114. *Historia Anglorum*, 2 p. 232, and note 6.

115. *Urkundenbuch des Hochstifts Halberstadt und seiner Bischofe*, ed. G. Schmidt, vol. 2, (Leipzig, 1884) nos. 1028, 1013.

116. *Pommersches Urkundenbuch*, ed. K. Conrad, R. Prümers, *et al.*, 10 vols. (Stettin and Cologne, 1868—1984) 2 nos. 696, 1352; cf. *Les registres d'Alexandre IV*, ed. C. Bourel de la Roncière *et al.*, 3 vols., BEFAR (Paris, 1896—1953) no. 482.

117. *Codex diplomaticus Brandenburgensis. Sammlung der Urkunden, Chroniken und sonstigen Geschichtsquellen für die Geschichte der Mark Brandenburg und ihrer Regenten*, ed. A. F. Riedel, 41 vols. (Berlin, 1838—69) A 19 p. 1 no. 1, 20 p. 182 no. 8, 24 pp. 1—2 no. 2.

118. See W. Kuhn, 'Kirchliche Siedlung als Grenzschutz, 1200 bis 1250 (am Beispiel des mittleren Oderraums)' *Ostdeutsche Wissenschaft* 9 (1962) 48—50.

119. Henry of Livonia, *Chronica Lyvoniae*, ed. W. Arndt, *MGHS* 23 pp. 246ff., especially p. 273 on Brothers Berthold and Arnold, p. 305 on Brother Rudolf.

120. *Cod. Dip. Boh.*, 5, 1 pp. 626—7, no. 422.

121. *Registrum visitationem archiepiscopi Rothomagensis: journal des visites pastorales d'Eude Rigord, archevêque de Rouen*, ed. T. Bonnin (Rouen, 1852) pp. 67, 85, 95, 247, 709, 716, 722.

122. Comte de Marsy, ed., 'Fragment d'un cartulaire de l'ordre de Saint-Lazare en Terre Sainte', *AOL* 2, 'Documents', pp. 154—5, nos. 37—8; *Règle*, p. 286, para. 546.

123. 'Eracles', p. 481.

124. *CGH* nos. 2934—5.

125. *Rotuli Roberti Grossetesti, episcopi Lincolniensis*, ed. F. N. Davis, Canterbury and York Society 10 (London, 1913) *passim*; *Rotuli Ricardi Gravesend diocesis Lincolniensis*, ed. F. N. Davis *et al.*, Canterbury and York Society 31 (Oxford, 1925) pp. 162—3; *CM* 5 p. 97.

126. *The register of Walter Giffard, lord archbishop of York 1266–1279*, ed. W. Brown, Surtees society 109 (Durham, London and Edinburgh, 1904) pp. 47—8.

127. *Councils and synods*, 2, 2 p. 1428 (index): councils at the New Temple, London: thirteen councils were held here 1250—1300, six of which were during Peckham's time. *Fratris Johannis Pecham quodam archiepiscopi Cantuariensis: Tractatus tres de paupertate*, ed. C. L. Kingsford, A. G. Little, F. Tocco (Aberdeen, 1910) p. 173 lines 293—6; cf. *Walter Map*, pp. 52—4, 112—4. Two manuscripts of the *Defensio* survive.

128. E.g., Wojtecki, 'Der Deutsche Orden unter Friedrich II', pp. 214—6.

129. *Urkundenbuch der Deutschordensballei Thüringen*, ed. K. H. Lampe, 1 (Jena, 1936) no. 298.

130. Printed by Bulst-Thiele, *Sacrae domus*, pp. 360—2, esp. 361.

131. *Monumenta ordinis fratrum praedicatorum historica, 3, Acta capitulorum generalium*, ed. B. M. Reichert, 1 (Rome and Stuttgart, 1898) p. 26; *CM* 6, *Liber Additamentorum*, pp. 203—7, nos. 100—2.

132. *The Sandford cartulary*, ed. A. M. Leys, 2 vols., Oxfordshire Record Society nos. 19, 22 (Oxford, 1938—41) no. 58 and note.

133. *UB Thüringen*, no. 259.

134. *CGH* no. 4028.

135. E.g. *Reg. Urb. IV*, no. 713.

136. Reginald of Durham, *Libellus de vita et miraculis S. Godrici heremitae de*

Finchale, ed. J. Stevenson, Surtees Society 20 (1844) p. 57.

137. *Sandford cartulary*, no. 335.
138. *CGH* nos. 4002, 4159; *Urkundenbuch der Deutschordensballei Hessen*, ed. A. Wyss, 3 vols., (1879—1899, reprinted Osnabruck, 1965) 1 no. 526.
139. S. Menache, 'Contemporary attitudes concerning the Templars' affair: propaganda's fiasco?' *Journal of Medieval History*, 8 (1982) 137—8, 140—1.
140. Walter Map, p. 68.

Chapter four

1. *L'histoire de Guillaume le Maréchal, comte de Striguil et de Pembroke*, ed. P. Meyer, 3 vols., SHF (Paris, 1891—1901) lines 18317—20, 18351—18442, especially 18433—442.
2. *CM* 4 pp. 44, 56.
3. *UB Thüringen* nos. 132, 137.
4. G. Duby, *The chivalrous society*, trans. C. Postan (London, 1977) pp. 78—9, 107, 178—85; cf., e.g., *Mort Artu*, pp. 24, 27, paras. 26, 29.
5. *RHGF* 24 p. 221, no. 1509; C. Perkins, 'The Knights Templars in the British Isles', *English historical review* 25 (1910) 217—8.
6. E.g., Lees, pp. clxxxiii, p. 57 (Lockridge); *La continuation de Guillaume de Tyr, (1184-1197)* ed. M. R. Morgan (Paris, 1982) pp. 135—7, para. 133.
7. M. Gervers, *The cartulary of the knights of St John of Jerusalem in England, secunda camera. Essex*, (Oxford, 1982) p. xxxviii; *CGH*, no. 89.
8. Gervers, ed., *Cartulaire*, p. xlv.
9. Gervers, ed., *Cartulaire*, pp. xlv—xlvi; *CGH*, no. 1973.
10. E.g., P. Gérard and E. Magnou, eds., *Cartulaires des Templiers de Douzens* (Paris, 1965) no. 115 (114) pp. 107—8 (1133); no. 40, pp. 50—1 (1133—4), etc.; *Sandford cartulary*, no. 247 p. 179 (1155—6), no. 1 pp. 3—4 (1240); *CGH* nos. 1365 (1211), 1464 (1218), 2883 (1257), 3718, 3744, 3897, 3762 (1280—1285); *UB Thüringen*, no. 473 (1289).
11. *The Burton Lazars cartulary: a medieval Leicestershire estate*. Burton Lazars research group, ed. T. Bourne and D. Marcombe (University of Nottingham, Dept. of adult education, 1987) p. 63, f.249; for date, see C. Tyerman, *England and the crusades, 1095-1588*, (Chicago and London, 1988) pp. 205—6.
12. Oliver, 'Historia Damiatina', p. 207.
13. J. Walker, 'The motives for patrons of the order of St Lazarus in England in the twelfth and thirteenth centuries', in J. Loades, ed., *Monastic studies I: the continuity of tradition* (Bangor, 1990) 171—181.
14. *UB Thüringen*, nos. 167, 263 (Henry I, vogt of Plauen), 203 (the counts of Eberstein) 310 (Heinemann of Dobena, steward of the kingdom of Bohemia) 397 (Otto IV, count of Orlamünde) 404 (Otto IV, count of Arnshaugk) 473 (Albrecht, landgrave of Thuringia).
15. The only example in *UB Thüringen* is no. 473; nos. 397 and 404 make an oblique reference.
16. *CGH* no. 3322, and see also 2860 and note, 2883, for a donation of Henry, count of Furstenburg, 1253.
17. D'Albon, ed., *Cartulaire*, nos. 17, 141, 205, 375; Osto of St Omer became a

prominent Templar in England in the twelfth century: Lees, pp. xlviii, li–liv.

18. M. Méras, *Le Beaujolais au moyen âge*, (Villefranche-en-Beaujolais, 1956) esp. pp. 32–3, 59; Bulst-Thiele, *Sacrae domus*, pp. 259–60, on William of Beaujeu, master of the Temple 1273–91.

19. H. d'Arbois de Jubainville, 'Catalogue d'actes des comtes de Brienne, 950–1356', *BEC* 33 (1872) nos. 37, 146–7, 151, 163, 165, 167, 169, 171, 189, 191, 192.

20. D. A. Greenway, ed., *Charters of the honour of Mowbray, 1107–1191*, (London, 1972) pp. 22–27, nos. 23–31, (St. Lazarus) pp. 124–5, nos. 170–1, (Hospital) pp. 182–5, nos. 270–6 (Temple); R. V. Taylor, ed., 'Ribston and the knights Templars', *Yorkshire archaeological and topographical journal*, 8 (1884) pp. 281–3, nos. 20–1.

21. *UB Thüringen*, no. 266. The title 'Vogt' originally meant 'governor' or 'bailiff' but by the thirteenth century it had become an hereditary lordship.

22. *UB Hessen*, 1 no. 218.

23. *Circa* 1163: Luchaire, ed., *Études*, nos. 485, 504, and index.

24. *Close Rolls*, 1242–47, p. 311.

25. Wojtecki, 'Der Deutsche Orden unter Friedrich II', pp. 187–207.

26. *UB Thüringen*, no. 263.

27. For a good summary, see Keen, *Chivalry*, pp. 51–7.

28. See D'Albon, ed., *Cartulaire*, nos. 18 (1128), 27, 28 (esp. Losbert de Vico Forti), 33 (1130), 61, 84, 139 (1137) etc.

29. *Ibid.*, no. 68.

30. See chapter five.

31. *Register Innocenz' III*, 2 no. 54.

32. See Barber, 'The origins of the order of the Temple', *Studia monastica* 12 (1970) 223, 227–8.

33. See below, chapter five, p. 89.

34. The evidence is discussed by Forey, 'Recruitment to the military orders (twelfth to mid-fourteenth centuries)' *Viator* 17 (1986) 143–144.

35. Discussed in *ibid.*, 165, 166.

36. *Acta Sanctorum*, ed. J. Bollandus *et al.*, (Antwerp, 1643ff., reprinted Brussels, 1966) May VI, p. 855f.

37. William fitz Stephen, 'Vita Sancti Thomae', in *Materials for the history of Thomas Becket*, ed. J. C. Robertson, 7 vols., RS 51 (London, 1875–85) 3 p. 105; W. L. Warren, *Henry II* (London, 1973) p. 216.

38. *CGH*, no. 649; see also nos. 299, 370, 382, 400 for this donor.

39. See C. T. Clay, 'The family of Amundeville', *Reports and papers of the Lincolnshire architectural and archaeological society*, 3 (1945) 128.

40. E.g., *Sandford cartulary*, nos. 74–6, 81, 87, 120, 125, 146, 162, 221; *CGH*, nos. 1785, 1788, 1817, 2112, 2963.

41. Walker, 'Motives of patrons', p. 177.

42. The evidence is summarized by F. L. Carsten, *The origins of Prussia*, (Oxford, 1954) pp. 13–14; Kuhn, 'Kirchliches Siedlung', 6–55.

43. *Pommersches UB*, 3 pp. 140–1, no. 1596.

44. *CGH* no. 3718.

45. *CGH* nos. 3744, 3897, and rephrased in 3762.

46. See above, chapter two, pp. 27—28.

47. *CGH* no. 3882; *Patent Rolls* (1281—92) pp. 120, 147, 225, 243—4, 343, 436, 486; *List of inquisitions ad quod damnum preserved in the Public Record Office,* 2 vols., P.R.O. lists and indexes 17 (reprinted New York, 1963) p. 20, no. 9, p. 23, no. 1, p. 25, no. 28, p. 26, no. 25, p. 27, nos. 10, 14. Some of these may be sales.

48. Schüpferling, pp. 240—1.

49. *CM* 5 pp. 108—9.

50. Siberry, *Criticism,* p. 196.

51. Housley, *Italian crusades,* pp. 62—70, 151—6, 158—9, 162—70, 252—3, 257.

52. Ricaut Bonomel, 'Ir'e dolors s'es dins mon cor asseza', ed. A. de Bastard, 'La colère et la douleur d'un templier en Terre Sainte', *Revue des langues romanes,* 81 (1974) 357, strophe V.

53. William of Tyre, *A history of deeds done beyond the sea,* trans. E. A. Babcock and A. C. Krey, 2 vols. (reprinted New York, 1976) 1 p. 43.

54. Morgan, *Chronicle of Ernoul,* p. 187.

55. J. Richard, 'Les Templiers et les Hospitaliers en Bourgogne et en Champagne meridionale (XII—XIII siècles)', in Fleckenstein and Hellmann, eds., *Geistlichen Ritterorden,* pp. 241—2.

56. J. C. Ward, 'Fashions in monastic endowment: the foundations of the Clare family, 1066—1314', *Journal of Ecclesiastical History,* 32 (1981) 446—51; cf. Raban, *Mortmain Legislation,* pp. 131—3

57. Arbois de Jubainville, 'Catalogue', (after 1250) nos. 189, 191, 192, and see note 19 above.

58. *CGH,* nos. 268, 600, 843 (Guy II, Guy III), 1431, 1453 (Renaud de Forez), 1599, 1666, 1938, 2233, 2234 (Guy IV), 3488, 3489 (Guy V).

59. D'Albon, ed., *Cartulaire,* nos. 47, 475; *CGH* nos. 36, 515, 855, 960, 1308, 3698*bis.*

60. D'Albon, ed., *Cartulaire,* no. 338; *CGH* nos. 1781, 3723, 3989, 4089; *Patent Rolls* (1247—58) p. 142.

61. See above, pp. 61—2.

62. Raoul de Houdenc, *Meraugis de Portlesguez,* ed. M. Friedwagner (reprinted Geneva, 1975) *passim; The continuations of the Old French Perceval of Chrétien de Troyes,* ed. W. Roach *et al.,* 5 vols. in 6 (Philadelphia, 1949—1983) 2 lines 1529—1531; *Le roman de Tristan en prose,* ed. P. Ménard *et al.,* 1ff. TLF 353 etc., (Geneva, 1987ff.) 1 p. 194, and pp. 174—5, 191—4; see also *ibid.,* 4 (1992) pp. 201—3 etc. ('railleries de Dinadan'); *La Queste del Saint Graal, roman du XIIIe siècle,* ed. A. Pauphilet, CFMA 33 (Paris, 1980) p. 54, pp. 229—32.

63. *Continuation de Guillaume de Tyr,* pp. 39—40, 41, chs. 26, 28.

64. Guiot of Provins, lines 1695—1739, especially lines 1722—3.

65. A. Långfors, A. Jeanroy and L. Brandin, eds., *Recueil général des jeux-partis français,* 2 vols. in 1, SATF (Paris, 1926) 2 p. 109 no. 128, strophe 3. William the Vinier, a married clerk and a burgess of Arras, died in 1245: 1 p. xliv. For Adam, see 1 p. xlvi; for Peter of Corbie see 1 p. xlvii. This debate survives in five manuscripts.

66. Gervers, ed., *Cartulaire,* p. xlvi.

67. E.g., *CGH.,* no. 3266; *Pommersches UB,* 2 nos. 891, 914, 1312, p. 536; *Reg.*

Nic. IV, no. 6096; cf. Kuhn, 'Kirchliche Siedlung', 46–53.

68. See above, notes 43–5.
69. E.g., Ambroise, lines 3021–3036, 4755–8, 7237–77, 7691–2; 'Du bon William Longespee', *passim*.
70. Ernoul, p. 149; Morgan, *Chronicle of Ernoul*, pp. 41–6, 78–136.
71. *Continuation de Guillaume de Tyr*, p. 39 para. 25, p. 87 para. 76, p. 99 paras. 96–8; p. 137, para. 133.
72. *Ibid.*, pp. 31–3, para. 17, p. 36, para. 23, pp. 43ff., para. 30–42, p. 39, para. 25, pp. 45–6, para. 33, para. 57, pp. 135–7, para. 133.
73. Philip of Nanteuil, 'En chantant veil mon duel faire', in J. Bédier and P. Aubry, eds., *Les chansons de croisade* (Paris, 1909, reprinted Geneva, 1974) p. 223, strophe 4; 'Rothelin', pp. 538–49; Matthew Paris, *Historia Anglorum*, 2 p. 433.
74. John of Joinville, pp. 195–6, paras. 540–2.
75. *Ibid.*, pp. 168–91, sections 412–4, pp. 161–3, sections 381–5.
76. See chapter three, pp. 00–00; *Preuß UB*, 1, 2 nos. 62, 65.
77. Kuhn, 'Ritterorden als Grenzhüter', 42–52.
78. Cf. *Preuß UB*, 1, 1 no. 94.
79. *Rotuli Hundredonum temp. Hen. III & Edw. I in turri Lond. et curia receptae Scaccarii Westm. asservati*, 2 vols. (London, 1812–8) e.g., 1 pp. 117, 129, 295, 378; 2 pp. 27, 226, 318, 320; Perkins, 'Knights Templars', 218–22.
80. *Ibid.*, 1 p. 58, 2 p. 228.
81. *Placita de Quo Warranto temporibus Edw. I, II & III in curia receptae Scaccarii Westm. asservata* (London, 1818) pp. 761–2.
82. E.g., acquittals, pp. 117, 129, 277, 280–1, 341, 353, 678, 747, 761, 762, 786, 787–8, 792; cf. amercements, e.g., pp. 251–2, 356, 375–6, 588, 596, 692, 761–2.
83. Siberry, *Criticism*, p. 11.
84. *Poésies complètes du troubadour Marcabru*, ed. J. M. L. Dejeanne (Toulouse, 1909, reprinted New York and London, 1971) no. xxv, p. 171. Dated 1146–7 or 1138–45: Constable, 'Second crusade', 230, note 94.
85. Peirol, 'Pus flum Jordan ai vist e.l monimon', in *Peirol, troubadour of Auvergne*, ed. S. C. Aston (Cambridge, 1953) pp. 3–4, 161–3, no. XXXII.
86. Rutebeuf, *Oeuvres complètes*, ed. E. Faral and J. Bastin, 2 vols. (Paris, 1959–60) 1 p. 508, lines 327–335, p. 502, line 134, p. 504, lines 219–20.
87. Bernart Sicart de Marvejols, 'Ab greu cossire', strophe 3.
88. Daspol, 'Seinhos, aujas, c'aves saber e sens', lines 41–56, in P. Meyer, 'Les derniers troubadours de la Provence d'après le chansonnier donné à la Bibliothèque impériale par M. Ch. Giraud', *BEC* 5 (6ème série) (1869) 289.
89. 'Pos de sa mar man cavalier del Temple', in Meyer, ed., 'Les derniers troubadours de la Provence', 497–8, and see 484–5.
90. *La 'Bible' au seigneur de Berzé*, ed. F. Lecoy (Paris, 1938) lines 261–293, 349-370, pp. 22–5.
91. *Poésies complètes du troubadour Peire Cardenal (1180–1278)* ed. R. Lavaud (Toulouse, 1957) pp. 388–93.
92. 'Sur les états du monde', in I. S. T. Aspin, ed., *Anglo-Norman political songs*, Anglo-Norman texts 11 (Oxford, 1953) pp. 117, 123, no. XI verses 24–5.
93. 'Ordre de Bel Ayre', in *ibid.*, pp. 130–1, 134, no. XII lines 71–8: remarking

on the Hospitallers' beautiful mounts.

94. Raoul de Houdenc, *Songe d'enfer*, ed. M. T. Mihm, (Tübingen, 1984) MS W, p. 146, lines 361—4.

95. See my article, 'Jacquemart Giélée's *Renart le nouvel*: the image of the military orders on the eve of the loss of Acre', in Loades, ed., *Monastic studies*, pp. 182—9.

96. *CGH* no. 3507.

97. Jacquemart Giélée, *Renart le nouvel*, ed. H. Roussel, SATF (Paris, 1961) pp. 7—10. The poem is written in the French of northeastern France, with some Flemish thrown in. It is therefore unlikely to have circulated outside this area.

98. *Renart le nouvel*, lines 7199—7330.

99. *Ibid.*, lines 7469—7666.

100. *Ibid.*, lines 7667—7720.

101. Hugh von Trimberg, *Der Renner*, ed. G. Ehrismann, 4 vols., BLVS 247, 248, 252, 256 (Tübingen, 1908—9) 2 p. 70 lines 11134—5.

102. See also below, chapter six, pp. 120—22.

103. E.g., Ernoul, p. 161; *Die Register Innocenz' III*, 2 no. 247; *PL* 216 col. 56 year 12 no. 45; Burton annals, in *Annales monastici* 1 p. 494; C. Kohler and Ch. V. Langlois, eds., 'Lettres inédits concernant les croisades (1275—1307)', *BEC* 52 (1891) p. 56.

104. Hugh, lord of Berzé, lines 261—6; Richard, earl of Cornwall: *CM* 4 p. 139; Matthew Paris, e.g., *CM* 4 pp. 167, 279, 291, 5 pp. 745—6; for the loss of Acre, see below, chapter 7, notes 7, 9.

105. One exception occurs in 1267: *Urkundenbuch der Stadt Friedburg* 1 (1216—1410) ed. M. Foltz (Marburg, 1904) pp. 17—8, no. 52.

106. H. von Hammerstein, 'Der Besitz der Tempelherren in Lotharingen', *Jahrbuch der Gesellschaft für Lothringische Geschichte und Altertumskunde*, 7, 1 (1895) 19 no. 38.

107. D. Wojtecki, *Studien zur Personengeschichte des Deutschenordens im 13 Jahrhundert*, (Wiesbaden, 1971) pp. 78—9, 88—90.

108. Richard, *Latin kingdom*, 2 pp. 365—7, 414; Bulst-Thiele, *Sacrae domus*, pp. 233—4, 240, 264; cf. p. 271.

109. W. Urban, *The Baltic crusade* (Decatur, 1975) pp. 131—2, 137, 141, 142, 145, 257ff.; cf. Alberic of Trois Fontaines, p. 930.

110. J. Piquet, *Des banquiers au moyen âge: les Templiers: Étude sur leurs opérations financières* (Paris, 1939) pp. 90—2.

111. Dunstable annals, pp. 222—3.

112. *Histoire et cartulaire des Templiers de Provins*, ed. V. Carrière (Paris, 1919) nos. 148, 151.

113. *Rot. Hund.*, 1 pp. 77, 96, and cf. 317.

114. *Ibid.*, 1 pp. 83, 291, 401.

115. P. Ménard, *Les fabliaux: contes à rire du moyen âge* (Paris, 1983) pp. 87—107.

116. W. Noomen and N. von den Boorgaard, eds., *Nouveau recueil complet des fabliaux*, 6 vols. to date, (Assen/Maastricht, 1983ff.) 3 no. 16, pp. 179, 197—8, lines 146—9.

117. Ménard, *Fabliaux*, pp. 72—5.

118. James of Vitry, sermon 38, pp. 419—420; on Waldensian non-violence, see

the Anonymous of Passau in *Quellen zur Geschichte der Waldenser*, ed. A. Patshovsky and K.-V. Selge (Gütersloh, 1973) p. 81; Kedar, *Crusade and mission*, p. 174.

119. Delaruelle, 'Templiers et Hospitaliers en Languedoc', 315–6; Peter of Vaux-de-Cernay, 'Historia Albigensium', *RHGF* 19, pp. 60, 71, 100–1; William of Puylaurens, *ibid.*, p. 218.

120. *RHGF* 24 pp. 320–1, no. 1, p. 363 no. 10.

121. William of Puy-Laurens, pp. 222–3.

122. *The itinerary of Benjamin of Tudela*, ed. M. N. Adler (London, 1907) pp. 22–3.

123. *Le chronique de Michel le Syrien, Patriarche Jacobite d'Antioche, 1166–1199*, ed. J. B. Chabot, 4 vols. (Paris, 1899–1910) 3 pp. 201–3; *RHC DocArm* 1 pp. 331–3; Riley-Smith, 'Cilician Armenia', pp. 99, 101–3, 105–8.

124. *The chronography of Gregory Abû'l-Faraj, 1225–1286, the son of Aaron, the Hebrew Physician, commonly known as Bar Hebraeus, being the first part of his political history of the world*, trans. E. W. Budge, 2 vols. (London, 1932, reprinted Amsterdam, 1976) 1 pp. 280, 282, 308–9, 381, 389, 396, 463; see chapter 7 for his continuator's description of the loss of Acre.

125. *The chronicle of Novgorod 1016–1471*, trans. R. Mitchell and N. Forbes, Camden 3rd series 25 (London, 1914) pp. 85–7, 93–4, 101–3.

126. *Preuß. UB*, 1, 1 nos. 298, 273, 274, 324; *Livländische Reimchronik*, ed. F. Pfeiffer, BLVS 7B (Stuttgart, 1844) lines 2448ff.

127. 'Imâd ad-Din al-Isfahânî, (519–597/1125–1201) *Conquête de la Syrie et de la Palestine par Saladin*, trans. H. Masse, (Paris, 1972) p. 31, and pp. 15–7, 29, 30–31, 36–7, 45, 97, 125, 142–4, etc.

128. *Ibid.*, pp. 41, 81–2.

129. Quoted from 'Imâd ad-Din by Abu Shamah, 'The book of the two gardens', in *RHC Or* 4–5, 4 p. 385 (read Kaukab for Safed); and by Ibn Alatyr, 'El-Kamel Altevarylch', *RHC Or* 1 p. 736.

130. Riley-Smith, *Knights*, pp. 75–76.

131. Abou 'L-Feda, 'Annals', *RHC Or* 1, pp. 161, 151, and also 112, 158; see also Riley-Smith, *Knights*, p. 141 for other Muslim comments on the Hospitallers of Margat.

132. E.g., *Memoirs of an Arab-Syrian gentleman, or, an Arab knight in the Crusades: memoirs of Usamah ibn-Munqidh*, trans. P. K. Hitti, (Beirut, 1964) pp. 161, 163–4; *CGH*, no. 2149 (also sent to the Temple); Innocent III in *PL* 215, col. 689, 8 no. 119; Abou 'L-Feda, p. 120; Riley-Smith, *Knights*, p. 78, note 1, p. 162; Bulst-Thiele, *Sacrae domus*, pp. 200, 221, 226–7, 276.

133. Cf. Perkins, 'Knights Templars', 215, 218–9, 221, 229–30.

Chapter five

1. See D. Tyson, 'Patronage of French vernacular history writers in the twelfth and thirteenth centuries', *Romania*, 100 (1979) 186–7; E. Baumgartner, 'Les techniques narratives dans le roman en prose', in N. J. Lacy, D. Kelly and K. Busby, eds., *The legacy of Chrétien de Troyes*, 2 vols. (Amsterdam, 1987) 1 pp. 167–8.

2. Davis, 'William of Tyre', pp. 70—1, 74—5.

3. J. M. A. Beer, *Narrative conventions of truth in the middle ages* (Geneva, 1981) esp. pp. 9, 11, 85.

4. Other versions appear in, for example, Gregory of Tours, *Histoire des Francs*, ed. H. Omont and G. Collon, 2 vols. (Paris, 1886—93) 1 pp. 133—4, Bk. 4 ch. 42; translated as *The history of the Franks*, trans. L. Thorpe (Harmondsworth, 1974) p. 238; 'Math, son of Mathonwy', in *The Mabinogion*, trans. J. Gantz (Harmondsworth, 1976) p. 101.

5. Gerhoh of Reichersberg, p. 377; Michael the Syrian, 3 p. 276; cf. Bar Hebraeus, 1 p. 274.

6. 'Annales Herbipolenses', p. 7; Ralph of Coggeshall, p. 12.

7. Roger of Howden, *Gesta Henrici Secundi*, ed. W. Stubbs, 2 vols., RS 49 (London, 1867) 1 pp. 130—1, note 10; *Chronica*, 2 pp. 131—2. The Christians were indeed bribed to abandon this siege, but the gold was genuine; Abou 'L—Feda, p. 48.

8. Otto of St Blasien, p. 327.

9. Gervase of Canterbury, *Historical Works*, ed. W. Stubbs, 2 vols., RS 75 (London, 1879—90) 1 pp. 137—8.

10. Davis, 'William of Tyre', p. 71. Some of William's tales were repeated by Walter Map before 1187; Walter Map pp. xxv—xxvi, xxix—xxx, 62—6. It is possible that Map heard them via the third Lateran council.

11. That is, M. R. Morgan's mss. A. B. and z: Morgan, *Chronicle of Ernoul*, pp. 11—13, 46—50; Ernoul, pp. 12—13.

12. Since the 1160s: see Forey, 'Militarisation', 88.

13. See Gerald of Wales, 8 p. 201.

14. *MGHES* 1 no. 79 pp. 57—8, no. 80 p. 60; *CGH* no. 1633.

15. Albert Milioli, 'Liber de temporibus et aetatibus et cronica imperatorum', ed. O. Holder-Egger, *MGHS* 31 pp. 639—40. Also printed as 'Codex Estensis', *PL* 213 cols. 511—2, note 23.

16. William of Tyre, 2 pp. 822—3. Bk. 18 ch. 9.

17. Abou 'L—Feda, pp. 30—31.

18. Walter Map, pp. 62—6.

19. 'Continuatio Premonstratensis', ed. D. L. C. Bethmann, *MGHS* 6 pp. 455—6; Guy of Bazoches in Alberic of Trois-Fontaines, p. 846 (erroneously recorded under 1162); Baldwin of Ninove, 'Chronicon', ed. O. Holder-Egger, *MGHS* 25, p. 534 (written in the second half of the thirteenth century: pp. 515—6).

20. William of Tyre, 2 pp. 953—5, Bk. 20 chs. 29—30.

21. Walter Map, p. 66; Guy of Bazoches in Alberic of Trois-Fontaines, p. 859; Thomas Tusci, p. 507; Oliver *Scholasticus*, p. 129.

22. James of Vitry, 'Historia Orientalis', col. 1063.

23. Abu Shamah, *RHC Or* 4, p. 185.

24. Robert of Torigny, *Chronicle*, in R. Howlett, ed., *Chronicles of the reign of Stephen, Henry II and Richard I*, 4 vols., RS 82 (London, 1884—9) 4 p. 288.

25. *Continuation de Guillaume de Tyr*, pp. 58—9.

26. Ernoul, pp. 255—6.

27. E.g. 'Annales Herbipolenses', p. 7.

28. Bartholomew of Neocastro, pp. 114—7; cf. *HDFS* 3 p. 491 note 1, 5 p. 708.

29. Matthew Paris, *CM*, 3 pp. 177—9; *Flores* 2 pp. 194—5; *Historia Anglorum*, 2 pp. 312—5 and p. 312 note 4, 3 p. 259.
30. *Règle*, p. 154 section 230 (before 1187), p. 230 para. 422 (first half of thirteenth century), pp. 296—7 paras. 568—70 (1257—1265); *Die Statuten des Deutschen Ordens nach die Altesten Handschriften*, ed. M. Perlbach (Halle, 1890) p. 86 no. 39, 'Very great faults' no. 5; *CGH* no. 2213 section 34 (*c*.1239).
31. William of Tyre, 2 p. 949, Bk. 20 ch. 26.
32. Roger of Howden, *Gesta*, 1 p. 341; *Chronica*, 2 p. 307. In medieval legends of the distant past and fairytales, succession is down the female line; hence the daughter of Saladin's sister is his heiress.
33. *CM* 5 p. 387.
34. Ernoul, p. 458; Alberic of Trois-Fontaines, pp. 925, 945.
35. Ralph of Coggeshall, pp. 134—5.
36. Walter Map, pp. 58—60; for Mary's involvement in this miracle, see *Catalogue of romances in the department of manuscripts, British Museum*, ed. H. L. D. Ward, 2 vols. (London, 1883—93) 2 p. 662; *Anecdotes historiques, légends et apologues tirés du recueil inédit d'Étienne de Bourbon, Dominicain du XIII siècle*, ed. A. Lecoy de la Marche, SHF (Paris, 1877) pp. 105—6, no. 123. Stephen of Bourbon was born at Belleville on the Saone, entered the Dominican convent at Lyons, and had become an inquisitor by 1235. He died in 1261 in Lyons.
37. L'abbé A. Guillotin de Corson, 'Traditions populaires concernant le Temple et l'Hôpital en Bretagne', *Bulletin archéologique de l'association Breton*, 19 (1901) 244—9.
38. *Récits d'un ménestrel de Reims au treizième siècle*, ed. N. de Wailly, SHF (Paris, 1876) pp. xxxiv, 104—9, 112, paras. 198—208, 213.
39. Winchester annals, *Annales monastici*, 2 p. 92; Ernoul, p. 36; *Itinerarium* p. 9.
40. *Raoul de Cambrai, chanson de geste*, ed. P. Meyer and A. Longnon, SATF (Paris, 1882) pp. xxxiii—lv; lines 3427—8.
41. *Orson de Beauvais, chanson de geste du XIIe siècle*, ed. G. Paris, SATF (Paris, 1899) lines 3319—3321, pp. lxii—lxviii, lxxviii—lxxx; *Itinerarium*, pp. 67, 122.
42. *La chevalerie d'Ogier de Danemarche*, ed. M. Eusebi (Milan and Varese, 1953) line 10427, and pp. 34—5; 5 manuscripts survive. *Renaus de Montauban, oder die Haimonskinder, Altfranzösisches Gedicht*, ed. H. Michelant, BLVS 67 (Stuttgart, 1862) p. 337 line 10; cf. *Renaut de Montauban*, ed. J. Thomas, line 11000, etc., and p. 9. *Renaut* survives in 13 manuscripts.
43. *La fille du comte de Ponthieu: nouvelle du XIIIe siècle*, ed. C. Brunel, CFMA 52 (Paris, 1926) p. 22, lines 305—310.
44. Jean Renart, *Le roman de la rose ou Guillaume de Dole*, ed. F. Lecoy, CFMA 91 (Paris, 1962) line 5589; *L'Escoufle, roman d'aventure*, ed. F. Sweetser, TLF 211 (Geneva, 1974) pp. vii—viii, xiii.
45. *L'Escoufle*, lines 2390—2395, pp. vii, xii.
46. *L'Histoire de Guillaume le Maréchal*, lines 18351—18378, 18233—18242.
47. M. Blaess, ed., 'L'abbaye de Bordesley et les livres de Guy de Beauchamp', *Romania*, 78 (1957) 514.
48. *Der festländische Bueve de Hantone, Fassung III*, ed. A. Stimming, 2 vols., GRL 34, 42 (Dresden, 1914—1920) 1 lines 16279—82, 16297—9, 2 pp. 1—11.

49. *The old French crusade cycle, vol. VII: the Jérusalem continuations, part 1: La chrétienté Corbaran*, ed. P. W. Grillo (Alabama, 1984) pp. xvi–xvii.

50. *The old French crusade cycle, vol. V: les chétifs*, ed. G. M. Myers (Alabama, 1981) lines 2147–2148, 3058; this is thought to have been written around 1180: S. Duparc Quioc, *La chanson d'Antioche: étude critique* (Paris, 1978) pp. 132–9; cf. G. Myers, 'Les chétifs — étude sur le développement de la chanson', *Romania*, 105 (1984) 65–75, where it is shown that the third part was a later interpolation written to extol the knights of Beauvais. Ten manuscripts survive.

51. *Old French crusade cycle vol VII*, p. xx, and note 24 on pp. xx–xxi.

52. *Gontier de Soignies: il canzoniere*, ed. L. Formisano (Milan and Naples, 1980) no. XVIII 'L'an quant voi esclarcir', p. 130, lines 63–4, and p. lx.

53. Ernoul, p. 114; 'Regni Iherosolymitani Brevis Historia', in *Annali Genovesi di Caffaro e de'suoi continuatori dal MXCIX al MCCXCIII*, ed. L. T. Belgrano and C. I. di Sant'Angelo, new edn, 5 vols. (Rome, 1890–1929) 1 pp. 137–8; *MGHS* 18 p. 3; *Continuation de Guillaume de Tyr (1184–97)*, p. 46 section 33.

54. *La Chastelaine de Vergi, poème du XIII siècle*, ed. G. Raynaud, 2nd edition revue par L. Foulet, CFMA 1 (Paris, 1912) p. iii and lines 941–3. One of these two manuscripts (from a total of ten) dates from the thirteenth century, the other from the fourteenth (pp. iv–v, 35).

55. *Sone von Nausay*, ed. M. Goldschmidt, BLVS 216 (Tübingen, 1899) lines 8705–6. The poem probably dates from after 1264, as it assumes that a lady rules Beirut: pp. 552–4.

56. *Sone*, lines 6437-6840, 17525–17662.

57. See King Mark's remarks on King Solomon in *Tristan*, ed. Ménard, 4 (1992) p. 159, 85 lines 13–17; and 1 Kings 11 verse 1.

58. *Der festländische Bueve de Hantone, Fassung II*, ed. A. Stimming, 2 vols., GRL 30, 41 (Dresden, 1912–1918) 1 line 17578; *Fassung III*, 1 lines 3180–3197, 3240–5, 3249.

59. *Fille du comte de Ponthieu*, pp. 39–40, lines 570–3.

60. *Sone*, lines 5995–6916.

61. *Li roman de Laurin, fils de Marques le sénéschal*, ed. L. Thorpe, 2 vols. (Cambridge, 1950–8) 2 p. 111, line 4614, and 1 p. 107. Eight manuscripts survive.

62. *Bueve de Hantone, Fassung III*, line 15828.

63. *Les chansons de Jaufré Rudel*, ed. A. Jeanroy, CFMA 15 (Paris, 1924) pp. vii, 21.

64. *Li romans de Claris et Laris*, ed. J. Alton, BLVS 169 (Tübingen, 1884; reprinted Amsterdam, 1966) lines 40–9.

65. *Ibid.*, lines 9863–9871, 9907–9922.

66. Jean Renart, *L'Escoufle*, lines 1060–1065.

67. Gautier de Tournay, *L'Histoire de Gille de Chyn*, ed. E. B. Place (Chicago, 1941) pp. 5–6, 10–11.

68. 'Du bon William Longespee', pp. 339–353.

69. Blaess, ed., 'L'abbaye de Bordesley', 513.

70. *Esclarmonde, Clarisse et Florent, Yde et Olive, drei Fortsetzungen der chanson von Hugh de Bordeaux*, ed. M. Schweigel (Marburg, 1889) lines 1942–2035, esp.

1944, 2010, 2013—4, 2020—1 (survives in only one manuscript); 'Rothelin', pp. 539—40.

71. Ulrich von Etzenbach, *Wilhelm von Wenden*, ed. H.-F. Rosenfeld, (Berlin, 1957) lines 3784—3793, 3841—3848.

72. F. W. Wentzlaff-Eggebert, *Kreuzzugsdichtung des Mittelalters. Studien zu ihrer Geschichtlichen und Dichterlichen Wirklichkeit* (Berlin, 1960) pp. 280—3, 393.

73. *Ortnit und die Wolfdietriche nach Müllenhofs vorarbeiten*, ed. A. Amelung and O. Jänicke, 2 vols., Deutsches Heldenbuch 3—4 (reprinted Dublin and Zurich, 1968) 3 pp. iii—iv, 4 p. xv, pp. 56—62 (V lines 106—140), p. 227 (X line 65.2), p. 229 (X line 79.1).

74. Wentzlaff-Eggebert, pp. 379—380; H. de Boor, *Geschichte der Deutschen Literatur 1: Der Deutsche Literatur von Karl dem Grossen bis zum Beginn der Höfischen Dichtung, 770-1170*, (Munich, 1949) pp. 256—7.

75. *Orendal*, ed. H. Steinger, (Halle, 1935) pp. iii—iv, and lines 836—43, 866—70, 884—91, 1201—4, 1340—1, 1676—1685, 1949—2016, 2161—2186.

76. Ottokar's *Reimchronik*, which criticizes all the military orders, dates from after the trial of the Temple: M. Fischer, 'Criticism of church and crusade in Ottokar's *Österreichische Reimchronik'*, *Forum for Modern Language Studies*, 22 (1986) 157, 162; and cf. *Die Kreuzfahrt des Landgrafen Ludwigs* written 1306 (*ibid.*, 162) which praises the order.

77. *Sone*, lines 17607—618, 17659—60.

78. *Ibid.*, lines 20527—20530, 20580—2, 20601—4.

79. *Der festländische Bueve de Hantone, Fassung I*, ed. A. Stimming, GRL 25 (Dresden, 1911) lines 10554—7 (one manuscript survives: p. xi); dated to 1220—1225 by Moisan, *Répertoire des noms propres de personnes et de lieux cités dans les chansons de geste françaises et les oeuvres étrangères dérivées*, 5 vols., (Geneva and Paris, 1986) p. 36; *Fassung III*, lines 15552—3.

80. Jean Renart, *L'Escoufle*, lines 798—801.

81. Eighty-six manuscripts survive, forty-four of which date from the thirteenth century: B. Schirok, *Parzivalrezeption im Mittelalter* (Darmstadt, 1982) p. 57. This testifies to the immense popularity of the poem.

82. Wolfram von Eschenbach, *Parzival*, ed. K. Lachmann and W. Spiewok, 2 vols. (Stuttgart, 1981) Book 16, 816.15.

83. *Parzival*, 2 Book 9:443.6—445.30, 468.23—30, Book 16: 792.20—24, 793.21—28, 797.13—15, 802.11—20, 804.4—7, 805.22—23, 816.5—6, 16—17, 821.18—21; *Wolframs von Eschenbach Parzival und Titurel*, ed. E. Martin 1 (Halle, 1920) p. 298, line 11.

84. Wolfram von Eschenbach, *Parzival*, trans. A. T. Hatto (Harmondsworth, 1980) pp. 421—3, 424, 428, 438.

85. *Parzival*, trans. Hatto, pp. 427—8; *The continuations of the Old French 'Perceval' 5: The Third Continuation by Manessier*, lines 42658—42668.

86. *Reinfrid von Braunschweig*, ed. K. Bartsch, BLVS 109 (Tübingen, 1871) lines 782—791; see also *Der Marner*, ed. P. Strauch (Strasbourg, 1876, reprinted Berlin, 1962) p. 127 XV 16: '*Ich sunge ouch wol wie Titurel/ templeise bi dem Grâle züge'*; cf. Schirok, *Parzivalrezeption*, p.65ff.

87. *Queste*, pp. 26—9, especially p. 28 line 9; *Perlesvaus: Le Haut Livre du Graal*, ed. W. A. Nitze and J. Atkinson Jenkins, 2 vols. (reprinted New York, 1972) 1 p. 388 lines 9588—9590; Upton-Ward, 'Attitudes', pp. 39—40;

Trotter, *Medieval French literature*, p. 157; the order in fact bore a black and white shield, with a red cross emblazoned on the white section, see Figure 6; the knights of Christ of Livonia bore a red cross on a white field, with a red sword, while the Prussian order bore a red sword and star on a white field: Kuhn, 'Ritterorden', 12, 27; the Militia of the Blessed Virgin Mary also bore a red cross: Housley, 'Politics and Heresy', 206; the Hospital bore a white cross on a red ground: see Figure 5.

88. *Queste*, pp. 220—226.
89. *Queste*, p. 54, but cf. pp. 229—233.
90. J. Frappier, 'Le Graal et la chevalerie', *Romania* 75 (1954) 207.
91. E.g. *Moniage Guillaume, passim; Moniage Rainouart, passim; Ornit*, p. 220ff., X 11 to end.
92. E.g. *Renaut de Montauban*, line 14095 to end; *Queste*, p. 279, lines 14—18; *Mort Artu*, pp. 260—263; Manessier, lines 42551—42637; *Perlesvaus*, 1 p. 408, lines 10179—10185; *Escanors*, ed. H. Michelant, BLVS 178 (Tübingen, 1886) lines 24811—25204.
93. E.g. *Mort Artu*, p. 225; Chrétien, *Guillaume de l'Angleterre, roman du XIIe siècle*, ed. M. Wilmotte, CFMA 55 (Paris, 1978) *passim*; also heroes such as Sone de Nausay, Bueve de Hantone.
94. Humbert de Romans, *De modo*, p. 472.
95. Cf. Trotter, *Medieval French literature*, p. 101, and P. Aebisher, ed., *Le voyage de Charlemagne à Jérusalem et à Constantinople*, TLF 115 (Geneva, 1965) p. 29. The crusade cycle was still being copied and adapted: Duparc-Quioc, *La Chanson D'Antioche*, pp. 63—8.
96. Blaess, 'L'abbaye de Bordesley', 511—8.
97. As the publication of *Tristan* by Philippe Ménard and his collaborators had not reached this point of the text at the time of writing, this assertion is based on E. Loseth, *Le roman en prose de Tristan, le roman de Palamède et la compilation de Rusticien de Pise. Analyse critique d'après les manuscrits de Paris* (Paris, 1891) pp. 349—51 paras. 494—502, p. 289 para. 405, p. 307 para. 448 (but cf. p. 307 note 2, where seven manuscripts depicted Galaad defeating Tristan in one encounter. Two of these are late thirteenth century or fourteenth century and the rest are fifteenth or sixteenth century.) It remains to be seen how far the published text will agree with Loseth's summary.
98. The *Perlesvaus*, which exalts the knight who serves God, survives in seven manuscripts or parts of manuscripts (1 pp. 3—12); in contrast *Lancelot*, ed. A. Micha, 9 vols., TLF 247 etc., (Geneva, 1978—83), exalting the knight who serves his lady (at least to immediate appearances), survives in 'around a hundred' manuscripts or fragments, 1 pp. ix—x; *Queste*, exalting the knight who serves God, survives in around forty manuscripts, pp. iii—v; *Mort Artu*, exalting the knights who love and give to the poor, in almost fifty manuscripts, pp. xxx—xxxiii; *Le roman de Tristan en Prose*, ed. R. Curtis, 3 vols. (Cambridge, 1985) continued in *Le roman de Tristan*, ed. Ménard, exalting the knight who serves his lady, in around 82 manuscripts (ed. Ménard, 1 p. 8). On the basis of manuscripts, the knight who served God was less interesting to audiences than the knight who served his lady.
99. *CM* 5 pp. 148—154; cf. 'Du bon William Longespee'; 'Rothelin', pp. 604—6,

Ménestrel de Reims, pp. 196–8, paras. 381–3.
100. Note 86, above; cf. Trotter, *Medieval French literature*, pp. 29, 33–4.
101. 'Rothelin', p. 604.
102. *Continuation de Guillaume de Tyr*, p. 45.
103. *CM*, 3 p. 177–9; and see above, pp. 43–4, 81–4.
104. Walter Map, p. 68.
105. E.g. Bertrand de Bar-sur-Aube, *Girart de Vienne*, ed. W. van Emden, SATF (Paris, 1977) lines 8–12; *Tristan*, ed. Curtis, 1 p. 39 lines 1–7; Beer, *Narrative conventions*, pp. 9, 11, 85.
106. Trotter, *Medieval French literature*, pp. 20–27; Lloyd, *English Society*, pp. 96–7.
107. *CM* 4, p. 291, 5 p. 118.
108. E.g. Hugo von Trimberg, 2 lines 11133–6; *Johannis Pecham, tractatus*, p. 173 lines 293–6: John later refutes this criticism.

Chapter six

1. This chapter is adapted from a paper which I read to the members of Jonathan Riley-Smith's crusade seminar on 21 May 1990. I am grateful for the various comments and suggestions made then, some of which have been included below.
2. John of Salisbury, *Policraticus*, 2 p. 196, Bk. 7 ch. 21, 694a; Walter Map, p. 110.
3. *CM* 5 p. 150; see also *UB Thüringen* no. 147, and *Preuß. UB* 1, 2 nos. 62, 65.
4. *CGH* no. 70.4; *Règle*, pp. 43–4, section 37.
5. *Règle*, pp. 291–2 para. 558.
6. E.g., see *Règle*, p. 286 para. 546.
7. *CGH* nos. 2213.75, 82 (*c.*1239), 3396.24 (1270), 3844.7, 8 (1283); *Règle*, p. 153 para. 225 (12th century, probably before 1187), p. 189 para. 326, p. 228 para. 418 (13th century, probably before 1250), p. 288 para. 550 (1257–65); *Statuten des Deutschen Ordens*, p. 83, 'greater crimes', no. 3 (before 1264).
8. *CGH* nos. 2186 (1238), 2213.82 (*c.*1239).
9. *Règle*, pp. 289–90, paras. 553–4.
10. Quoted by A. Forey, 'A thirteenth-century dispute between Templars and Hospitallers in Aragon', *Durham University journal* 80 (1988) 185–6.
11. Riley-Smith, *Knights*, pp. 379–80.
12. Strehlke, no. 560.
13. Lees, Royal charters no. 5; *Rotuli chartarum in Turri Londonensis asservati*, ed. T. D. Hardy (London, 1837) pp. 2b–3.
14. *HDFS* 1, 2 pp. 438–40.
15. G. Servois, ed., 'Emprunts de S. Louis en Palestine et en Afrique. Appendice', *BEC* 19 (1858) 291f: *RRH* no. 1347.
16. *Reg. Urb. IV*, no. 946.
17. Primat, pp. 50–1, 55, 56.
18. R. C. Smail, 'Latin Syria and the west, 1149–1187', *TRHS* 5th series 19

(1969) 1–21; Lloyd, *English society*, pp. 232ff., and appendices 1–2.

19. This has been discussed in detail by Smail, 'Latin Syria'; Lloyd, *English Society*, pp. 27–31, 36ff., 248ff., 256–60; B. J. Cook, 'The transmission of knowledge about the Holy Land through Europe, 1271–1314', unpublished Ph.D. thesis (University of Manchester, 1985) p. 402ff., especially pp. 419ff., 453ff., 477–488, 490ff.

20. Amaury's brother Simon had married the earl's sister Eleanor. The earl was himself about to set out on crusade.

21. *CM* 4, pp. 25–6.

22. Letters from the Holy Land appear in *CM* 4 pp. 288–91, 307–11, 6 pp. 152–4, 155–62, 167–9, 191–7, 203–7.

23. *RRH* no. 926.

24. *RRH* no. 1299.

25. 'De constructione castri Saphet', ed. R. B. C. Huygens, *Studi Medievali*, 3rd series, 6 (1965) 355–387.

26. 'Chronicon Lemovicense', *RHGF* 21 pp. 773–4; 'Chronicon Rothomagensis', *RHGF* 23, p. 340; 'Continuatio 1 minoritae Erphod.', ed. O. Holder-Egger, *MGHS* 24 p. 403; 'Cronica S. Petri Erphod.', p. 403.

27. *CGH*, no. 3308, 4 p. 292.

28. Oliver *Scholasticus*, pp. 290–1, 169–174.

29. 'Annales Colonienses Maximi', p. 832; 'Gesta crucigerorum Rhenanorum', p. 36; Roger of Wendover, 2 pp. 206–7.

30. 'Annales S. Rutberti', p. 780 (brief notice); 'Cronica S. Petri Erfordiensis Moderna', p. 386 (brief notice); Matthew Paris (from Roger of Wendover), *CM* 3 p. 14.

31. *MGHL* p. 264.

32. Strehlke, no. 72, pp. 56–7.

33. *Reg. Nich. IV*, no. 5209.

34. Cf. *CM* 3 p. 178.

35. Forey, 'St. Thomas of Acre', 494.

36. *CM* 5 p. 745; Salimbene de Adam, *Cronica*, ed. G. Scalla, 2 vols. (Bari, 1966) pp. 255, 14; Joinville, pp. 195–6.

37. Schüpferling, p. 110.

38. *Burton Lazars cartulary* p. 38 f.73 (1261), p. 44 f.117, p. 55 f. 201, *bis*; *Patent Rolls*, (1266–72) p. 526 (1271), (1281–92) p. 137 (1284), p. 431 (1291).

39. *The journey of William of Rubruck to the eastern parts of the world, 1253–65, as narrated by himself*, trans. and ed. W. W. Rockhill, Hakluyt Society, 2nd series 4 (London, 1900, reprinted Nendeln, 1967) p. 94.

40. *CM* 4 p. 291; 5 p. 118.

41. Prawer, 'Military orders', pp. 223–4.

42. 'Nouveau monuments de croisiés recueilliés en Terre Sainte', ed. Clermont-Ganneau, *AOL* 2, C 462–3.

43. Bulst-Thiele, *Sacrae Domus*, plate 1a, facing page 416; Matthew Paris, *Historia Anglorum* 1 pp. 223.

44. Riley-Smith, *Knights*, p. 279.

45. M. Gervers, 'Donations to the Hospitallers in England in the wake of the second crusade', in M. Gervers, ed., *The second crusade and the Cistercians* (New York, 1991) p. 159.

46. See Figures 4 and 6.
47. James of Vitry, sermon 37 pp. 412–3, 38 p. 420; *Anecdotes d'Étienne de Bourbon*, p. 164, section 188.
48. Sermons, 37 p. 412, 38 p. 420.
49. *Caesarii Heisterbachensis monachi ordinis Cisterciensis Dialogus miraculorum*, ed. J. Strange, 2 vols. (Cologne, Bonn and Brussels, 1851) 2 p. 119.
50. *Ibid.*, p. 360.
51. S. Schein, 'The image of the crusader kingdom of Jerusalem in the thirteenth century', *Revue Belge de philologie et d'histoire* 64 (1986) 712.
52. *Livländische Reimchronik*, ed. F. Pfeiffer, BLVS 7B (Stuttgart, 1844).
53. *Itinerarium*, Book I, chapters two, pp. 6–8, and five, pp. 16–17.
54. For these, see the letter from grand-preceptor Thierry to Henry II of England, *PL* 201, cols. 1409–10, and 'Imâd ad-Din, p. 125.
55. J. Folda, *Crusader manuscript illumination at Saint-Jean d'Acre, 1275–91*, (Princeton, 1976) p. 60ff.
56. *Anecdotes*, pp. 105–6, no. 123; *Ménestrel de Rheims*, pp. 104–9, 112, paras. 198–208, 213.
57. Extracts from the *Vitas Patruum*, and *Thais*, in P. Mayer, 'Notice sur le manuscrit Fr. 24862 de la Bibliothèque Nationale contenant divers ouvrages composés ou écrits en Angleterre', *Notices et extraits des manuscrits de la Bibliothèque Nationale et autres bibliothèques publiés par l'Académie des inscriptions et de belles-lettres*, 35 (1896) 131–168; 'Poème sur Antéchrist', in R. Fawtier and E. C. Fawtier-Jones, 'Notice sur manuscrit 'French 6' de la John Rylands library, Manchester', *Romania* 49 (1923) IX, 331–340; L. E. Kastner, 'Les versions françaises inédites de la descente de Saint Paul en enfer: 1) version d'Henri d'Arcy' *Revue des langues romanes* 48 (1905) 385–395; and see M. D. Legge, *Anglo-Norman literature and its background*, (Oxford, 1963) pp. 191–2.
58. *Le livre des Juges. Les cinq textes de la version française faite au XIIe siècle pour les chevaliers du Temple*, ed. le Marquis d'Albon (Lyons, 1913), pp. i–iii, p. 46 chapter 11 verse 45, p. 6 chapter 1 verse 21, and *passim*.
59. Folda, *Crusader manuscript*, pp. 66, 71.
60. K. Helm and W. Ziesemer, *Die Literatur des Deutschen Ritterordens*, (Giessen, 1951) p. 41ff.
61. In the eleventh century, the abbey of Vézelay in Burgundy claimed to possess the relics of St Mary Magdalene. In the thirteenth century this legend was elaborated to claim that Mary and her brother and sister Lazarus and Martha had come to Provence to spread the Gospel and that Mary had died as a hermit in the Maritime Alps. 'Research has shown the tale is unreliable': *Butler's Lives*, 3 pp. 162–3; in 1164 some relics were brought to Cologne from Milan, reputedly originally from Constantinople, which were identified with the Three Kings of Matthew 2, verses 1–2: *ibid.*, 3 pp. 168–9. There are many other examples.
62. Walter Map, p. 124.
63. Gerhoh of Reichersberg, p. 378.
64. *Hospitallers' Riwle*, lines 1–368.
65. *CGH* no. 911.
66. *CGH* no. 2654.

67. *CGH* no. 3562, p. 317.
68. *CGH* no. 3002. I am grateful to Tony Luttrell and Karl Borchardt for drawing my attention to the two unpublished letters of the Franconian Hospitallers. At the time of writing, Karl Borchardt was editing these letters for publication.
69. William of San Stefano, 'Comment la sainte maison de l'Hospital de S. Johan de Jerusalem commença', *RHC Occ* 5 p. 424, ch. 2.
70. *Livre des Juges*, p. 6 chapter 1 verse 21, pp. 31–2 chapter 8, verse 27.
71. *Queste*, p. 221.
72. *Libellus*, pp. 211–2.
73. A. Micha, *Essais sur le cycle du Lancelot-Graal* (Geneva, 1987) p. 12, dates the cycle to 1225–30 or possibly 1215–1235.
74. See S. Schein, 'Between Mount Moriah and the Holy Sepulchre: the changing traditions of the Temple Mount in the central middle ages', *Traditio*, 40 (1984) 175–195.
75. 'La chanson de Jérusalem — a critical edition', ed. N. R. Thorpe, unpublished Ph.D. thesis (Reading, 1980) line 7681. This has now been published as *La chanson de Jérusalem*, ed. N. R. Thorpe (Alabama, 1991), but I have not yet been able to obtain access to a copy.
76. *Jerusalem pilgrimage, 1099–1185*, ed. J. Wilkinson, J. Hill and W. F. Ryan, Hakluyt society, 2nd series, 167 (London, 1988) p. 240. The pool was the scene of a miracle in the Gospel of John, chapter 5, verses 2–9.
77. See *Burton Lazars cartulary*, p. 2; P. Bertrand de la Grassière, *L'ordre militaire et hospitalier de Saint-Lazare de Jérusalem* (Paris, 1960) p. 15 claims that this was accepted in 1151, but gives no reference. Cf. *Jerusalem Pilgrimage*, p. 200, which indicates that the reference was to the first hospital in Jerusalem, not the hospital of St Lazarus, stating that it was founded by John Hircan, who was a nephew of Judas Maccabaeus and ruled Judaea from 133–106 BC. The order of St Lazarus seems to have distorted this story.
78. 'Narratio de primordiis ordinis Theutonici', in *Statuten des Deutschen Ordens*, pp. 22–3, 159–60 (Frederick, Duke of Swabia); Jacques de Vitry, 'Historia Orientalis', cols. 1084–5.
79. *HDFS* 1 p. 288, 2 p. 224, 282, 3 pp. 154–5, 497, 4 p. 393.
80. 'Annales Colmarienses minores', ed. P. Jaffé, *MGHS* 17 p. 189 (began 1212); 'Rebus de Alsaticis ineuntis saeculis XIII', ed. P. Jaffé, *MGHS* 17, pp. 232, 235 (began *c.*1211); 'Chronicon Montis Sereni', ed. E. Ehrenfeuchter, *MGHS* 23 p. 163 (began 1190, in the time of Frederick, duke of Swabia); 'Cronica S. Petri Erphod.', p. 355 (founded 1200, by the emperor Henry VI at Acre). William of Andres thought that it began in 1127, at the same time as the order of the Temple: *MGHS* 26 p. 209. James of Vitry believed that it began at Jerusalem, but gave no date: 'Historia Orientalis', cols. 1084–5.
81. Humbert of Romans, 'De eruditione', p. 473.
82. Forey, 'St Thomas of Acre', 481–2, 492, 494.
83. *UB Thüringen*, no. 121.
84. *Itinerarium*, Bk. 1 ch. 2, p. 7; *Quinti Belli Sacri*, pp. 99–100, 130–1, 157.
85. See, for example, M. Dygo, 'The political role of the cult of the Virgin Mary in Teutonic Prussia in the 14th and 15th centuries', *Journal of Medieval History* 15 (1989) 63–80.

86. Boockmann, *Deutsche Orden*, p. 34.
87. *Livländische Reimchronik*, lines 8430—59, 10686—7.
88. Dusberg, p. 260, section 32; see also pp. 112—4, section 12.
89. Humbert de Romans, *De eruditione*, p. 473.
90. D'Albon, ed., *Cartulaire*, nos. 45, 95; see also nos. 119, 120, 124, 125 etc.
91. *Ibid.*, no. 139.
92. *Cartulaire de la commanderie de Richerenches de l'ordre du Temple (1136–1214)*, ed. le Marquis de Ripert-Monclar (Avignon, 1907) nos. 67, 69, 206—7, 227.
93. W. A. Neumann, ed., 'Drei mittelalterliche Pilgerschriften III: Philippi Descriptio Terrae Sanctae', *Oesterreichische Vierteljahresschrift für katholische Theologie* 11 (1872) 76.
94. P. Devos, 'Les premières versions occidental de la légende de Saïdnaia', *Analecta Bollandiana*, 65 (1947) 255—6, 258, 273.
95. C. H. Cheney, ed., 'The downfall of the Templars and a letter in their defence', in C. H. Cheney, ed., *Medieval texts and studies* (Oxford, 1973) p. 326.
96. 'Philippi Descriptio' p. 76.
97. *Acta Sanctorum*, Sept V p. 252ff.
98. Dusberg, pp. 138—40, section 36.
99. *CGH* no. 2008; *Reg. Greg. IX* nos. 1998—9.
100. 'Annales Colonienses Maximi', p. 845.
101. F. Tommasi, 'L'ordine dei Templari a Perugia', *Bolletino della deputazione di Storia Patria per L'Umbria*, 78 (1981) 9—10, 49—50, no. 5.
102. *Reg. Nich. IV*, no. 897.
103. *Reg. Greg. IX*, no. 1536.
104. *Jerusalem pilgrimage*, pp. 21, 239, 11, 178.
105. *CGH*, no. 3797.
106. *Acta SS.*, May V pp. 270—1; *Bibliotheca sanctorum*, Istituto Giovanni XXIII nella pontificia Università Lateranense, 12 vols. (Rome, 1961—70) 6 pp. 845—6; L. de Mas Latrie, *Histoire de l'Ile de Chypre sous le règne des princes de la maison de Lusignan*, 3 vols. (Paris, 1852—61) 1 p. 344.
107. See A. Luttrell in J. Azzopardi, *The order's early legacy in Malta* (Valletta, 1989) p. 45. I am grateful to Jonathan Riley-Smith for drawing my attention to this reference.
108. William of Tyre, 1 p. 375, Bk. 7 ch. 23.
109. *Ibid.*, 2 p. 812, Bk. 18 ch. 3.
110. *Acta SS.*, May VI pp. 854—9.
111. *Ibid.*, Oct IV pp. 362—4.
112. Riley-Smith, *Knights*, pp. 271—2.
113. *Butler's Lives*, 4 pp. 38—9.
114. On Nicasius, see I. Bosio, *Dell'Istoria della sacra religione et illustrissima militia di S. Giovanni Gierosol^{no}*. 3 parts, new ed. (Rome, 1621—84) 1 pp. 622—4; V. Venuti, 'Dell'esistenza, professione e culto di S. Nicasio martire. Discorso storico-critico', in F. Testa, ed., *Opuscoli di auctori Siciliani* 7 (Palermo, 1762) esp. pp. 22—3, 47, 99. no. 4.
115. *HDFS* 4 pp. 956—7.
116. *Acta SS.* June III p. 651ff.

117. *Ibid.*, May III p. 246ff; *Butler's Lives*, 2 pp. 378–9.
118. Venuti claimed that Nicasius died at Hattin, but no contemporary source mentions him. Perhaps Venuti confused Nicasius with the Templar Nicholas, a martyr of Hattin: *Itinerarium* p. 16.
119. *Libellus*, pp. 214, 215–6.
120. *Itinerarium*, Bk. 1 ch. 2 pp. 7–8.
121. Perhaps Hospitallers were favoured over Templars and Teutonic brothers because they were more famous for these peaceful virtues, but it is more likely that the preference reflects the Hospital's later predominance. Any saint known to have been connected with a military order would be assigned to the Hospitallers.
122. *CGH* no. 438.
123. *CGH* nos. 2257, 2258.
124. *CGH* no. 3308.
125. *CGH* no. 3002.
126. *CGH* no. 4149; *Reg. Nich. IV* no. 4635.
127. Riley-Smith, 'Crusading as an act of love', *History*, 65 (1980) 177–92; Forey, 'Emergence', 187.
128. John of Würzburg, col. 1087.
129. Amargier, ed., 'La défense du Temple', pp. 495–500.
130. *Le Dossier de l'affaire des Templiers*, ed. G. Lizerand (Paris, 1923) p. 2.
131. See above, p. 74.
132. E.g., *CGH* no. 558 (1179), no. 2117 (1235), no. 2784 (1256), no. 2902 (1258), no. 2943 (1260), nos. 3026–9, 3032, 3044, 3045 (1262), no. 3239 (1267). These were between the Hospital and Temple, except for no. 2902, which also included the Teutonic order.
133. Prawer, 'Military orders', pp. 223–4.
134. Kuhn, 'Ritterorden als Grenzhüter', 42–52.
135. *CGH*, no. 3308 (vol. 4).
136. Jacquemart Giélée, *Renart le Nouvel*, lines 7599–7650.
137. *CGH* no. 2120.
138. *CM* 4 p. 291.

Chapter seven

1. See S. Schein, *Fideles Crucis: Europe, the papacy and the crusade, 1274–1314* (Oxford, 1990).
2. *CGH* no. 4157.
3. 'Cronica S. Petri Erford.', pp. 424–5.
4. Geoffrey of Callone, 'Chronicon', RHGF 22 p. 9 (writing up to 1294); Jacobo d'Oria, in *Annali Genovesi*, 5 p. 130 (writing up to 1293).
5. *Magistri Thadei Neapolitani, Historia de desolacione et conculcacione civitatis Acconensis et tocius terrae sanctae, in AD MCCXCI...*, ed. P. Riant (Geneva, 1873) pp. 18–25, esp. p. 24.
6. See Eberhard of Ratisbon, p. 594.
7. 'De excidio urbis Acconis libri II', in E. Martène and U. Durand, eds., *Veterum scriptorum et monumentum*, 5 (Paris, 1729) col. 766.

8. *Dossier*, p. 4.
9. Dunstable annals, p. 366; Bartholomew of Neocastro, p. 132, but cf. p. 108ff., where he blames the pope. See Schein, *Fideles Crucis*, p. 76.
10. Bartholomew Cotton, p. 216; *Registrum Johannis de Pontissara, episcopi Wyntoniensis AD MCCLXXXII–MCCCXIV*, ed. C. Deedes, 2 vols., Canterbury and York Society 19 and 30 (London, 1915–24) 2 pp. 481–2.
11. Thaddeo of Naples, pp. 20–22, 23.
12. 'De excidio', Temple: pp. 781, 782–4, Hospital: pp. 772–3, 779, 781–2.
13. E.g., William of Nangis, 'Chronicon', *RHGF* 20 pp. 573–4; see also Morgan, 'Rothelin continuation', pp. 256–7.
14. *Renart le Nouvel*, lines 7558–7581.
15. Thaddeo of Naples, pp. 18–20.
16. Rutebuef, 1 p. 508, lines 327–335; Bar Hebraeus, pp. 492–3; *Cronica di Giovanni Villani*, ed. G. Antonelli, 4 vols. (Firenze, 1823) 2 pp. 353–4.
17. 'Lettres de Ricoldo de Monte Cruce', ed. R. Röhricht, *AOL* 2 292; 1 Kings chapters 16 verse 29 to 22 verse 40, especially 21 verse 25.

Conclusion

1. *Close Rolls*, (1251–1253) p. 428.
2. *UB Thüringen*, no. 147.
3. *CGH*, no. 4014.
4. *Renart le Nouvel*, lines 7571–5.
5. Case quoted by G. Barrow, 'The aftermath of war; Scotland and England in the late thirteenth and early fourteenth centuries', *TRHS* 28 (1978) 112–4. Walter Scott based the villainous Templar of *Ivanhoe*, Brian de Bois-Gilbert, on the character of Brian of Jay recorded in this case.
6. *CGH*, no. 3788.
7. *CGH*, nos. 2139, 3656; cf. Strehlke, nos. 104, 106; *Rot. Hund.*, 1 pp. 58, 83, 291, 401, 2 p. 320; Brand, 'Control of mortmain alienation', pp. 35–6; Forey, 'Thirteenth century dispute', 182–5, 186.
8. Joinville, pp. 168–9, paras. 412–4.
9. Menko, p. 555; Matthew Paris, *CM*, 4 pp. 139, 291, 5 pp. 745–6; *Flores*, 2 p. 264; *Historia Anglorum*, 2 p. 472; Bartholomew of Neocastro, p. 132; Hugh, lord of Berzé, lines 261–266; Fidenzio of Padua, p. 15, para. 10; Gilbert of Tournai, p. 57, para. 17; Ramon Lull, pp. 407–8, Book 4, chapter 80, para. 7.
10. Cf. Riley-Smith, *Knights*, pp. 150–1, 469, 443–50; Bulst-Thiele, *Sacrae Domus*, pp. 235, 282, 191–2.
11. *CGH* no. 3577; *Urkundenbuch für die Geschichte Niederrheins*, ed. T. J. Lacomblet, 4 vols., (reprinted Aalen, 1960) 2 p. 88, no. 171, note 2.
12. *The Anglo-Saxon chronicle*, ed. D. Whitelock, D. C. Douglas and S. I. Tucker (London, 1961) pp. 194–5.
13. *CM*, 5 p. 150.
14. *Gestes des Chyprois*, pp. 235, 240.
15. *PL* 215 col. 689, 8 no. 119.
16. Otto of St. Blasien, p. 327.

17. Gregory IX in *CGH.*, no. 2149; the emperor Frederick II in *CM*, 4 p. 302; Robert of Artois in *ibid.*, 5 pp. 149–50; Odo, bishop of Tusculanum, in *Spicilegium*, 3 p. 625; repeated by John of Columna, p. 119, and William of Nangis, 'Gesta Ludovici', *RHGF* 20, pp. 366–8.

18. *Reg. Greg. IX*, no. 2287; *CGH.*, no. 2186.

19. E.g., Roger of Howden, *Gesta*, 1 p. 131 note 10 (MS.B).; Otto of St Blasien, p. 327; Gervase of Canterbury, 1 pp. 137–8; Ernoul, pp. 12–3; Albert Milioli, pp. 639–40.

20. E.g., Philip de Nanteuil, p. 223, strophe 4; 'Rothelin,' pp. 538–49; Ambroise, lines 7691ff.; *Itinerarium*, Bk. 4 ch. 35, Bk. 5 ch. 1, pp. 305–9, Bk.6 ch. 1, pp. 379–82, ch. 7 pp. 393–4; Roger of Wendover, 1 p. 209.

21. William of Tyre, e.g., 2 p. 1008, Bk. 22 ch. 2.

22. *Fontes Egmundenses*, p. 161.

23. 'Sur les états du monde,' in *Anglo-Norman political songs*, p. 123, XI verse 25.

24. E.g., William of Tyre, 1 p. 554, Bk. 12 ch. 7, 2 p. 817, Bk. 18 ch. 6; Walter Map, p. 60; Bernart Sicart de Marvejols, 'Ab greu cossire', strophe 3, lines 42-3; *CM*, 4 p. 291.

25. *Règle*, p. 337 para. 658, p. 339 para. 661.

26. Roger of Howden, *Chronica*, 4 pp. 76–77; Gerald of Wales, 4 p. 54, 6 p. 44; Matthew Paris, *Flores*, 2 p. 117; cf. Frederick II in Winkelmann, ed., *Acta inedita*, p. 370, no. 437, lines 18–9, where the 'white brethren', presumably Cistercians, are accused of *luxure*.

27. Cf. Kedar, *Crusade and mission*, especially pp. 111–2.

28. Nigel of Longchamps, lines 2064–8; *CM* 3 p. 405; cf. Odo of Deuil, pp. 124–8.

29. See above, chapter three, p. 39; *Reg. Greg. IX*, nos. 2287, 3792–5; *Preuß. UB*, 1, 1 no. 134, 1, 2 no. 65.

30. *Preuß. UB*, 1, 1 no. 134, p. 101.

31. *CGH*, no. 3039.49; Kedar, *Crusade and mission*, pp. 48, 53, 146–151.

32. *CM*, 3 p. 178, 4 p. 291; *Councils and synods*, 2, 2 pp. 815, 1112 (14); Bartholomew Cotton, pp. 208–9, 213; John of Thilrode, p. 581.

33. E.g., Burton annals, pp. 493–4; *CGH.*, no. 3308.

34. See above, chapter six, pp. 102–3.

35. *CGH*, no. 2186.

36. E.g., *CGH*, nos. 2213.34, 3844.9; *Règle*, pp. 153–4, para. 231, p. 229 para. 418, p. 230 para. 422, pp. 297–8 paras. 571–3; *Die Statuten*, p. 86f., para. 39.

37. John of Salisbury, *Policraticus*, 2 p. 199, Bk. 7 ch. 21, 695c–d, and note on line 21; Walter Map, p. 80.

38. *Règle*, p. 156 para. 236, p. 243 para. 452, p. 309 para. 594; *CGH*, no. 70 Sections 4,9, no. 2186; *Statuten des Deutschen Ordens*, p. 50 no. 28, p. 52 no. 31, pp. 80 no. 2.

39. M. Barber, 'Propaganda in the Middle Ages: the charges against the Templars', *Nottingham Medieval Studies*, 17 (1973) 42–57.

40. *Renart le nouvel*, lines 7559–60.

41. Hugo von Trimberg, lines 11133–6; John Peckham, *Tractatus tres de paupertate*, p. 173 lines 293–6.

42. Forey, 'The military orders in the crusading proposals of the late thirteenth and early fourteenth centuries', *Traditio* 36 (1980) 317–345.

BIBLIOGRAPHY

Primary sources

Works are listed in alphabetical order, by the first name of the original author, or, if anonymous, by the first letter of the title (excluding the article).

'L'abbaye de Bordesley et les livres de Guy de Beauchamp,' ed. M. Blaess, *Romania* 78 (1957) 511–518.

Abou 'L-Feda, 'Annals', in *RHC Or* 1.

Abu Shamah, 'The book of the two gardens', in *RHC Or* 4–5.

Acta Imperii adhuc inedita: Acta Imperii inde ab Henrico I ad Henricum VI usque adhuc inedita. Urkunden des Kaiserreiches aus dem X, XI, und XII Jahrhunderts, ed. K. F. Stumpf-Brentano, 2 vols. (Innsbrück, 1865–1881): vol. 3 of K. F. Stumpf-Brentano, *Die Reichkanzler vernehmlich des X, XI und XII Jahrhunderts nebst einem Beitrage zu den Regesten und zur Kritik der Kaiserurkunden dieser Zeit.*

Acta inedita seculi XIII: Urkunden und Briefe zur Geschichte des Kaiserreichs und des Königreichs Sicilien in den Jahren 1198 bis 1273, ed. E. Winkelmann (Innsbrück, 1880).

Actes du Parlement de Paris, ed. E. Boutaric, 2 vols (Paris, 1863–7, reprinted Hildesheim/New York, 1975).

Alberic of Trois-Fontaines, 'Chronicon', ed. P. Scheffer-Boichorst, *MGHS* 23.

Albert von Beham: C. Höfler, ed., *Albert von Beham und Regesten Innocenz IV*, BLVS 16b (Stuttgart, 1847).

Albert Milioli, 'Liber de temporibus et aetatibus et chronica imperatorum', ed. O. Holder-Egger, *MGHS* 31.

Alexander III, 'Epistolae', in *PL* 200.

Alexander IV, *Registres*, ed. C. Bourel de la Roncière, *et al.*, 3 vols., BEFAR (Paris, 1896-1953).

Alexander Minorita, *Expositio in Apocalypsim*, ed. A. Wachtel, *MGH* Die Deutschen Geschichtsquellen des Mittelalters 500–1500, Quellen zur Geistesgeschichte des Mittelalters 1 (Weimar, 1955).

Aliscans, chanson de geste, ed. F. Guessard and A. de Montaiglon (Paris, 1890, reprinted Nendeln, 1966).

Alphonse de Poitiers, *Correspondance administrative*, ed. A. Molinier, 2 vols., Collection des documents inédits sur l'histoire de France (Paris, 1894–1900).

Ambroise, *Estoire de guerre sainte: Histoire en vers de la troisième croisade*, ed. G. Paris,

Collection des documents inédits sur l'histoire de France, (Paris, 1897).

Anglo-Norman political songs, ed. I. S. T. Aspin, Anglo-Norman Texts 11 (Oxford, 1953).

The Anglo-Saxon chronicle: a revised translation, ed. D. Whitelock, D. C. Douglas and S. Tucker (London, 1965).

'Annales Casinenses', ed. G. H. Pertz, *MGHS* 19.

Annales Cestrienses, or the chronicle of the abbey of St Werburg at Chester, ed. R. C. Christie, Lancashire and Cheshire Record Society, 14 (1886).

'Annales Colmarienses maiores', ed. P. Jaffé, *MGHS* 17.

'Annales Colmarienses minores', ed. P. Jaffé, *MGHS* 17.

'Annales Colonienses Maximi', ed. K. Pertz, *MGHS* 17.

'Annales Herbipolenses', ed. G. H. Pertz, *MGHS* 16.

'Annales Ianuenses', in *Annali Genovesi di Caffaro* 3.

Annales monastici, ed. H. R. Luard, 5 vols., RS 36 (London, 1864–1869).

'Annales S. Pataleonis Coloniensis', ed. H. Cardauns, *MGHS* 22.

'Annales S. Rutberti Salisburgensis', ed. D. W. Wattenbach, *MGHS* 9.

'Annales de Terre Sainte', ed. R. Röhricht and G. Raynaud, *AOL* 2 427–461.

Annali Genovesi di Caffaro e de'suoi continuatori dal MXCIX al MCCXCIII, ed. L. T. Belgrano and C. I. di Sant'Angelo, new edn, 5 vols., Fonti per la Storia Italia nos. 11–14*bis* (Rome, 1890–1929) and ed. G. H. Pertz, *MGHS* 18.

Annals of Walden, in *Monasticon Anglicanum* 4.

Anonymous of Béthune, *RHGF* 24 pp. 750–775.

Anonymous of Passau, in *Quellen zur Geschichte der Waldenser*, ed. A. Patschovshy and K.-V. Selge, Texte zur Kirchen und Theologiegeschichte, Heft 18 (Gütersloh, 1973).

Anonymous Pilgrim 5, 2 in *Anonymous pilgrims I-VIII (11th and 12th centuries)* trans. A. Stewart, PPTS 6 (London, 1894).

Anselm, bishop of Havelburg, 'Dialogi', in *PL* 188.

Arnold, Abbot of Lübeck, 'Chronicon Slavorum', ed. B. Lappenberg, *MGHS* 21.

'Aucharium Aquicinense', ed. D. L. C. Bethmann, *MGHS* 6.

Baldwin of Ninove, 'Chronicon', ed. O. Holder-Egger, *MGHS* 25.

Bar Hebraeus: *The chronography of Gregory Abû'l-Faraj (1225–1286) the son of Aaron, the Hebrew Physician, commonly known as Bar Hebraeus, being the first part of his history of the world*, trans. E. A. W. Budge, 2 vols. (London, 1932, reprinted Amsterdam, 1976) 1.

Bartholomeo of Neocastro, 'Historia Sicula', ed. G. Paladino, *RIS NS* 13.3.

Bartholomew Cotton, *Historia Anglicana*, ed. H. R. Luard, RS 16 (London, 1859).

Benjamin of Tudela, *Itinerary*, ed. M. N. Adler (London, 1907).

Bernard of Clairvaux, 'Liber ad milites Templi de laude novae militiae', in *Opera*, ed. J. Leclerq and H. M. Rochais, 8 vols. (Rome, 1957–77) 3 pp. 205–239.

— 'Epistolae', *PL* 182.

Bernart Sicart de Marvejols, 'Ab greu cossire', in *Choix des poésies originales des troubadours*, ed. M. Raynouard, 4.

Bertrand de Bar-sur-Aube, *Girart de Vienne*, ed. W. van Emden, SATF (Paris, 1977).

'du bon William Longespee', in A. Jubinal, ed., *Nouveau recueil de contes, dits, fabliaux, et autres pièces inédits des XIIIe, XIVe et XVe siècles, pour faire suite aux collections legrand d'Aussy, Barbazan et Méon, mis au jour pour la première fois*, 2 vols. (Paris, 1839–42) 2 pp. 339–353.

Bruno, bishop of Olmütz, 'Bericht am Papst Gregor X,' in C. Höfler, 'Analecten zur Geschichte Deutschlands und Italiens', part 1, *Abhandlungen der philosophisch-historischen Klasse der Königlich Bayerischen Akademie der Wissenschaften*, series 3, 4 part 3 (1846).

Bueve de Hantone:
— *Der anglonormannische Bueve de Haumtone*, ed. A. Stimming, Bibliotheca Normannica, 7 (Halle, 1899).
— *Der festländische Bueve de Hantone: Fassung I*, ed. A. Stimming, GRL 25 (Dresden, 1911).
— *Fassung II*, ed. A. Stimming, 2 vols., GRL 30, 41 (Dresden, 1912–1918).
— *Fassung III*, ed. A. Stimming, 2 vols., GRL 34, 42 (Dresden, 1914–1920).

Burton Annals, in *Annales monastici* 1.

The Burton Lazars cartulary: a medieval Leicestershire estate, Burton Lazars research group, ed. T. Bourne and D. Marcombe (University of Nottingham, Dept. of Adult Education, 1987).

Caesarius of Heisterbach: *Caesarii Heisterbachensis monachi ordinis Cisterciensis Dialogus miraculorum*, ed. J. Strange, 2 vols. (Cologne, Bonn and Brussels, 1851).

Calendar of the Charter Rolls preserved in the Public Record Office, 1ff., 1226ff. (London, 1903ff.).

Calendar of the Close Rolls preserved in the Public Record Office. Edward I, vols. 1–3 (London, 1900–4).

Calendar of the Liberate Rolls preserved in the Public Record Office: Henry III, 6 vols. (London, 1916–64).

Calendar of the Patent Rolls preserved in the Public Record Office, 1216ff. (London, 1901ff.).

Cartulaire de la commanderie de Richerenches de l'ordre du Temple (1136–1214) ed. le Marquis de Ripert-Monclar (Avignon, 1907).

Cartulaire général de l'ordre des Hospitaliers de S. Jean de Jérusalem, 1100–1310, ed. J. Delaville le Roulx, 4 vols., (Paris, 1894–1905).

Cartulaire général de Paris, ed. R. de Lasteyrie, 1 (528–1180) (Paris, 1887).

Cartulaire général de l'ordre du Temple, 1119?–1150, ed. le Marquis d'Albon (Paris, 1913).

Cartulaire Normand de Philippe-Auguste, Louis VIII, Saint Louis et Philippe le Hardi, ed. L. Delisle (Caen, 1882, reprinted Geneva, 1978).

Cartulaires des Templiers de Douzens, ed. P. Gérard and E. Magnou, Collection des documents inédits sur l'histoire de France, série in 8°, 3 (Paris, 1965).

Cartulaire des Templiers de Vaour (Tarn), ed. C. Portal and E. Cabié, Archives Historiques de l'Albigeois, fasc.1 (Albi, 1894).

A cartulary of Buckland Priory in the county of Somerset, ed. F. W. Weaver, Somerset record society, 25 (1909).

The Cartulary of the Knights of St John of Jerusalem in England, Secunda Camera. Essex, ed. M. Gervers, Records of social and economic history, new series 6, published for the British Academy (Oxford, 1982).

'Casus monasterii Petrihusensis', ed. O. Abel and L. Weiland, *MGHS* 20.

La chanson de Roland, ed. F. Whitehead (Oxford, 1946).

Charters of the Honour of Mowbray, 1107–1191, ed. D. Greenway, Records of social and economic history, new series 1 (London, 1972).

'Chartes de la commanderie de Beauvoir, de l'ordre Teutonique', in L'Abbé Lalore, ed., *Collection des principaux cartulaires du diocèse de Troyes*, 7 vols. (Paris/Troyes, 1875ff.) 3.

'Chartes de départ et de retour des comtes de Dampierre-en-Astenois, IVe et Ve croisades', ed. A. de Barthélemy, *AOL* 2 184–207.

'Chartes du Terre Sainte', ed. J. Delaville le Roulx, *ROL* 11 (1908) 181–191.

La chastelaine de Vergi, poème du XIII siècle, ed. G. Raynaud, 2nd edn revised by L. Foulet, CFMA 1 (Paris, 1912).

La chevalerie d'Ogier de Danemarche, ed. M. Eusebi (Milan and Varese, 1953).

Choix des poésies originales des troubadours, ed. M. Raynouard, 6 vols. (Paris, 1816–21).

Chrétien, *Guillaume de l'Angleterre, roman du XII siècle*, ed. M. Wilmotte, CFMA 55 (Paris, 1978).

Chrétien de Troyes, *Cligès*, ed. A. Micha, CFMA 84 (Paris, 1982).

Chronica Buriensis, the chronicle of Bury St Edmunds 1212–1301, ed. A. Gransden (London and Edinburgh, 1964).

The chronicle of Melrose: a facsimile edition, ed. A. O. and M. O. Anderson (London, 1936) and extr. ed. R. Pauli in *MGHS* 27.

The chronicle of Novgorod 1016–1471, trans. R. Mitchell and N. Forbes, Camden 3rd series 25 (London, 1914).

Chronicles of the Reigns of Stephen, Henry II, and Richard I, ed. R. Howlett, 4 vols., RS 82 (London, 1884–89).

'Chronicon Hanoniense quod dicitur Balduini Avennensis', ed. J. Heller, *MGHS* 25, and extr. *RHGF* 21.

'Chronicon Lemovicense', *RHGF* 21.

'Chronicon Montis Sereni', ed. E. Ehrenfeuchter, *MGHS* 23.

'Chronicon Rotomagensis', extr. *RHGF* 23.

'Chronicon Turonense, auctore anonymo, S. Martini Turon. canonico', extr. *RHGF* 18.

Chronique d'Ernoul et de Bernard le trésorier, ed. L. de Mas Latrie, SHF (Paris, 1871).

'Chroniques de St Denis', extr. *RHGF* 12, 17, 21.

Clement IV, *Registres*, ed. E. Jordan, BEFAR (Paris, 1893–1945).

Close Rolls of the reign of Henry III preserved in the Public Record Office, 1227ff. (London, 1902ff.).

Codex Diplomaticus Brandenburgensis. Sammlung der Urkunden, Chroniken und sonstigen Geschichtsquellen für die Geschichte der Mark Brandenburg und ihrer Regenten, ed. A. F. Riedel, 41 vols. (Berlin, 1838–69).

Codex Diplomaticus et Epistolaris regni Bohemiae, ed. G. Friedrich *et al.*, 5 vols. in 7 (Prague, 1904–1981).

'de constructione castri Saphet', ed. R. B. C. Huygens, *Studi Medievali*, 3rd series, 6 (1965) 355–387.

'Continuatio Aquicinctina', ed. D. L. C. Bethmann, *MGHS* 6.

'Continuatio Cuonradi praepositi Urspergensis', ed. O. Abel and L. Weiland, *MGHS* 23.

'Continuatio 1 Minoritae Erphordiensis', ed. O. Holder-Egger, *MGHS* 24.

'Continuatio Premonstratensis', ed. D. L. C. Bethmann, *MGHS* 6.

La continuation de Guillaume de Tyr, (1184–97), ed. M. R. Morgan (Paris, 1982).
'La continuation de Guillaume de Tyr, de 1228 à 1261, dit du manuscrit de Rothelin', in *RHC Occ* 2.
The continuations of the Old French Perceval of Chrétien de Troyes, ed. W. Roach *et al.*, 5 vols. in 6 (Philadelphia, 1949–83).
'The council of Pisa, 1135: a re-examination of the evidence for the canons', ed. R. Somerville, *Speculum* 45 (1970) 98–114.
Councils and synods with other documents relating to the English Church, ed. D. Whitelock, F. M. Powicke *et al.*, 2 vols. in 4, (Oxford, 1964–81).
Le couronnement de Louis: chanson de geste du XIIe siècle, ed. E. Langlois, CFMA 22 (Paris, 1984).
'Cronica S. Petri Erfordiensis Moderna', ed. O. Holder-Egger, *MGHS* 30.
Crusaders as conquerors. The chronicle of the Morea, translated from the Greek, by H. E. Lurier (New York and London, 1964).
Daspol, 'Seinhos, aujas, c'aves saber e sen', in 'Les derniers troubadours de la Provence'.
'La Défense du Temple devant le concile de Lyons en 1274', ed. P. Amargier, in *1274: L'année charnière: mutations et continuités, Lyon–Paris 30 Septembre–5 Octobre 1974*, Colloques internationaux du Centre national de la recherche scientifique (Paris, 1977) pp. 495–501.
'Les derniers troubadours de la Provence d'après le chansonnier donné à la Bibliothèque impériale par M. Ch. Giraud', ed. P. Meyer, *BEC* 5, 6ème série (1869) 245–97, 461–531, 649–87.
'Descente de Saint Paul en enfer', in 'Les versions françaises inédites de la descente de Saint Paul en enfer: 1', ed. L.-E. Kastner, *Revue des Langues Romanes* 48 (1905) 385–95.
Diplomatarium Suecarum, ed. J. G. Lijegren, 1 (Holm, 1829).
Diplomatic documents preserved in the Public Record Office, 1 (1101–1272) ed. P. Chaplais (London, 1964).
Le dossier de l'affaire des Templiers, ed. G. Lizerand (Paris, 1923).
'The downfall of the Templars and a letter in their defence', ed. C. H. Cheney, in C. H. Cheney, ed., *Medieval texts and studies* (Oxford, 1973) pp. 314–327.
Dunstable annals, in *Annales monastici* 3.
Eberhard, archdeacon of Ratisbon, 'Annales', ed. P. Jaffé, *MGHS* 17.
'Emprunts de Saint Louis en Palestine et en Afrique. Appendice', ed. G. Servois, *BEC* 19 (1858) 283–293.
Escanors, ed. H. Michelant, BLVS 178 (Tübingen, 1886).
Esclarmonde, Clarisse et Florent, Yde et Olive, drei Fortsetzungen der chanson von Hugh de Bordeaux, ed. M. Schweigel, Ausgaben und Abhandlungen aus dem Gebiete für romanische Philologie, ed. E. Stengel, 83 (Marburg, 1889).
'Estoire de Eracles empereur et la conqueste de la Terre d'Outremer', in *RHC Occ* 2.
Études sur les actes de Louis VII, ed. A. Luchaire (Paris, 1885).
Eudes Rigord, *Registrum visitationum archiepiscopi Rothomagensis: Journal des visites pastorales d'Eudes Rigaud, archevêque de Rouen*, ed. T. Bonnin (Rouen, 1852).
'De Excidio urbis Acconis libri II', in E. Martène and U. Durand, eds., *Veterum scriptorum et monumentum*, 5 (Paris, 1729) col. 757ff.
Fidenzio de Padua, 'Liber recuperationis Terrae Sanctae', in P. G. Golubovich,

Bibliotheca Bio-Bibliographia della Terra Sancta e dell'oriente francescano, 2 (Quarrachi, 1913) pp. 9—60.

La fille du comte de Ponthieu, nouvelle du XIIIe siècle, ed. C. Brunel, CFMA 52 (Paris, 1926).

Foedera, conventiones, litterae et cuiuscumque generis acta publica inter reges Angliae et alios quosvis imperatores, reges, pontifices, principes vel communitates, ed. T. Rymer, R. Sanderson, enlarged and amended by A. Clark and F. Holbrooke, 4 vols. in 7 parts (Record Commission, London, 1816—69).

Fontes Egmundenses, ed. O. Oppermann, Werken uitgegeven door het Historisch Genootschap (Gevestigd te Utrecht) derde Serie, no. 61 (Utrecht, 1933), also ed. G. H. Pertz, in *MGHS* 16.

'Fragment d'un cartulaire de l'ordre de Saint-Lazare en Terre Sainte', ed. Comte de Marsy, *AOL* 2, Documents, 121—157.

'Fragmentum de captione Damiatae', in *Quinti Belli Sacri Scriptores*.

Gautier de Tournai, *L'histoire de Gille de Chyn*, ed. E. B. Place (Chicago, 1941, reprinted New York, 1970)

Geoffrey de Callone, 'Chronicon', extr. *RHGF* 22.

Gerald of Wales, *Opera*, ed. J. S. Brewer *et al.*, 8 vols., RS 21 (London, 1861—91).

Gerhoh of Reichersberg, 'De investigatione Antichristi', ed. E. Sackur, *MGH Libelli de Lite Imperatorum et Pontificum*, 3 (Hanover, 1897).

Gervase of Canterbury, *Historical works*, ed. W. Stubbs, 2 vols., RS 73 (London, 1879—90).

'Gesta crucigerorum Rhenanorum', in *Quinti belli sacri scriptores*.

'Gesta obsidionis Damiatae', in *Quinti belli sacri scriptores* and ed. O. Holder-Egger, in *MGHS* 31.

Les Gestes des Chyprois, recueil de chroniques françaises écrites en orient en XIII et XIV siècles, ed. G. Raynaud, SOL (Paris, 1887, reprinted Osnabrück, 1968).

Ghislebert, 'Chronicon Hanoniense', ed. W. Arndt, *MGHS* 21.

Gilbert Foliot, *Letters*, ed. Z. N. Brooke, A. Mory, C. N. L. Brooke (Cambridge, 1962).

Gilbert of Tournai, 'Collectio de Scandalis Ecclesiae', ed. A. Stroick, *Archivum Franciscanum historicum*, 24 (1931) 33—62.

Giovanni Villani, *Cronica*, ed. G. Antonelli, 4 vols. (Firenze, 1823).

Godfrey of Viterbo, 'Pantheon', ed. G. Waitz, *MGHS* 22.

Gontier de Soignies: *Gontier de Soignies: il canzoniere*, ed. L. Formisano (Milan and Naples, 1980).

Gregory IX, *Registres*, ed. L. Auvray, 4 vols., BEFAR (Paris, 1896—1955).

Gregory X, *Registres*, ed. J. Guiraud, BEFAR (Paris, 1892—1960).

Gregory of Tours, *Histoire de Francs*, ed. H. Omont and G. Collon, Collection de textes pour servir à l'étude et à l'enseignement de l'histoire, 2 vols. (Paris, 1886—1893).

Guigues, abbot of La Grande Chartreuse, letter to the order of the Temple, in *Lettres des premiers Chartreux*, I, Sources Chrétiennes no. 88 (Paris, 1962).

Guilhem de Berguedan: 'El testamento de trovador Guilhem de Berguedan', ed. M. de Riquier, *Mélanges de linguistique et de littérature romanes à la mémoire d'Istvan Frank, Annales Universitatis Sarraviensis* 6 (1957) 573—583.

Guilhem Figueira, ein provenzlischer Troubadour, ed. E. Levy (Berlin, 1880).

Guillaume le Clerc, *Le besant de Dieu*, ed. P. Ruelle (Brussels, 1973).

Guiot of Provins, 'La Bible', in *Les oeuvres de Guiot de Provins, poète lyrique et satirique*, ed. J. Orr (Manchester, 1915).

Guy of Bazoches: in Alberic of Trois-Fontaines' chronicle.

Hadrian IV, 'Epistolae', in *PL* 188.

Henry of Livonia, 'Chronicon Lyvoniae', ed. W. Arndt, *MGHS* 23.

Histoire et cartulaire des Templiers de Provins, ed. V. Carrière (Paris, 1919).

L'histoire de Guillaume le Maréchal, comte de Striguil et de Pembroke, ed. P. Meyer, 3 vols., SHF (Paris, 1891−1901).

Historia diplomatica Fridericii Secundi, ed. J. L. A. Huillard-Bréholles, 6 vols. in 11 (Paris, 1852−61, reprinted Turin, 1963).

Historia pontificum et comitum Engolismensium, ed. J. Boussard, Bibliothèque Elzévirienne (Paris, 1957).

Historical documents of Ireland, ed. J. T. Gilbert, RS 53 (London, 1878).

Honorius III, *Regesta*, ed. P. Pressutti, 2 vols. (Rome, 1888−95, reprinted Hildesheim/New York, 1978).

Honorius IV, *Registres*, ed. M. Prou, BEFAR (Paris, 1888).

The Hospitallers' riwle (Miracula et regula Hospitalis Sancti Johannis Jerusolimitani), ed. K. V. Sinclair, Anglo-Norman texts 42 (Oxford, 1984).

Hugh, lord of Berzé: *La 'Bible' au seigneur de Berzé*, ed. F. Lecoy (Paris, 1938).

Hugh of Neville: M. S. Giuseppe, 'On the testament of Sir Hugh de Neville, written at Acre, 1267' *Archaeologia*, 56 (1899) 351−370.

Hugh 'Peccator', in J. Leclerq, ed., 'Un document sur les débuts des Templiers', *Revue de l'histoire ecclesiastique*, 52 (1957) 81−91; and C. Sclafert, ed., 'Lettre inédite de Hugues de Saint-Victor aux chevaliers du Temple', *Revue d'ascétique et de mystique*, 34 (1958) 275−299.

Hugo von Trimberg, *Der Renner*, ed. G. Ehrismann, 4 vols., BLVS 247−8, 252, 256 (Tübingen, 1909).

Humbert de Romans, 'De eruditione praedictorum, Liber II: de modo prompte cudiendi sermones ad omne hominum et negotiorum genus', in M. de la Bigne, ed., *Maxima bibliotheca veterum patrum et antiquorum scriptorum ecclesiasticorum*, 27 vols. (Lyons, 1677) 25, p. 424ff.

— 'Opus Tripartium', in *Fasciculus rerum expetendarum et fugiendarum*, 2, *appendix*, ed. E. Brown, 2 vols. (London, 1690) p. 185ff.

Ibn Alatyr, 'El-Kamel Altevarylch', in *RHC Or* 1.

Ibn al-Qalanisi, 'Chronicle', extr. and trans. in *The Damascus chronicle of the crusades*, by H. A. R. Gibb (London, 1932).

'Imâd ad-Dîn al-Isfahânî, *Conquête de la Syrie et de la Palestine par Saladin (al-Fath al-qwsî fî l-fath al qudsî)*, trans. H. Mascé (Paris, 1972).

Innocent III, *Letters concerning England and Wales. A calendar with an appendix of texts*, ed. C. R. Cheney and M. G. Cheney (Oxford, 1967).

— 'Liber registorum sive epistolarum', 3 vols., *PL* 214−216.

— *Die Register Innocenz' III*, ed. O. Hageneder and A. Haidacher, 2 vols. in 4 (Graz−Cologne, 1964−8, Rome−Vienna, 1979−83).

Innocent IV, *Registres*, ed. E. Berger, 4 vols., BEFAR (Paris, 1884−1921).

— Letters: P. Sambin, *Problemi politici attraverso lettere inedite di Innocenzo IV*, Istituto Veneto di scienze, lettere ed arti Venezia, Memorie classe di scienze morali e lettere, 31 fasc. 3 (Venice, 1955).

Isaac of l'Étoile, 'Sermones', in *PL* 194.

Itinerarium peregrinorum et gesta Regis Ricardi, in W. Stubbs, ed., *Chronicles and memorials of the reign of Richard I*, 2 vols., RS 38 (London, 1864–5) 1.

Jacobo d'Oria, 'Annales', in *Annali Genovesi* 5.

Jacquemart Giélée, *Renart le Nouvel*, ed. H. Roussel, SATF (Paris, 1961).

James I, King of Aragon, *Chronicle*, trans. J. Forster, 2 vols. (London, 1883).

James of Vitry, 'Historia Orientalis', in J. Bongars, ed., *Gesta Dei per Francos*, 2 vols. in 3 (Hanover, 1611) 1, 2 pp. 1047–1124.

— (attrib.) 'Historia Damiatina', in *Gesta Dei per Francos* 1, 2 pp. 1125–1145.

— *Lettres*, ed. R. B. C. Huygens (Leiden, 1960).

— 'Sermones vulgares', in J. B. Pitra, ed., *Analecta novissima spicilegii Solesmensis: altera continuatio 2, Tusculana* (Paris, 1888).

Jaufré Rudel, *Chansons*, ed. A. Jeanroy, CFMA 15 (Paris, 1924).

Jean Renart, *L'Escoufle, roman d'aventure*, ed. F. Sweetser, TLF 211 (Geneva, 1974).

— *Le roman de la rose, ou Guillaume de Dole*, ed. F. Lecoy, CFMA 91 (Paris, 1962).

Jerusalem pilgrimage, 1099–1185, ed. J. Wilkinson, J. Hill and W. F. Ryan, Hakluyt Society, 2nd series, 167 (London, 1988).

Johannes de Tulbia, 'de domino Johanne Rege Ierusalem', in *Quinti belli sacri scriptores.*

John of Columna, 'Mare historiarum', extr. *RHGF* 23.

John of Fordun, *Chronica gentis Scotorum*, ed. W. F. Skerne, The Historians of Scotland, 1 (Edinburgh, Edmonton and Douglas, 1871).

John of Joinville: *La vie de Saint Louis: le témoignage de Jehan, seigneur de Joinville. Texte du XIVe siècle*, ed. N. L. Corbett (Quebec, 1977).

John Peckham, archbishop of Canterbury, *Registrum epistolarum*, ed. C. T. Martin, 3 vols., RS 77 (London, 1882–5).

— *Tractatus tres de paupertate*, ed. C. L. Kingsford, A. G. Little, and F. Tocco (Aberdeen, 1910).

John of Pontoise: *Registrum Johannis de Pontissara, episcopi Wyntoniensis AD MCCLXXXII–MCCCXIV*, ed. C. Deedes, 2 vols., Canterbury and York Society 19, 30 (London, 1915–24).

John le Romeyn: *The register of John Le Romeyn, lord archbishop of York, 1286–1296*, ed. W. Brown, 2 vols, Surtees Society 123, 128 (Durham, London and Berlin, 1913–16).

John of Salisbury, *Policraticus*, ed. C. C. J. Webb, 2 vols. (Oxford, 1909).

— *Historia pontificalis*, ed. M. Chibnall (London and Edinburgh, 1956).

— *Letters*, ed. W. J. Miller, *et al.*, 2 vols. (London, 1955 and Oxford, 1979).

John Thilrode, 'Chronicon', ed. J. Heller, *MGHS* 25.

John of Würzburg, 'Descriptio Terrae Sanctae', in *PL* 155.

Die Königsaaler Geschichts-Quellen, mit den zusätzen und der Fortsetzung des Domherrn Franz von Prag, ed. J. Loserth, Fontes rerum Austricarum 1, 8 (Vienna, 1875).

Lambert Waterlos, 'Annales Cameracenses', ed. G. H. Pertz, *MGHS* 16.

Lancelot, roman en prose du XIIIe siècle, ed. A. Micha, 9 vols., TLF 247 etc. (Geneva, 1978–83).

Layettes du trésor des chartes, ed. A. Teulet *et al.*, 5 vols. (Paris, 1863–1909).

The legend of Duke Ernst, trans. J. W. Thomas and C. Dussère (Lincoln (Neb.) and London, 1979).

'Lettre des Chrétiens de Terre-Sainte à Charles d'Anjou, (22 avril 1260)', ed.

H. F. Delaborde, *ROL* 2 (1894) 206—215.

'Lettres inédits concernant les croisades (1275—1307)', ed. Ch. Kohler and Ch. V. Langlois, *BEC* 52 (1891) 46—63.

Lettres de rois, reines et autres personnages des cours de France et d'Angleterre depuis Louis VII jusqu'à Henri IV, ed. Champollion—Figeac, 1 (Paris, 1839).

Libellus de expugnatione Terrae Sanctae per Saladinum, in Ralph of Coggeshall, *Chronicon Anglicanum*.

'Liber duelli Christiani in obsidione Damiate exacti', in *Quinti belli sacri scriptores* and ed. O. Holder-Egger, *MGHS* 31.

Livländische Reimchronik, ed. F. Pfeiffer, BLVS 7B (Stuttgart, 1844).

Le Livre des Juges. Les cinq textes de la version française faite au XII siècle pour les chevaliers du Temple, ed. le Marquis d'Albon, Société des bibliophiles Lyonnais (Lyons, 1913).

The Mabinogion, trans. J. Gantz (Harmondsworth, 1976).

Manessier, *The third continuation*, in *Continuations of the Old French Perceval*, 5.

Marcabru, *Poésies complètes*, ed. J. M. L. Dejeanne (Toulouse, 1909, reprinted New York and London, 1971).

Der Marner, ed. P. Strauch (Strasbourg, 1876, reprinted Berlin, 1965).

Martin IV, *Registres*, ed. F. Oliver-Martin, BEFAR (Paris, 1913—1935).

Materials for the history of Thomas Becket, ed. J. C. Robertson, 7 vols., RS 51 (London, 1875—85).

Matthew Paris, *Chronica majora*, ed. H. R. Luard, 7 vols., RS 57 (London, 1872—83).

— *Flores historiarum*, ed. H. R. Luard, 3 vols., RS 95 (London, 1890).

— *Historia Anglorum, sive . . . Historia minor, item . . . Abbreviatio chronicorum Angliae*, ed. F. Madden, 3 vols., RS 44 (London, 1866—9).

Menko, 'Chronicon', ed. L. Weiland, *MGHS* 23.

Michael the Syrian: *Le chronique de Michel le Syrien, patriarche Jacobite d'Antioche, 1166-1199*, ed. J. B. Chabot, 4 vols. (Paris, 1899—1910).

— Armenian translation in *RHC DocArm* 1.

Monasticon Anglicanum: a history of the abbies and other monasteries, hospitals, friaries, and cathedral and collegiate churches, with their dependencies, in England and Wales . . . ed. W. Dugdale, new edn ed. J. Caley, H. Ellis and B. Bandinel, 6 vols. in 8 (London, 1817—30).

Le moniage Guillaume: Les deux rédactions en vers du moniage Guillaume, chansons de geste du XIIe siècle, ed. W. Cloetta, 2 vols. SATF (Paris, 1906—11).

Le moniage Rainouart 1: publié d'après les manuscrits de L'Arsenal et de Boulogne, ed. G. A. Bertin, SATF (Paris, 1973).

Monumenta Corbeiensia, ed. P. Jaffé, Bibliotheca rerum Germanicarum, 1 (Berlin, 1864).

Monumenta Germaniae Historica, ed. G. H. Pertz et al. (Hanover, Weimar, Stuttgart and Cologne, 1826ff.)

MGH Constitutiones et acta publica imperatorum et regum, ed. L. Weiland, 3 vols. (Hanover, 1893), in *MGH Legum sectio IV (Leges 2. Quarto)*.

MGH Epistolae saeculi XIII e regestis pontificum Romanorum selecti, ed. G. H. Pertz and K. Rodenburg, 3 vols. (Berlin, 1883—94).

MGH Legum, series in folio, ed. G. H. Pertz, vol. 2 (Hanover, 1887).

MGH Scriptores, ed. G. H. Pertz et al., 32 vols. (Hanover, 1826—1934).

Monumenta ordinis Fratrum Praedicatorum historica, 3: acta capitulorum generalium, ed. B. M. Reichert, 1 (Rome and Stuttgart, 1898).

Monuments historiques, ed. J. Tardif (Paris, 1866).

La mort le roi Artu, roman du XIIIe siècle, ed. J. Frappier, TLF 58 (Geneva, 1964).

Niccolò da Calvi, 'La vita d'Innocenzo IV', ed. F. Pagnotti, *Archivio della R. società Romana di storia patria* 21 (1898) 7—120.

Nicholas III, *Registres*, ed. J. Gay, BEFAR (Paris, 1938).

Nicholas IV, *Registres*, ed. E. Langlois, 1 vol. in 2, BEFAR (Paris, 1905).

Nigel of Longchamps, *Speculum stultorum*, ed. J. H. Mozley and R. R. Raymo (Berkeley and Los Angeles, 1960).

'Notice sur le manuscrit Fr 24862 de la Bibliothèque Nationale contenant divers ouvrages composés ou écrits en Angleterre', ed. P. Meyer, *Notices et extraits des manuscrits de la Bibliothèque Nationale et autres Bibliothèques publiés par l'Académie des inscriptions et de belles-lettres*, 35 (1896) 131—168.

'Un Nouveau manuscrit de la Règle du Temple', ed. J. Delaville le Roulx, *Annuaire-bulletin de la société de l'histoire de France* 26 pt. 2 (1889) 185—214.

Nouveau recueil complet des fabliaux, ed. W. Noomen and N. von den Boorgaard, 1ff. (Assen/Maastricht, 1983ff.).

'Nouveaux monuments des croisiés recueillés en Terre Sainte', ed. Clermont-Ganneau, *AOL* 2, C, 457—64.

Odo de Deuil, *De profectione Ludovici VII in orientem*, ed. V. G. Berry (New York, 1948).

Odo, bishop of Tusculanum, letter to Innocent IV, in *Spicilegium* 3.

The Old French crusade cycle, vol.V: Les chétifs, ed. G. M. Myers (Alabama, 1981).

— vol. VII: the Jérusalem continuations, Part 1: La chrétienté Corbaran, ed. P. W. Grillo (Alabama, 1984).

Les Olim ou registres des arrêts rendus par la cour du Roi, ed. le comte Beugnot, 4 vols. (Paris, 1839—48).

Oliver *Scholasticus*, 'Historia regum Terrae Sanctae', and 'Historia Damiatina', in *Die Schriften des Kölner Domscholasters, Späteren Bischofs von Paderborn und Kardinalbischofs von S. Sabina, Oliverus*, ed. H. Hoogeweg, BLVS 202 (Tübingen, 1894).

Oliver Sutton, *The rolls and register of Bishop Oliver Sutton, 1280–1299*, ed. R. T. Hill, 8 vols., Lincoln Record Society 39, 43, 48 etc. (1948—86).

Oliver le Templer, 'Estat aurai lonc temps en pessamen', in Raynouard, *Choix de poésies*, 5.

Orderic Vitalis, *The ecclesiastical history*, ed. M. Chibnall, 6 vols. (Oxford, 1969—80).

Orendal, ed. H. Steinger, Altdeutsches Textbibliothek 36 (Halle, 1935).

Orneit und Wolfdietrich nach der Wiener Piaristenhandschrift, ed. J. Lunzer, BLVS 239 (Tübingen, 1906).

Orson de Beauvais, chanson de geste du XIIe siècle, ed. G. Paris, SATF (Paris, 1899).

Ortnit und die Wolfdietriche nach Müllenhofs vorarbeiten, ed. A. Amelung and O. Jänicke, Deutsches Heldenbuch 3—4 (reprinted Dublin/Zurich, 1968).

Osney Annals, in *Annales monastici*, 4.

Otto, bishop of Freising, 'Chronicon', ed. R. Wilmans, *MGHS* 20.

Otto of St Blasien, 'Continuatio Sanblasiana', ed. R. Wilmans, *MGHS* 20.

Papsturkunden für Templer und Johanniter, ed. R. Hiestand, Abhandlungen der

Akademie der Wissenschaften in Göttingen, Phil.-hist. Klasse, dritte Folge no. 77 (Göttingen, 1972).

Patrologiae cursus completus, series Latina, ed. J. P. Migne, 217 vols., and 4 vols. of indexes (Paris, 1834—64).

Peire Cardenal, 'Mon chanter vueil retraire', in Poésies complètes, ed. R. Lavaud (Toulouse, 1957).

Peirol, troubadour of Auvergne, ed. S. C. Aston (Cambridge, 1953).

Peregrinatores medii aevi quatuor, ed. J. C. M. Laurent, 2nd edn (Leipzig, 1873).

Perlesvaus: le haut livre du Graal, ed. W. A. Nitze and J. Atkinson Jenkins, 2 vols. (reprinted New York, 1972).

Peter von Dusberg, Chronik des Preussenlandes, ed. K. Scholz and D. Wojtecki, Ausgewählte Quellen zur Deutschen Geschichte des Mittelalters, Freiherr von Stein-Gedächtnisausgabe, Band 25 (Darmstadt, 1984).

Peter of Vaux-de-Cernay, 'Historia Albigensium', RHGF 19.

Peter the Venerable, Letters, ed. G. Constable, 2 vols. (Cambridge, Mass., 1967).

Philip Mousket, 'Historia regum Francorum', extr. ed. A. Tobler, MGHS 26, and as 'chronique rimée', extr. in RHGF 22.

Philip de Nanteuil, 'En chantant veil mon duel faire', in J. Bédier and P. Aubry, eds., Les chansons de croisade (Paris, 1909, reprinted Geneva, 1974).

Philip of Novara, 'Memoirs', in Les gestes des Chyprois.

Philippus, 'Descriptio Terrae Sanctae', in W. A. Neumann, ed., 'Drei mittelalterliche Pilgerschriften III', Oesterreichische Vierteljahresschrift für katholische Theologie 11 (1872) 1—78.

Placita de Quo Warranto temporibus Edw. I, II & III in curia receptae Scaccarii Westm. asservata (London, 1818).

Les plus anciennes chartes en langue Provençale: recueil des pièces originales antérieures du XIIIe siècle, ed. C. Brunel, 2 vols. (Paris, 1926—52).

'Un poème contemporain sur Saladin', ed. G. Paris, ROL 1 (1893) 433—444.

'Poème sur Antéchrist', in 'Notice du manuscrit French 6' de la John Rylands Library, Manchester', ed. R. Fawtier and E. C. Fawtier-Jones, Romania 49 (1923) IX, 331—340.

Pommerellisches Urkundenbuch, ed. M. Perlbach (Danzig, 1881—1916).

Pommersches Urkundenbuch, ed. K. Conrad, R. Prümers, et al., 10 vols. (Stettin and Cologne, 1868—1984).

Le premier budget de la monarchie française, ed. F. Lot and R. Fawtier, Bibliothèque de l'école des Hautes-Etudes (Paris, 1932).

'Les premiers versions occidental de la légende de Saïdnaia', ed. P. Devos, Analecta Bollandiana 65 (1947) 245—278.

Preußisches Urkundenbuch, ed. A. Philipps et al., 6 vols. (Königsberg, Aalen and Marburg, 1882—1986).

Primat, 'Chronique', trans. Jean du Vignay, RHGF 23.

La queste del Saint Graal, roman du XIIIe siècle, ed. A. Pauphilet, CFMA 33 (Paris, 1980).

Quinti belli sacri scriptores minores, ed. R. Röhricht, SOL (Geneva, 1879).

Ralph of Coggeshall, Chronicon Anglicanum, ed. J. Stevenson, RS 66 (London, 1875).

Ralph of Diceto, Historical works, ed. W. Stubbs, 2 vols., RS 68 (London, 1876).

Ralph Niger, *De re militari et triplici via peregrinationis ierosolymitane*, ed. L. Schmugge (Berlin, 1977).

Ramon Lull, 'Blanquerna', in *Obras Literarias*, ed. M. Batllori and M. Caldentey (Madrid, 1948).

Ramon Muntaner, *Chronik des Edlen en Ramon Muntaner*, ed. K. Lanz, BLVS 8 (Stuttgart, 1844).

Raoul de Cambrai, chanson de geste, ed. P. Meyer and A. Longnon, SATF (Paris, 1882).

Raoul de Houdenc, *Meraugis de Portlesguez*, ed. M. Friedwagner (reprinted Geneva, 1975).

— *La songe d'Enfer*, ed. M. T. Mihm, Beiheft zur Zeitschrift für romanische Philologie, Band 190 (Tübingen, 1984).

'Rebus de Alsaticis ineuntis saeculis XIII', ed. P. Jaffé, *MGHS* 17.

The Receipt Roll of the Exchequer for Michaelmas Term xxxi Henry II, AD 1185, ed. H. Hall, Studies in Economics and Political Science 7 (London, 1899).

Récits d'un ménestrel de Reims au treizième siècle, ed. N. de Wailly, SHF (Paris, 1876).

Records of the Templars in England in the twelfth century; the inquest of 1185 with illustrative charters and documents, ed. B. A. Lees, Records of social and economic history of England and Wales, 9 (London, 1935).

Records of the Wardrobe and Household, 1285-89, ed. B. F. Byerly and C. R. Byerly, 2 vols. (London, 1977—86).

Recueil des actes de Henri II, roi d'Angleterre et Duc de Normandie, concernant les provinces françaises et les affaires de France, ed. L. Delisle and E. Berger, Introduction (Paris, 1906) and 3 vols. (Paris, 1916—27).

Recueil des actes de Philippe Auguste, roi de France, ed. H.-Fr. Delaborde, C. Petit-Dutaillis *et al.*, 4 vols. (Paris, 1916—79).

Recueil général des jeux-partis français, ed. A. Långfors, A. Jeanroy and L. Brandin, 2 vols. in 1, SATF (Paris, 1926).

Recueil des historiens des croisades, pub. Académie des Inscriptions et de Belles-Lettres, 16 vols. (Paris, 1841—1906).

Recueil des historiens des Gaules et de la France, ed. Bouquet *et al.*, new edition ed. L. Delisle, 24 vols. (Paris, 1878).

Regesta Imperii, ed. J. Böhmer, 5: *Die Regesten des Kaiserreichs unter Philipp, Otto IV, Friedrich II, Heinrich (VII), Conrad IV, Heinrich Raspe, Wilhelm und Richard, 1190–1271*, ed. J. F. Böhmer, J. Ficker *et al.*, 4 vols. (Innsbrück, Cologne and Vienna, 1881—1983).

— 6: *Die Regesten des Kaiserreichs unter Rudolf, Adolf, Albrecht, Heinrich VII, 1273–1313*, ed. J. F. Böhmer, O. Redlich and V. Samanek, 2 vols. (Innsbrück, 1898—1948).

Regesta pontificum Romanorum ab condita Ecclesia ad Annum post Christum natum MCXCVIII, ed. P. Jaffé, 2nd edn ed. G. Wattenbach *et al.*, 2 vols. (Leipzig, 1885—8).

Regesta regni Hierosolymitani, and *Additamentum*, ed. R. Röhricht (Innsbrück, 1893, 1904).

Regesta regum Anglo-Normannorum, 1066-1154, 3, (1135—1154) ed H. A. Cronne, R. H. C. Davis (Oxford, 1968).

Regesta regum Scottorum, 1153-1424, 1: *The acts of Malcolm IV, king of Scots 1153–1165*, ed. G. W. S. Barrow (Edinburgh, 1960).

— 2: *The acts of William I, king of Scots 1165–1214*, ed. G. W. S. Barrow and W. W. Scott (Edinburgh, 1971).

Reginald of Durham, *Libellus de vita et miraculis S. Godrici, heremitae de Finchale*, ed. J. Stevenson, Surtees Society 20 (London and Edinburgh, 1844).

I registri della cancelleria Angioina, ed. R. Filangieri, 1ff., (Naples, 1950ff.).

La règle du Temple, ed. H. de Curzon, SHF (Paris, 1886).

'Regni Iherosolymitani brevis historia,' in *Annali Genovesi* 1.

Reinfrid von Braunschweig, ed. K. Bartsch, BLVS 109 (Tübingen, 1871).

Renaus de Montauban oder die Haimonskinder, Altfranzösisches Gedicht, ed. H. Michelant, BLVS 67 (Stuttgart, 1862).

Renaut de Montauban. Edition critique du manuscrit Douce, ed. J. Thomas, TLF 371 (Geneva and Paris, 1989).

Rerum Italicarum scriptores: raccolta degli storici Italiani dal cinquecento ad millecinquecento, ed. L. Muratori, new edition ed. G. Carducci, V. Fiorini, P. Fedele (Citta di Castello, Bologna, 1900ff.).

'Ribston and the Knights Templars,' ed. R. V. Taylor, *Yorkshire archaeological and topographical journal*, 7 (1882) 429–52, 8 (1884) 259–99, 9 (1886) 71–98.

Ricaut Bonomel, 'Ir'e dolors s'es dins mon cor asseza', ed. A. de Bastard, 'La colère et la douleur d'un templier en Terre Sainte', *Revue des langues romanes*, 81 (1974) 333–373.

Riccardus de S. Germano, 'Chronico', ed. G. H. Pertz, *MGHS* 19; also in *Rerum Italicarum scriptores*, ed. L. A. Muratori, 25 vols. (Milan, 1723–51) 7.

Richard Gravesend: *Rotuli Ricardi Gravesend diocesis Lincolniensis*, ed. F. N. Davis, *et al.*, Canterbury and York Society 31 (Oxford, 1925).

Richard of Poitou, 'Chronica', extr. ed. G. Waitz, *MGHS* 26.

Ricoldo de Monte Cruce, 'Lettres', ed. R. Röhricht, *AOL* 2, Documents, 258–96.

Robert the canon of St Marianus of Auxerre, 'Chronicon', ed. O. Holder-Egger, *MGHS* 26.

Robert Grosseteste: *Rotuli Roberti Grosseteste, episcopi Lincolniensis*, ed. F. N. Davis, Canterbury and York Society, 10 (London, 1913).

Robert of Torigny, *Chronicle*, in *Chronicles of the reigns of Stephen, Henry II and Richard I*, 4.

Roger Bacon, *Opus maius*, ed. J. H. Bridges, 3 vols. (Oxford, 1877–1900, reprinted Frankfurt, 1964).

Roger of Howden, *Gesta regis Henrici Secundi: The chronicle of the reigns of Henry II and Richard I*, ed. W. Stubbs, 2 vols., RS 49 (London, 1867).

— *Chronica*, ed. W. Stubbs, 4 vols., RS 51 (London, 1868–71).

Roger of Wendover, *Flores historiarum*, ed. H. R. Hewlett, 3 vols., RS 84 (London, 1886–9).

Roll of divers accounts for the early years of the reign of Henry III . . . ed. F. A. Cazel, Publications of the Pipe roll society 82 (new series, 44) (London, 1982).

Le roman de Laurin, fils de Marques le sénéchal, ed. L. Thorpe, 2 vols. (Cambridge, 1950–8).

Le roman de Tristan en prose, ed. R. Curtis, 3 vols. (Cambridge, 1985).

Le roman de Tristan en prose, ed. P. Ménard *et al.*, 1 ff., TLF 353, 387, etc., (Geneva, 1987ff.).

Li romans de Claris et Laris, ed. J. Alton, BLVS 169 (Tübingen, 1884; reprinted Amsterdam, 1966).

Li romanz du reis Yder, ed. A. Adams (Cambridge, 1982).

Rostanh Berenguier, 'Pos de sa mar man cavalier del Temple', in P. Meyer, 'Les derniers troubadours'.

'Rothelin,' in *RHC Occ* 2.

Rotuli chartarum in Turri Londonensi asservati, ed. T. D. Hardy, 1 vol, (1199—1216) (London, 1837).

Rotuli hundredonum temp. Hen. III & Edw. I in turri Lond. et curia receptae Scaccarii Westm. asservati, 2 vols. (London, 1812—8).

Rotuli litterarum clausarum in Turri Londonensi asservati, ed. T. D. Hardy, 2 vols. (London, 1833—44).

Rotuli litterarum patentium in Turri Londonensi asservati, ed. T. D. Hardy (London, 1835).

Rotuli parliamentorum: ut et petitiones et placita in parliamento, 6 vols. (Record Commission, London 1767—77) 1 (*tempore Edwardi R.I*).

Royal and other historical letters illustrative of the reign of Henry III, from the originals in the Public Record Office, ed. W. W. Shirley, 2 vols., RS 27 (London, 1862—66).

'The rule of the Templars and a courtly ballade', ed. J. Oliver, *Scriptorium* 35 (1981) 303—6.

Rutebuef, *Oeuvres complètes*, ed. E. Faral and J. Bastin, 2 vols. (Paris, 1959—60).

Sacrorum conciliorum nova et amplissima collectio, ed. J. D. Mansi, *et al.*, 55 vols. (Florence, Venice, Paris, Arnhem, Leipzig, 1759—1962).

Salimbene de Adam, *Cronica*, ed. G. Scalia, 2 vols. (Bari, 1966) and ed. O. Holder-Egger, *MGHS* 32.

The Sandford cartulary, ed. A. M. Leys, 2 vols., Oxfordshire record society nos. 19, 22 (Oxford, 1938, 1941).

Schlesiches Urkundenbuch, ed. H. Appelt *et al.*, vol. 1ff. (Graz, Vienna and Cologne, 1963ff).

A Scottish chronicle known as the chronicle of Holyrood, ed. M. O. and A. O. Anderson, Publications of the Scottish history society, 3rd series 30 (Edinburgh, 1938).

Simon of St Bertin, 'Gesta abbatum Sancti Bertini Sithensium', ed. O. Holder-Egger, *MGHS* 13.

Sone von Nausay, ed. M. Goldschmidt, BLVS 216 (Tübingen, 1899).

Spicilegium sive collectio veterum aliquot scriptorum qui in Galliae bibliothecis delituerant, ed. L. d'Achery, new edn ed. L. F. T. de la Bavre, 3 (Paris, 1723).

Die Statuten des Deutschen Ordens nach den Ältesten Handschriften, ed. M. Perlbach (Halle, 1890).

Stephen of Bourbon: *Anecdotes historiques, légendes et apologues tirés du recueil inédit d'Etienne de Bourbon, Dominicain du XIIIe siècle*, ed. A. Lecoy de la Marche, SHF (Paris, 1877).

Suger, Abbot of St Denis: 'Epistolae', *PL* 186.

Tabulae ordinis Theutonici ex tabularii regii Berolinensis codice potissimum, ed. E. Strehlke, new edition with preface by H. E. Mayer (Jerusalem, 1975).

Tewkesbury Annals, in *Annales monastici* 1.

Thadeo of Naples, *Historia de desolacione et conculcacione civitatis Acconensis et tocius terre sancte, in AD MCCXCI*, ed. P. Riant (Geneva, 1873).

'Thais', ed. P. Meyer in 'Notice sur le manuscrit Fr 24862' 147—151.

Theodoric, *Libellus de locis sanctis*, ed. M. L. and W. Bulst (Heidelberg, 1976).

Thomas Aquinas, *Summa theologica*, Blackfriars edition, 60 vols. (London, 1964–76).

Thomas of Spalato, 'Historia pontificum Salonitanorum et Spalatinorum', ed. L. von Heinemann, *MGHS* 29.

Thomas Tuscus, 'Gesta imperatorum et pontificum', ed. E. Ehrenfeuchter, *MGHS* 22.

Thomas Wykes, *Annales*, in *Annales monastici*, 4.

'A twelfth century Oxford disputation concerning the privileges of the Knights Hospitallers', ed. J. A. Brundage, *Medieval Studies* 24 (1962) 153–160.

Ulger, bishop of Anjou, 'Epistolae', *PL* 180.

Ulrich von Etzenbach, *Wilhelm von Wenden*, ed. H.-F. Rosenfeld, Deutsche Texte des Mittelalters 49 (Berlin, 1957).

Urban IV, *Registres*, ed. J. Guiraud, *et al.*, 5 vols., BEFAR (Paris, 1899–1958).

Urkundenbuch der Deutschordensballei Hessen, ed. A. Wyss, 3 vols., Publicationen aus den K. Preußischen Staatsarchiven, nos. 3, 19, 73: Hessisches Urkundenbuch 1 (1879–1899, reprinted Osnabrück, 1965) 1.

Urkundenbuch der Deutschordensballei Thüringen, ed. K. H. Lampe, vol. 1, Thüringische Geschichtsquellen, neue Folge 7 (Jena, 1936).

Urkundenbuch für die Geschichte Niederrheins, ed. T. J. Lacomblet, 4 vols. (reprinted Aalen, 1840–56).

Urkundenbuch des Hochstifts Halberstadt und seiner Bischöfe, ed. G. Schmidt, vol. 2, Publicationen aus den K. Preußischen Staatsarchiven, 21 (Leipzig, 1884).

Urkundenbuch der Stadt Friedburg 1 (1216–1410) ed. M. Foltz (Marburg, 1904).

Usamah ibn-Munqidh, *Memoirs*, in *Memoirs of an Arab-Syrian Gentleman, or, an Arab knight in the crusades: the memoirs of Usamah ibn-Munqidh*, trans. P. K. Hitti (Beirut, 1964).

'Vitas Patrum', extr. ed. P. Meyer, 'Notice sur le manuscrit Fr. 24862'.

Le Voyage de Charlemagne à Jérusalem et à Constantinople, ed. P. Aebisher, TLF 115 (Geneva, 1965).

Walter Giffard: *The register of Walter Giffard, lord archbishop of York 1266–1279*, ed. W. Brown, Surtees society 109 (Durham, London and Edinburgh, 1904).

Walter Gray, *The register, or rolls, of Walter Gray, lord archbishop of York*, ed. J. Raine, Surtees Society 56 (Durham, London and Edinburgh, 1872).

Walter of Guisborough, *Chronicle*, ed. H. Rothwell, Camden Society 3rd series, 89 (London, 1957).

Walter Map, *De nugis curialium*, ed. M. R. James, C. N. L. Brooke and R. A. B. Mynors (Oxford, 1983).

Waverley Annals, in *Annales monastici* 2.

'Wenceslai I regis historia', ed. D. R. Köpke, *MGHS* 9.

William of Andres, 'Chronica', ed. J. Heller, *MGHS* 24, and interpolating the 'Historia regum Francorum' of Andrew of Marchian, ed. G. Waitz, *MGHS* 26.

William the Breton, 'Gesta Philippi Augusti', in *Oeuvres de Rigord et de Guillaume le Breton, historiens de Philippe Auguste*, ed. H. F. Delaborde, 2 vols. (Paris, 1882–5).

William de Nangis, 'Gesta Ludovici IX', in *RHGF* 20.

— 'Gesta Philippi tertii Francorum regis', in *RHGF* 20.

— 'Chronicon', in *RHGF* 20.

William of Newburgh, *Historia rerum Anglicarum*, in *Chronicles of the Reigns of Stephen, Henry II and Richard I*, 1—2.

William of Puylaurens, 'Historia Albigensium', *RHGF* 19.

William Rishanger, *Chronica et annales*, ed. H. T. Riley, RS 28, 2 (London, 1865).

William of Rubruck: *The Journey of William of Rubruck to the eastern parts of the world, as narrated by himself*, trans. and ed. W. W. Rockhill, Hakluyt Society, 2nd series 4 (London, 1900, reprinted Nendeln, 1967).

William of San Stefano, 'Comment la sainte maison de l'Hospital de S. Johan de Jerusalem commenca', in *RHC Occ* 5.

William fitz Stephen, 'Vita Sancti Thomae', in *Materials for the History of Thomas Becket*, 3.

William, Archbishop of Tyre, *Chronicon*, ed. R. B. C. Huygens, 2 vols., Corpus Christianorum — continuatio medievalis 63 (Turnholt, 1986).

— translated as, *A history of deeds done beyond the sea*, ed. E. A. Babcock and A. C. Kray, 2 vols. (reprinted New York, 1976).

William Wickwane, *The register of William Wickwane, lord archbishop of York 1279–1285*, ed. W. Brown, Surtees Society 114 (Durham, London and Berlin, 1907).

Winchester Annals, in *Annales monastici*, 2.

Wolfram von Eschenbach, *Parzival*, ed. K. Lachmann and W. Spiewok, 2 vols. (Stuttgart, 1981).

— trans. A. T. Hatto (Harmondsworth, 1980).

— *Titurel*, in *Wolframs von Eschenbach Parzival und Titurel*, ed. E. Martin, part 1 (Halle, 1920).

'Ein zeitgenössisches Gedicht auf die Belagerung Accons', ed. H. Prutz, *Forschungen zur Deutschen Geschichte*, 21 (1881) 449—494.

Secondary sources

Acta Sanctorum, ed. J. Bollandus *et al.*, (Antwerp, 1643ff., reprinted Brussels, 1966).

H. d'Arbois de Jubainville, 'L'ordre Teutonique en France', *BEC* 32 (1871) 63—83.

— 'Catalogue d'actes des comtes de Brienne, 950—1356', *BEC* 33 (1872) 141—186.

B. Arnold, *German Knighthood 1050-1300* (Oxford, 1985).

U. Arnold, 'Enstehung und Frühzeit des Deutschen Ordens, zu Gründung und innerer Struktur des Deutschen Hospitals von Akkon und des Ritterordens in der ersten Hälfte des 13 Jahrhunderts', in Fleckenstein and Hellmann, eds., *Geistlichen Ritterorden*, pp. 81—107.

M. Barber, 'The origins of the order of the Temple', *Studia Monastica*, 12 (1970) 219—240.

— 'Propaganda in the middle ages: the charges against the Templars', *Nottingham Medieval Studies*, 17 (1973) 42—57.

— *The trial of the Templars* (Cambridge, 1978).

— 'The social context of the Templars', *TRHS* 34 (1984) 27—46.

Barrow, 'The aftermath of war: Scotland and England in the late thirteenth and early fourteenth centuries', *TRHS* 28 (1978) 103—125.

E. Baumgartner, 'Les techniques narratives dans le roman en prose', in N. J. Lacy, D. Kelly and K. Busby, eds., *The Legacy of Chrétien de Troyes*, 2 vols. (Amsterdam, 1987) 1 pp. 167—190.

J. M. A. Beer, *Narrative conventions of truth in the Middle Ages* (Geneva, 1981).

K. H. Bender, ed., *Les Epopées de la Croisade: premier colloque international*, Zeitschrift für französische Sprache und Literatur. Beiheft 11 (Stuttgart, 1987).

P. Bertrand de la Grassière, *L'ordre militaire et hospitalier de Saint-Lazare de Jérusalem* (Paris, 1960).

Biblotheca Sanctorum, Istituto Giovanni XXIII nella pontificia Università Lateranense, 12 vols. (Rome, 1961—70).

B. Bolton, 'A mission to the Orthodox? The Cistercians in Romania', in D. Baker, ed., *Studies in Church History, 13: The Orthodox Churches and the West* (Oxford, 1976) pp. 169—181.

— 'Via Ascetica: a papal quandary', in W. J. Sheils, ed., *Studies in Church History 22: Monks, Hermits and the ascetic tradition* (Oxford, 1985) pp. 161—191.

G. Bonath, 'Reflets des croisades dans la littérature allemand', in K. H. Bender, ed., *Les Épopées de la croisade*, pp. 105—118.

H. Boockmann, *Der Deutsche Orden: Zwölf Kapitel aus seiner Geschichte* (Munich, 1982).

H. de Boor, ed., *Geschichte der Deutschen Literatur 1: Der Deutsche Literatur von Karl dem Grossen bis zum Beginn der Höfischen Dichtung, 770–1170* (Munich, 1949).

I. Bosio, *Dell'Istoria della sacra religione et illustrissima militia di S. Giovanni Gierosol^no*, 3 parts, new ed. (Rome, 1621—1684).

C. B. Bouchard, *Sword, Miter and Cloister: nobility and the Church in Burgundy, 980–1198* (Ithaca and London, 1987).

A. Boutémy, *Nigellus de Longchamp dit Wireker* (Paris, 1959).

P. A. Brand, 'Control of Mortmain alienation in England, 1200—1300', in J. H. Baker, ed., *Legal Records and the Historian*, (London, 1978) pp. 29—40.

M. L. Bulst-Thiele, 'Templer in Königlichen und Päpstlichen Diensten', in P. Classen and P. Scheibert, eds., *Festschrift Percy Ernst Schramm*, 2 vols. (Wiesbaden, 1964) pp. 289—308.

— Review of H. Mayer, ed., 'Das Itinerarium Peregrinorum', *Historische Zeitschrift* 198 (1964) 380—387.

— 'Noch einmal das Itinerarium Peregrinorum', *Deutsches Archiv für Erforschung des Mittelalters* 21 (1965) 593—606.

— 'Zur Geschichte der Ritterorden und des Königreichs Jerusalem im 13 Jahrhundert bis zur Schlacht bei la Forbie am 17 Okt 1244', *Deutsches Archiv für Erforschung des Mittelalters* 22 (1966) 197—226.

— *Sacrae domus militiae Templi Hierosolymitani magistri: Untersuchungen zur Geschichte des Templerordens 1118/9–1314.* Abhandlungen der Akademie der Wissenschaften in Göttingen. Philologisch-Historische Klasse, Dritte Folge, nr. 86 (Göttingen, 1974).

— 'Der Prozeß gegen der Templerorden', in Fleckenstein and Hellmann, eds., *Geistlichen Ritterorden*, pp. 375—402.

R. I. Burns, *The crusader kingdom of Valencia: reconstruction on a thirteenth-century frontier*, 2 vols. (Cambridge, Mass., 1967).

Butler's Lives of the Saints, edited, revised and supplemented by H. Thurston and D. Attwater, 4 vols. (London, 1956).

F. L. Carsten, *The origins of Prussia* (Oxford, 1954).

Catalogue of romances in the department of manuscripts, British Museum, ed. H. L. D. Ward, 2 vols. (London, 1883—93).

E. Christiansen, *The northern crusades: the Baltic and the Catholic frontier 1100–1525* (London, 1980).

C. T. Clay, 'The family of Amundeville', *Reports and papers of the Lincolnshire architectural and archaeological society*, 3 (1945) 109—136.

G. Constable, 'The second crusade as seen by contemporaries', *Traditio* 9 (1953) 213—279.

D. Corner, 'The *Gesta Regis Henrici Secundi* and *Chronica* of Roger, parson of Howden', *Bulletin of the Institute of Historical Research* 56 (1983) 126—144.

I. B. Cowan, P. H. R. Mackay, A. Macquarrie, eds., *The knights of St John of Jerusalem in Scotland*, Scottish history society, 4th series, 19 (Edinburgh, 1983).

H. E. J. Cowdrey, 'The eleventh century peace and truce of God', *Past and Present* 46 (1970) 42—67.

L. Dailliez, *Bibliographie du Temple* (Paris, 1972).

R. H. C. Davis, 'William of Tyre', in D. Baker, ed., *Relations between east and west in the middle ages* (Edinburgh, 1987) pp. 64—76.

E. Delaruelle, 'Templiers et Hospitaliers en Languedoc pendant la croisade contre les Albigeois', *Cahiers de Fanjeaux, 4: paix de Dieu et guerre sainte en Languedoc au XIIIe siècle* (1969) 315—334.

H. Delehaye, 'Saints de Chypre', *Analecta Bollandiana* 26 (1907) 161—301.

L. Delisle, 'Mémoire sur les opérations financières des Templiers', *Mémoires de l'Institut National de France, Académie des Inscriptions et Belles-Lettres*, 33, 2 (1889).

A. Demurger, *Vie et mort de l'ordre du Temple, 1118–1314* (Paris, 1985).

M. A. Du Bourg, *Ordre de Malte: histoire du grand prieuré de Toulouse* (Toulouse, 1883).

G. Duby, *The chivalrous society*, trans. C. Postan (London, 1977).

— *The three orders: feudal society imagined*, trans. A. Goldhammer (Chicago, 1980).

S. Duparc-Quioc, *La chanson d'Antioche – étude critique* (Paris, 1978).

M. Dygo, 'The political role of the cult of the virgin Mary in Teutonic Prussia in the fourteenth and fifteenth centuries', *Journal of medieval history* 15 (1989) 63—80.

P. W. Edbury and J. G. Rowe, *William of Tyre: historian of the Latin east* (Cambridge, 1988).

K. Eistert, 'Der Ritterorden der Tempelherren in Schlesien', *Archiv für Schlesische Kirchengeschichte*, 14 (1956) 1—23.

C. Eubel, *Hierarchia Catholica medii aevi, sive summorum pontificum SRE cardinalium ecclesiarum antistitum series. Ab anno 1198 usque ad annum 1431 perducta* (Munster, 1898, second edition 1913).

M. L. Favreau-Lilie, 'The Teutonic knights in Acre after the fall of Montfort (1271): some reflections', in Kedar *et al.*, eds., *Outremer*, pp. 272—284.

M. Fischer, 'Criticism of Church and crusade in Ottokar's Österreichische Reimchronik', *Forum for modern language studies*, 22 (1986) 157—171.

J. Fleckenstein, ed., *Probleme um Friedrich II*, Vorträge und Forschungen, 16 (Sigmaringen, 1974).

J. Fleckenstein and M. Hellmann, eds., *Die Geistlichen Ritterorden Europas*, Vorträge und Forschungen, 26 (Sigmaringen, 1980).

J. Flori, 'La notion de chevalerie dans les chansons de geste du XIIe siècle. Étude historique de vocabulaire', *Le moyen âge*, 81 (1975) 211—44, 407—45.

— 'Chevalerie et liturgie. Remise des armes et vocabulaire «chevaleresque» dans les sources liturgiques du IXe au XIVe siècles', *Le moyen âge* 84 (1978) 247—278, 409—442.

— 'Pour une histoire de la chevalerie: l'adoubement dans les romans de Chrétien de Troyes', *Romania* 100 (1979) 21—53.

— 'La chevalerie selon Jean de Salisbury (nature, fonction, idéologie)', *Revue de l'histoire ecclésiastique* 77 (1982) 35—77.

— *Idéologie du glaive: préhistoire de la chevalerie* (Geneva, 1983).

— *L'Essor de la chevalerie, XIe-XIIe siècles* (Geneva, 1986).

J. Folda, *Crusader manuscript illumination at Saint-Jean d'Acre, 1275-91* (Princeton, 1976).

A. J. Forey, 'The order of Mountjoy', *Speculum* 46 (1971) 250—66.

— 'The crusading vows of Henry III', *Durham University journal* 65 (1972—3) 229—247.

— *The Templars in the 'Corona de Aragon'* (London, 1973).

— 'The military order of St Thomas of Acre', *English historical review*, 92 (1977) 481—503.

— 'The military orders in the crusading proposals of the late thirteenth and early fourteenth centuries', *Traditio* 36 (1980) 317—345.

— 'Constitutional conflict and change in the Hospital of St John during the twelfth and thirteenth centuries', *Journal of ecclesiastical history* 33 (1982) 15—29.

— 'The failure of the siege of Damascus in 1148', *Journal of medieval history*, 10 (1984) 13—23.

— 'The militarisation of the Hospital of St John', *Studia monastica*, 26 (1984) 75—89.

— 'The military orders and the Spanish reconquest in the twelfth and thirteenth centuries', *Traditio* 40 (1984) 197—234.

— 'The emergence of the military order in the twelfth century', *Journal of ecclesiastical history*, 36 (1985) 175—195.

— 'Recruitment to the military orders (twelfth to mid-fourteenth centuries)', *Viator* 17 (1986) 139—171.

— 'Novitiate and instruction in the military orders during the twelfth and thirteenth centuries', *Speculum* 61 (1986) 1—17.

— 'Women and the military orders in the twelfth and thirteenth centuries', *Studia monastica* 29 (1987) 63—92.

— 'A thirteenth century dispute between Templars and Hospitallers in Aragon', *Durham University journal* 80 (1988) 181—192.

— 'The military orders and holy war against Christians in the thirteenth century', *English historical review*, 104 (1989) 1—24.

J. Frappier, 'Le Graal et la chevalerie', *Romania* 75 (1954) 165—210.

R. Frydrychowicz, 'Der Ritterorden von Calatrava in Tymau bei Mewe', *Altpreussische Monatschrift*, neue Folge 27 (1890) 315—320.

M. Gervers, 'Donations to the Hospitallers in England in the wake of the second crusade', in M. Gervers, ed., *The second crusade and the Cistercians*, (New York, 1991) pp. 155—161.

A. Grabois, 'Christian pilgrims in the thirteenth century and the Latin kingdom of Jerusalem: Burchard of Mount Sion', in Kedar *et al.*, eds., *Outremer*, pp. 285–296.

A. Gransden, *Historical writing in England c.550 to c.1307* (London, 1974).

C. V. Graves, 'The economic activities of the Cistercians in medieval England, 1128–1307', *Analecta Sacri Ordinis Cisterciensis* 13 (1957) 3–60.

L'Abbé A. Guillotin de Corson, 'Traditions populaires concernant le Temple et l'Hôpital en Bretagne', *Bulletin archéologique de l'association Breton* 19 (1901) 215–266.

E. Hallam, 'Henry II, Richard I and the order of Grandmont', *Journal of medieval history*, 1 (1975) 165–186.

— 'Royal burial and the cult of kingship in France and England, 1060–1330', *Journal of medieval history*, 8 (1982) 359–380.

B. Hamilton, *The Latin Church in the crusader states: the secular Church* (London, 1980).

— *Religion in the medieval west* (London, 1986).

H. von Hammerstein, 'Der Besitz der Tempelherren in Lotharingen', *Jahrbuch der Gesellschaft für lothringische Geschichte und Altertumskunde* 7, 1 (1895) 1–29.

F. Hellwald, *Bibliographie méthodique de l'ordre souv. de St Jean de Jérusalem* (Rome, 1885).

K. Helm and W. Ziesemer, *Die Literatur des Deutschen Ritterordens* (Giessen, 1951).

R. Hiestand, 'Die Anfänge der Johanniter', in Fleckenstein and Hellmann, eds., *Geistlichen Ritterorden*, 31–80.

J. W. Hillgarth, *Ramon Lull and Lullism in fourteenth century France* (Oxford, 1971).

J. C. Holt and R. Mortimer, eds., *Acta of Henry II and Richard I: Handlist of documents surviving in the original in repositories in the United Kingdom*, List and index society, special series, 21 (London, 1986).

N. Housley, *The Italian crusades. The papal-Angevin alliance and the crusades against Christian lay powers, 1254-1343* (Oxford, 1982).

— 'Politics and heresy in Italy: anti-heretical crusades, orders and confraternities, 1200–1500', *Journal of ecclesiastical history*, 33 (1982) 193–208.

W. Hubatsch, 'Der Johanniterorden in Ost- und Westpreußen', *Zeitschrift für Ostforschung Länder und Völker im östlichen Mitteleuropa* 21 (1972) 1–19.

P. Jackson, 'The crisis in the Holy Land in 1260', *English historical review* 95 (1980) 481–513.

— 'The end of Hohenstaufen rule in Syria', *Bulletin of the Institute of Historical Research* 59 (1986) 20–36.

— 'The crusades of 1239–41 and their aftermath', *Bulletin of the School of Oriental and African Studies* 50 (1987) 32–60.

H. Johnstone, 'Poor relief in the royal households of thirteenth century England', *Speculum* 4 (1929) 148–167.

B. Z. Kedar, H. E. Mayer and R. C. Smail, eds., *Outremer: Studies in the history of the crusading kingdom of Jerusalem presented to Joshua Prawer* (Jerusalem, 1982).

B. Z. Kedar, 'Gerald of Nazareth: a neglected twelfth-century writer in the Latin east. A contribution to the intellectual monastic history of the crusader states', *Dumbarton Oaks Papers*, 37 (1983) 55–77.

— *Crusade and mission: European approaches towards the Muslims*, (Princeton, 1984).

M. Keen, *Chivalry* (New Haven and London, 1984).

E. Kennan, 'Innocent III, Gregory IX and political crusades: a study in the disintegration of papal power', in G. F. Lytle, ed., *Reform and authority in the medieval and reformation Church* (Washington D.C., 1981) pp. 15—35.

Ch. Kohler, 'Rerum et personarum quae in Actis Sanctorum Bollandistis et analectis Bollandianis obviae ad orientem latinum spectant. Index analyticus', *ROL* 5 (1897) 460—561.

H. Krauss, 'La chanson de geste dans le système des genres littéraires', in K. H. Bender, ed., *Les épopées de la croisade*, pp. 170—176.

W. Kuhn, 'Ritterorden als Grenzhüter des Abendlandes gegen das östliche Heidentum', *Ostdeutsche Wissenschaft* 6 (1959) 7—70.

— 'Kirchliche Siedlung als Grenzschutz 1200 bis 1250, (am Beispiel des mittleren Oderraumes)', *Ostdeutsche Wissenschaft* 9 (1962) 6—55.

G. Labuda, 'Die Urkunden über die Anfänge des Deutschen Ordens im Kulmerland und in Preußen in den Jahren 1226—1243', in Fleckenstein and Hellmann, eds., *Geistlichen Ritterorden*, pp. 299—316.

J. L. La Monte, *Feudal monarchy in the Latin kingdom of Jerusalem 1100–1291* (Cambridge, Mass., 1932).

E. Langlois, *Table des noms propres de toute nature compris dans les chansons de geste* (Paris, 1904).

C. H. Lawrence, *Medieval monasticism: forms of religious life in western Europe in the middle ages* (London and New York, 1984).

L. von Ledebur, 'Die Tempelherren und ihre Besitzungen im Preußischen Staate. Ein Beitrag zur Geschichte und Statistik des Ordens', *Allgemeines Archiv für die Geschichtskunde des Preußischen Staates* 16 (1835) 97—120, 242—268, 289—336.

M. D. Legge, *Anglo-Norman literature and its background*, (Oxford, 1963).

List of ancient correspondence of the Chancery and Exchequer preserved in the Public Record Office, PRO. Lists and Indexes 15 (reprinted New York, 1968).

List of inquisitions ad quod damnum preserved in the Public Record Office, 2 vols., PRO. Lists and Indexes 17 (London, 1892—1912, reprinted New York, 1963).

S. Lloyd, *English society and the crusade, 1216–1307* (Oxford, 1988).

J. Loades, ed., *Monastic studies I: the continuity of tradition* (Bangor, 1990).

E. Loseth, *Le roman en prose de Tristan, le roman de Palamède et la compilation de Rusticien de Pise. Analyse critique d'après les manuscrits de Paris* (Paris, 1891, reprinted New York, 1970).

E. Lourie, 'The will of Alfonso I, "El Batallador", king of Aragon and Navarre: a reassessment', *Speculum*, 50 (1975) 635—651.

F. Lundgreen, *Wilhelm von Tyrus und der Templerorden*, Historische Studien veröffentlicht von E. Ebering, Heft 97 (Berlin, 1911).

H. Lüpke, *Untersuchungen zur Geschichte des Templerordens im Gebiet der nordostdeutschen Kolonisation: Inaugural-Dissertation* (Bernburg, 1933).

— 'Das Land Tempelburg. Ein historisch-geographische Untersuchung', *Baltische Studien*, 35 (1933) 43—97.

A. Macquarrie, *Scotland and the crusades, 1095–1560* (Edinburgh, 1985).

E. Magnou, 'Oblature, classe chevaleresque et servage dans les maisons méridionales du Temple au XIIe siècle,' *Annales du Midi* 73 (1961) 377—97.

L. de Mas Latrie, *Histoire de l'Ile de Chypre sous le règne des princes de la maison de Lusignan*, 3 vols. (Paris, 1852—61).

E. Mason, 'Timeo barones et dona ferentes', in D. Baker, ed., *Studies in Church history 15: religious motivation: biographical and sociological problems for the Church historian* (Oxford, 1978) pp. 61—75.

— 'Fact and fiction in crusading tradition: the earls of Warwick in the 12th century', *Journal of medieval history* 14 (1988) 81—95.

H. E. Mayer, 'Studies in the history of Queen Melisende of Jerusalem', *Dumbarton Oaks papers* 26 (1972) 93—182.

— 'Henry II of England and the Holy Land', *English historical review*, 97 (1982) 721—739.

— *The crusades*, trans. J. Gillingham, 2nd edn (Oxford, 1988).

M. Melville, *La vie des Templiers* (Paris, 1951).

S. Menache, 'Contemporary attitudes concerning the Templars' affair: propaganda's fiasco?', *Journal of medieval history*, 8 (1982) 135—147.

P. Ménard, *Les Fabliaux: contes à rire du moyen âge* (Paris, 1983).

M. Méras, *Le Beaujolais au moyen âge* (Villefranche-en-Beaujolais, 1956).

A. Moisan, *Répertoire des noms propres de personnes et de lieux cités dans les chansons de geste françaises et les oeuvres étrangères dérivées*, 5 vols. (Geneva/Paris, 1986).

M. R. Morgan, *The chronicle of Ernoul and the continuations of William of Tyre* (Oxford, 1973).

— 'The Rothelin continuation of William of Tyre', in Kedar *et al.*, eds., *Outremer*, pp. 244—257.

C. Morris, 'Propaganda for war: the dissemination of the crusading ideal in the twelfth century', in W. J. Sheils, ed., *Studies in Church history 20: The Church and war* (Oxford, 1983) pp. 79—101.

— *The papal monarchy. The western church from 1050 to 1250* (Oxford, 1989).

G. M. Myers, '*Les Chétifs* — étude sur le développement de la chanson', *Romania* 105 (1984) 63—87.

H. J. Nicholson, 'Jacquemart Giélée's *Renart le nouvel*: the image of the military orders on the eve of the loss of Acre', in Loades, ed., *Monastic studies*, pp. 182—189.

— 'Templar attitudes towards women', *Medieval history* 1, 3 (1991) 74—80.

P. Noble, 'Attitudes to social class as revealed by some of the older *chansons de geste*,' *Romania* 94 (1973) 359—85.

Z. Nowak, 'Milites Christi de Prussia. Der Orden von Dobrin und seine Stellung in der preußischen Mission', in Fleckenstein and Hellmann, eds., *Geistlichen Ritterorden* pp. 339—352.

P. Partner, *The lands of St Peter — the papal state in the middle ages and the early renaissance* (London, 1972).

— *The murdered magicians: the Templars and their myth*, (Oxford, 1982).

C. Perkins, 'The Knights Templars in the British Isles', *English historical review* 25 (1910) 209—230.

E. Petit, *Histoire des ducs de Bourgogne de la race Capétienne, avec des documents inédits et des pièces justificatives*, 9 vols. (Paris, 1885—1905).

C. Petit-Dutaillis, *L'Étude sur la vie et le règne de Louis VIII, (1187—1226)* (Paris, 1894).

J. Piquet, *Des banquiers au moyen âge: Les Templiers: Étude sur leurs opérations financières* (Paris, 1939).

J. Prawer, *The Latin Kingdom of Jerusalem* (Jerusalem, 1972).

— 'Military orders and crusader politics in the second half of the XIIIth century', in Fleckenstein and Hellmann, eds., *Geistlichen Ritterorden*, pp. 217—229.

M. Purcell, *Papal crusading policy: the chief instruments of papal crusading policy and crusade to the Holy Land from the final loss of Jerusalem to the loss of Acre (1244—1291)* (Leiden, 1975).

S. Raban, *Mortmain legislation and the English Church, 1279—1500*, (Cambridge, 1982).

W. Rees, *A History of the order of St John of Jerusalem in Wales and on the Welsh Border, including an account of the Templars* (Cardiff, 1947).

— 'The Templar manor of Llanmadoc', *Bulletin of the Board of Celtic Studies* 13 (1949) 144—5.

C. Régnier, review of H. Roussel's thesis, 'Étude sur Renart le Nouvel du poète lillois Jacquemart Giélée' (Lille, 1956), *Revue du nord* 41 (1959) 116—119.

P. Riant, *Expéditions et pèlerinages des Scandinaves en Terre Sainte au temps des croisades*, 2 vols. (Paris, 1865—9).

J. Richard, *Le comté de Tripoli sous la dynastie Toulousaine (1102—1187)* (Paris, 1945).

— *The Latin kingdom of Jerusalem*, trans. J. Shirley, 2 vols. (Amsterdam, 1979).

— 'Les Templiers et les Hospitaliers en Bourgogne et en Champagne méridionale (XIIe—XIIIe siècles), in Fleckenstein and Hellmann, eds., *Geistlichen Ritterorden*, pp. 231—242.

J. Riley-Smith, *The knights of St John in Jerusalem and Cyprus, c.1050—1310* (London, 1967).

— 'The Templars and the castle of Tortosa in Syria: an unknown document concerning the acquisition of the fortress', *English historical review* 84 (1969) 278—289.

— 'A note on confraternities in the Latin kingdom of Jerusalem', *Bulletin of the Institute of Historical Research* 44 (1971) 301—8.

— *What were the crusades?* (London and Basingstoke, 1977).

— 'The Templars and the Teutonic knights in Cilician Armenia', in T. S. R. Boase, ed., *The Cilician kingdom of Armenia*, (Edinburgh, 1978) pp. 278—289.

— 'Crusading as an act of love', *History*, 65 (1980) 177—192.

I. S. Robinson, 'Gregory VII and the soldiers of Christ', *History* 58 (1973) 169—192.

J. H. Round, 'Garnier de Nablous, prior of the Hospital of England, and grand master of the order of Jerusalem', *Archaeologia* 58 (1903) 383—390.

E. Roy, 'Les dates et les allusions historiques dans les chansons d'Ogier le Danois', in *Mélanges de linguistique et de littérature offerts à M. Alfred Jeanroy par ses élèves et ses amis* (Paris, 1928) pp. 415—25.

F. H. Russell, *The just war in the middle ages* (Cambridge, 1975).

A. Sandys, 'The financial and administrative importance of the London Temple in the thirteenth century', in A. G. Little and F. M. Powicke, eds., *Essays in medieval history presented to Thomas Frederick Tout* (Manchester, 1925) pp. 147—162.

H. M. Schaller, 'Die Kaiseridee Friedrichs II', in Fleckenstein, ed., *Probleme um Friedrich II*, pp. 109—134.

S. Schein, 'Between Mount Moriah and the Holy Sepulchre: the changing traditions of the Temple Mount in the central middle ages', *Traditio* 40 (1984) 175—195.

— 'The image of the crusader kingdom of Jerusalem in the thirteenth century', *Revue Belge de philologie et d'histoire* 64 (1986) 704—717.

— *Fidelis Crucis: the papacy, the west and the recovery of the Holy Land, 1274–1314* (Oxford, 1991).

B. Schirok, *Parzivalrezeption im Mittelalter* (Darmstadt, 1982).

M. Schüpferling, *Der Tempelherren-Orden in Deutschland. Dissertation zur Erlangung der Doktorwürde von der philos. Fakultät der Universität Freiburg in der Schweiz* (Bamberg, 1915).

K. Setton, ed., *A history of the crusades*, 1: M. W. Baldwin, ed., *The first hundred years* (Philadelphia, 1958). — 2: R. L. Wolff and H. W. Hazard, ed., *The later crusades, 1189–1311* (Madison and London, 1969). — 5: N. P. Zacour and H. W. Hazard, eds., *The impact of the crusades on the near east* (Madison and London, 1985).

E. Siberry, *Criticism of crusading, 1095–1274* (Oxford, 1985).

K. V. Sinclair, 'The Anglo-Norman miracles of the foundation of the Hospital of St John in Jerusalem', *Medium aevum* 55 (1986) 102–8.

R. C. Smail, 'Latin Syria and the west, 1149–1187', *TRHS* 5th series 19 (1969) 1–21.

R. C. Stacey, *Politics, policy and finance under Henry III, 1216–1245* (Oxford, 1987).

I. Sterns, 'Crime and punishment among the Teutonic knights', *Speculum* 57 (1982) 84–111.

— 'The Teutonic knights in the crusader states', in Setton, ed., *A history of the crusades*, 5 pp. 315–378.

E. Stickel, *Der Fall von Akkon. Untersuchungen zum Abklingen des Kreuzzugsgedankens am Ende des 13 Jahrhunderts* (Frankfurt/Munich, 1975).

E. A. Synan, 'St Thomas Aquinas and the profession of arms', *Medieval studies* 50 (1988) 404–437.

B. B. Szczesniak, *The Knights Hospitallers in Poland and Lithuania* (The Hague and Paris, 1969).

S. Thiolier-Mejean, *Les poésies satiriques et morales des troubadours du XIIe siècle à la fin du XIIIe siècle* (Paris, 1978).

P. A. Throop, 'Criticism of papal crusade policy in Old French and Provençal', *Speculum*, 13 (1938) 379–412.

F. Tommasi, 'L'ordine dei Templari a Perugia', *Bolletino della deputazione di Storia Patria per l'Umbria* 78 (1981) 1–79.

D. A. Trotter, *Medieval French literature and the crusades, 1100–1300* (Geneva, 1987).

P. M. Tumler, *Der Deutsche Orden in Werden, Wachsen und Wirken bis 1400 mit einem Abriß der Geschichte des Ordens von 1400 bis zur neuesten Zeit* (Montreal and Vienna, 1955).

C. Tyerman, *England and the crusades, 1095–1588* (Chicago and London, 1988).

D. B. Tyson, 'Patronage of French vernacular history writers in the twelfth and thirteenth centuries', *Romania* 100 (1979) 180–222.

W. Ullmann, *A short history of the papacy in the middle ages* (London, 1972).

W. Urban, *The Baltic crusade* (Decatur, 1975).

— *The Prussian crusade* (Lanham, 1980).

J. C. Van Cleve, *The emperor Frederick II of Hohenstaufen: Immutator Mundi* (Oxford, 1972).

R. Vaughan, *Matthew Paris* (Cambridge, 1958).

V. Venuti, 'Dell'esistenza, professione e culto di S. Nicasio martire. Discorso storico-critico', in F. Testa, ed., *Opuscoli di auctori Siciliani*, 7 (Palermo, 1762).

J. Walker, 'The motives for patrons of the order of St Lazarus in England in the twelfth and thirteenth centuries', in Loades, ed., *Monastic studies* pp. 171—181.

J. C. Ward, 'Fashions in monastic endowment: the foundations of the Clare family, 1066—1314', *Journal of ecclesiastical history,* 32 (1981) 427—51.

W. L. Warren, *King John* (London, 1961).

— *Henry II* (London, 1973).

F.-W. Wentzlaff-Eggebert, *Kreuzzugsdichtung des Mittelalters. Studien zu ihrer Geschichtlichen und Dichterischen Wirklichkeit* (Berlin, 1960).

W. E. Wightman, *The Lacy family in England and Normandy, 1066-1194* (Oxford, 1966).

E. Winkelmann, *Jahrbücher der Deutschen Geschichte: Philippe von Schwaben und Otto IV von Braunschweig,* 2 vols. (Leipzig, 1873—8).

— *Kaiser Friedrich II,* 2 vols. (Leipzig, 1889—1897).

D. Wojtecki, *Studien zur Personengeschichte des Deutschenordens im 13 Jahrhundert,* Quellen und Studien zur Geschichte des östlichen Europa, 3 (Wiesbaden, 1971).

— 'Der Deutsche Orden unter Friedrich II', in Fleckenstein, ed., *Probleme um Friedrich II,* pp. 187—224.

H. Wood, 'The Templars in Ireland', *Proceedings of the Royal Irish Academy,* 26C (1907) 327—377.

M. M. Wood, *The Spirit of protest in Old French literature* (New York, 1917).

Unpublished Theses

B. Beebe, 'Edward I and the Crusades', (Ph.D., St Andrew's, 1970).

B. J. Cook, 'The transmission of knowledge about the Holy Land through Europe, 1271—1314', (Ph.D., Manchester, 1985).

E. Hallam, 'Aspects of the monastic patronage of the English and French royal houses, c.1130—1270', (Ph.D., London, 1976).

S. S. Rovik, 'The Templars in the Holy Land during the XIIth century', (Ph.D., Oxford, 1986).

N. Thorpe, ed., 'La chanson de Jérusalem — a critical edition', (Ph.D., Reading, 1980) (now published as *La chanson de Jérusalem* (Alabama, 1991)).

J. Upton-Ward, 'Attitudes towards the Templars (c.1119 to 1312)', (M.A., Reading, 1986).

INDEX